T0247953

Praise for
SON OF BIRMINGHAM

"Being from the South, I know the power of legacy and tradition. Mayor Randall Woodfin embodies that. He's taken on challenges that many shy away from, pushing Birmingham toward a brighter future with grit and style. Seeing someone like Randall step up for the community is what keeps the South's spirit alive—he's not just about talk, he's about change. *Son of Birmingham* is a love letter to *Southernplayalisticadillacmuzik*, and I'm honored that Mayor Woodfin accredits such significant inspiration to Outkast."

—ANTWAN "BIG BOI" PATTON,
Grammy-winning member of Outkast

"Mayor Woodfin's *Son of Birmingham* is the compelling story of one of our nation's most captivating young political leaders. A voice from the '*new* new South,' Woodfin's election as mayor of Birmingham heralded a transformation in the story of the region. In this book, with deep insight, integrity, and incisive prose, he speaks to the challenges of twenty-first century America and offers a clear-eyed assessment of how we must step into our collective future."

—DR. IMANI PERRY, National Book Award winner and *New York Times* bestselling author of *South to America: A Journey Below the Mason-Dixon to Understand the Soul of a Nation*

"*Son of Birmingham* isn't just the story of Mayor Randall Woodfin, it's the story of a city in the midst of evolution. Birmingham's legacy is rooted in the Civil Rights Movement, and, under Mayor Woodfin's leadership, it's become a modern-day model for making a fairer and more just society. It's a story worth reading."

—MARYLAND GOVERNOR WES MOORE, *New York Times* bestselling author of *The Other Wes Moore: One Name, Two Fates*

"Grit and hard work are leadership traits that pay off no matter the field of play."

—NICK SABAN, six-time NCAA Football Champion head coach of the Alabama Crimson Tide

"One word comes to mind—*authentic*. Randall Woodfin has never sacrificed his core beliefs; and his intense love of music, community, and the people of Birmingham is what makes him a visionary leader."

—BAKARI SELLERS, *New York Times* bestselling author of *My Vanishing Country* and *The Moment*

"Randall Woodfin is one of the most dynamic young leaders of his time. *Son of Birmingham* is an engrossing story of a man with a deep love of his hometown and a progressive vision for its future."

—MICHAEL TUBBS, former mayor of Stockton, California, author of *Deeper the Roots: A Memoir of Hope and Home*

"Woodfin tells Birmingham's story of victory and redemption by combining modern hope with the wisdom of generations before him. He reminds us that culture and joy need not be lost in the pursuit of justice, and he challenges us all to eradicate the sin of poverty—one resilient city at a time. America needs this new generation of servant leaders."

—GEOFFREY CANADA, president and CEO of the Harlem Children's Zone, winner of the First Annual Heinz Award in the Human Condition, author of *Fist Stick Knife Gun: A Personal History of Violence*

"*Son of Birmingham* is a raw and inspiring story of our nation's future. It is about the light that comes when we entrust the next generation to lead our communities. It is about endless possibilities when people from divergent backgrounds unify behind a Black-majority city. It is about progress and perseverance in the face of constant adversity. Randall Woodfin has given us a moving memoir and a path toward racial justice and opportunity that runs through the people of the South. We are all sons and daughters of Birmingham."

—AMY LIU, former president of Brookings, cofounder of Brookings Metro

"Randall Woodfin continues in a long line of Alabamians who could've very well taken their talents and gifts to other places but instead chose to lay anchor in the place that anchored them. If ever there is a future not only for Birmingham but also for the state of Alabama to overcome the ghosts of its past and meet its true potential, then there has to be a precise dissection of its problems to find solutions. Randall Woodfin remains one of Alabama's most important societal surgeons."

—ROY WOOD JR., journalist, comedian, former correspondent on Comedy Central's *The Daily Show*, current host of CNN's *Have I Got News for You*, host of the 2023 White House Correspondents' Dinner

"My friend, Mayor Randall Woodfin, born and raised in Birmingham, Alabama, is a man for the people. He personally understands the obstacles faced by the majority of his constituents, and he leads with forward-facing vision, his eyes locked on justice, opportunity, and collective victory. He is a special leader of and for our times, rooted in integrity and brimming with vision for his Birmingham city and her people. Read his book."

—JOHN HOPE BRYANT, founder, chairman, and CEO of Operation HOPE, bestselling author of *Financial Literacy for All*

"I continue to be struck by the far-reaching effects of George Floyd's murder, from Northern cities like mine to Mayor Randall Woodfin's Birmingham, Alabama, and beyond. Most striking has been the leadership that has fought to change systemic racism and has battled to earn the people's trust in government. In *Son of Birmingham*, you will get to know a shining example of that leadership and the forces that influenced him—from family trauma to family love, from the Black Church to hip-hop, and from peaceful protest to destructive unrest. I am a true believer in the power of hope, and his story fills my heart with hope. Woodfin is a servant-leader for our times."

—MEDARIA ARRADONDO, former Minneapolis police chief, author of *Chief Rondo: Securing Justice for the Murder of George Floyd*

"Randall Woodfin has proven to be a rare and valuable gift of dynamic leadership for Birmingham. A Birmingham native son, he is the example of the new generation of political leadership our city and nation need. In his first run for mayor, he went door to door citywide, sharing his vision for Birmingham and won overwhelmingly. Now he is revitalizing Birmingham and Putting People First."

—RICHARD ARRINGTON, the first Black mayor of Birmingham, Alabama

SON OF
BIRMINGHAM

A MEMOIR

RANDALL WOODFIN

WITH EDWARD T. BOWSER

DIVERSION
BOOKS

Diversion Books
A division of Diversion Publishing Corp.
www.diversionbooks.com

Diversion Books and colophon are registered trademarks of
Diversion Publishing Corp.

For more information, email info@diversionbooks.com

Hardcover ISBN: 979-8-89515-002-3
e-ISBN: 979-8-89515-003-0

Cover design by Jonathan Sainsbury
Design by Neuwirth & Associates, Inc.

Printed in the United States of America
1   3   5   7   9   10   8   6   4   2

Diversion books are available at special discounts for bulk purchases
in the US by corporations, institutions, and other organizations.
For more information, please contact admin@diversionbooks.com

The publisher does not have any control over and does not assume any
responsibility for author or third-party websites or their content.

I dedicate this book to my family:
Kendra, Love, Aubrey, and Mason

CONTENTS

HOLD ON, BE STRONG

Tell me the truth: When you hear the words *Birmingham* and *Alabama*, what are the first things that jump to mind? If you've never stepped foot onto my hometown's red clay and your knowledge of the Magic City is confined to history books and Southern stereotypes, I bet I know what you're thinking.

You're probably envisioning struggle. Anguish. Black folk in their Sunday best cowering in the presence of attack dogs. Bodies buckling to violence. A city with the boot of Jim Crow on its neck.

All saturated in a black-and-white Instagram filter.

Birmingham has long been viewed by outsiders—and some within our borders, too—as a city frozen in the year 1963.

Our narrative is almost always a story about victims, never a story about victory.

As a son of Birmingham, I know the real story of our city. Its beauty. Its intricacies. Its strength. But I have to admit, on the night of May 31, 2020, as I stood in a crowd and literally watched part of my hometown burn, the most traumatic parts of our past echoed in our present.

Frustration. Violence. Fear. All rooted around a symbol of hatred.

On that last day of May 2020, a few months into the COVID pandemic, six days after police in Minneapolis killed George Floyd during an arrest over a suspected counterfeit twenty-dollar bill, my people were again in pain and outraged.

I had been among the crowd in Kelly Ingram Park, part of a peaceful rally protesting the murder of Mr. Floyd. Within hours, some among us turned their attention to the Confederate Soldiers and Sailors monument that stood in nearby Linn Park. Peaceful protest quickly turned to historical demolition.

That monument had long stood as a mockery to Birmingham's story, literally casting a shadow of oppression over a city that stood in defiance of it. That night, Birmingham had enough. Its people were sick of the lives of Black men being unjustly snuffed out. They were tired of symbols of white supremacy standing in mockery of them. They wanted to take their story into their own hands.

Crowds hammered away at the fifty-two-foot obelisk with pickaxes and sledgehammers. They defaced it with spray paint.

It would not budge.

Protesters brought a truck to the scene and hitched ropes to the monument, attempting to drag it from its foundation.

It still would not budge.

I despised the Confederate Soldiers and Sailors monument as much as anyone there that night. As mayor of Birmingham, my team and I had sought that eyesore's removal from our city for several years. But this method was too dangerous. If protesters had succeeded, that truck would have been crushed. People injured, possibly killed.

I could sense the desperation in the crowd. I had to take control. Not for the sake of that disgusting monument, but for the sake of the people I served.

I marched into that angry crowd, but I wasn't afraid. They were furious, hurt, and desperate—but they were my people. They chanted for me to stand with them, to remove the blight that hovered over their city. They were sick of being victims. I felt them.

I told the crowd to disperse for their own safety, and asked them to give me a few days to remove the monument. They balked.

New deal: I told them to give me twenty-four hours and I'd tear that monument down for good.

They agreed. But that wasn't enough to lower tensions. Crowds pounced on a nearby statue of Thomas Jefferson. One man tried to burn it down. The crowd targeted a monument to Confederate naval captain Charles Linn, the park's namesake.

They then turned their attention to the heart of downtown—shattering windows, raiding storefronts, even assaulting journalists who were simply doing their jobs. Birmingham's historic Black business district, a cherished area of our city that represented progress in the face of adversity, was left mangled and scarred.

As our first responders scrambled to regain control, I was awash in sorrow. While I shared the same pain, anger, and frustration as these protesters, I knew this was not the path to redemption.

All I had to do was look at that damn monument. It still stood arrogantly as our city burned, mocking us all.

I had twenty-four hours to tear down that hateful pillar once and for all.

I refused to let us be victims in this story once again.

In a city whose legacy since the 1960s has been built on breaking down systemic racism, that monument's existence was outright treasonous.

It had to fall.

For years, Birmingham mayor William Bell's administration—and later, mine—had engaged in an exhaustive court battle over the removal.

We made our position clear: Birmingham, Alabama, a city whose population is nearly 70 percent Black—refused to recognize a monument that celebrates a regime that aimed to suppress those same Black residents. However, the state attorney general fired back. The state filed a lawsuit against the city, citing the Alabama Memorial Preservation

Act of 2017, which prohibits local governments from removing, altering, or renaming monuments that are more than forty years old.

The people of Birmingham—by May 31, 2020—were damn tired of being told what should be in our city by people who don't even live here. I had watched the same footage of George Floyd that they did, and it hit far too close to home.

As our response teams fanned out downtown to protect our residents that night, I went live on social media trying to ease tensions. I can't remember exactly what I said, but I remember the sense of crushing, agonizing disappointment. I empathized with the anger—trust me, I was just as furious—but I couldn't justify the methods. Not when innocent people were being hurt and Black businesses were being victimized.

That was the only night of my tenure as mayor that I didn't sleep at all. But I'm a man of faith, and if it's one thing the church taught me, it's that joy comes in the morning.

The next morning saw residents and business owners standing side by side in cleanup efforts. Hometown heroes like comedian Roy Wood Jr. returned to join in the efforts. There was no finger-pointing, no outrage, no victim-blaming. There was just a city coming together, literally picking itself up in the face of adversity.

When people hear the words *Birmingham, Alabama*, this is the picture I hope they envision. The adversity, the violence, the tears of the past—that's just half of the story. Birmingham is a living, breathing redemption story, one that shines brightest in the second half.

As encouraging as that next morning was, I knew I had a job to do. We had less than twenty-four hours to remove that monument forever. I had made a promise, and I couldn't let Birmingham down. I had to let the world know that our story doesn't end with violence. It ends with victory.

CHAPTER 1

MYINTROTOLETUKNOW

I t was September 26, 2014, at Atlanta's Centennial Olympic Park, and the stars were out in force. But me? I had my eyes on a comet.

On the bill that night was one of three shows dubbed #ATLast weekend, featuring a reunion of the iconic rap duo Outkast (at the time of this writing, one of the last times they performed together).

Rap has had many incredible duos: 8Ball & MJG out of Memphis. The Underground Kingz, Bun B and Pimp C, reppin' Houston. But in my opinion, no two artists have meant more to Southern hip-hop—my favorite flavor of hip-hop—than Antwan "Big Boi" Patton and André "3000" Benjamin, a.k.a. 3 Stacks.

Prior to this show, the duo had amicably parted ways to pursue other projects, still proclaiming their brotherhood the whole time. It had been nearly a decade since their last album, *Idlewild*. (That album gets too much hate, by the way. It's got a few cuts I can rock with.)

It had been far too long since the Mighty O had blessed us with their presence. So, I gathered up a group of close friends to join me at the show, including my college roommate John Cox.

I wasn't missing that show for nuthin'. It was hip-hop history in the making.

2 Chainz hit the stage, dropping his addictive bars. He's a punchline machine, raining down absurd metaphors with effortless charisma. Janelle Monae was there, too, singing, rapping, dancing, and captivating. Janelle has Prince Rogers Nelson's showmanship wrapped in Ms. Lauryn Hill's God-given talent with a dash of Parliament-Funkadelic's intergalactic flow. If Wakanda had a Heritage Festival, Ms. Monae would be the headliner.

But nothing prepared us for the highlight of the night.

Big Boi and André 3000 reunited, and it felt so good.

This is the part where I should tell you about all the dope songs Outkast performed. What the stage set looked like. How the audience hung on every syllable, chanting along to every generation-defining hit song and introspective deep cut.

But I can't. I've attended a gazillion concerts in my life; this was the only time I felt like I was in a trance. There I was, shoulder to shoulder with my closest friends and thousands of hip-hop fans, but I was completely oblivious to them all. I couldn't hear them, I couldn't see them, I couldn't smell them (even though there was a lot of weed in the air, trust).

It was just me and those Two Dope Boyz in a Cadillac onstage.

Big Boi is a criminally underrated MC. He doesn't get enough props for being a technically proficient lyricist and storyteller who can take relatable situations and mold them into sonic masterpieces. I'd put him up against any rapper in the game today.

But I've always felt a kinship with André 3000. He isn't just a rapper; he's an artist in every sense of the word. He's thoughtful, creative, and in tune with the art of making music. There's a reason why he's mostly become a musical recluse, focusing on film projects and wandering around random towns serenading passersby with his flute. He doesn't care about fame. He just wants to create.

Like I said, I don't remember specific songs from that show, but I do remember Outkast's presence. Their aura. It was the best concert I've ever attended. I was honored to be in the presence of stars.

Scratch that—André never wanted to be a star. He often compared himself to a comet. Fiery. Untamable. Perpetual motion.

Stars shine bright. But comets keep it moving.

Back in 1995, during that year's now-infamous Source Awards, Outkast were rising players on the Southern stage. By the end of the night, they were prophets.

Let me set the scene: Hip-hop was in a very transformative space in 1995. For most of its existence, New York's gritty East Coast sounds and stars dominated the landscape. They were the trend-setters, the leaders of the pack. But by the early '90s, we had seen the emergence of West Coast stars like Snoop Dogg and Dr. Dre with their G-Funk sounds, which leaned on '70s-era samples and the influence of Parliament-Funkadelic. The dynamics of power began to shift, as did the tensions between East and West Coast artists.

Meanwhile, there was a Third Coast bubbling—groups like UGK and 8Ball & MJG gained ground, dropping albums that spoke specifically to the Southern experience. We rocked with them heavy here in the South. By '95, the whole nation began to take notice, which led to Outkast being selected as Best New Rap Group during the Source Awards event.

When hip-hop legends Christopher "Kid" Reid of Kid 'n Play and Cheryl James and Sandra Denton of Salt-N-Pepa presented Outkast with the award, the crowd erupted in boos.

At that very moment, 'Kast was caught in the middle of rap's civil war. The duo were outsiders—not seen as worthy contenders to rap's throne. But it was André 3000's acceptance speech that would signify an eventual shift in hip-hop's landscape:

> But it's like this, tho. I'm tired of folks . . . those close-minded folks. . . . It's like we have a demo tape and nobody wants to hear it. But it's like this—the South got something to say.

Those final six words refused to be drowned out in the chorus of boos and catcalls.

Nearly three decades later, the South would be the preeminent power in hip-hop, with Southern artists, Southern producers, and Southern flavor touching every part of American pop culture. Trap music, a production style that leans on sparse hi-hat patterns that was once a Southern rap staple, has manifested itself in R&B, pop, K-pop, and even country.

Southern hip-hop isn't considered a subgenre of hip-hop anymore. It *is* hip-hop. The Dirty South is in its DNA. The South reshaped the world of music in its image. But that's far from the first time we've made change down here.

My city, Birmingham, Alabama, has a reputation.

If you're on the outside looking in, the word *Birmingham* often conjures up visions of black-and-white photos of dogs attacking peaceful protesters. Of high-pressure water hoses tearing at the flesh of well-dressed men and women marching for their God-given rights. Of hateful, ignorant racists screaming threats at little Black boys and girls heading to integrated schools to better themselves. Of bombed Birmingham churches where cowards stole the lives of four little girls attending Sunday school.

We hear the boos, and I get it. They're justified. But that's not the whole story.

Our story is not one of pain. It's one of resilience. Many cities—including Selma, Alabama; Montgomery, Alabama; and Atlanta, Georgia, claim to be the cradle of the Civil Rights Movement. But if you ask me, Birmingham is the main battleground of the Movement.

On the streets of Birmingham our faith leaders teamed with activists and residents to push for change. Children, dubbed the Civil Rights Foot Soldiers, stood defiantly in the face of hatred, marching and rallying for a brighter future—for themselves and for generations like mine.

On these streets we helped attain voting rights for all people. We helped desegregate schools and buses. We ousted generations of racist leadership.

We were the first to pluck the feathers off Jim Crow. Black lives always mattered on our streets.

On the same streets today we fight to erase the specter of segregation by making sure every resident has a shot at a quality education. We fight for the rights of women and defiantly push back against unjust laws that threaten the LGBTQ+ community.

Birmingham, and *all* our brothers and sisters of the South, taught the world how to fight.

Yeah, the South got something to say. It wasn't just a declaration. It was a spoiler.

My love of Outkast's music traces all the way back to 1994 and their debut video, "Player's Ball." Oddly, the main thing that stuck out to me was watching André play pool at the table. There was just something so . . . *real* about it.

Their platinum-selling debut album, *Southernplayalisticadillacmuzik,* captivated me. These rappers felt like two guys from my hood, and I could relate to every lyric they spit. I'm also pretty sure they helped trigger my love of Cadillacs.

By the time Outkast came back on the scene for their second album, *ATLiens*, in 1996, their style had completely changed, and it caught people off guard. It was a complete 180 from two guys playing pool in the basement. The production was darker, more alien—literally, with intergalactic sound effects and stuff. A lot of fans thought it was wack, but I think the naysayers were distracted by the bells and whistles. 'Kast's messages of family and Southern culture were still there, and they had only gotten stronger. Big Boi and André 3000 had evolved but they hadn't lost themselves.

By 1998, I was growing up, and so was Outkast. I remember talking slick to my mom one day—and if you're reading this and know my mother, Cynthia Woodfin-Kellum (affectionately known as Mama Woodfin in our city), you already know where this is going.

Man, she told me, "Oh, you wanna be grown? Go live with your daddy."

Mama Woodfin don't play, y'all.

I went to live with my dad—who was divorced from my mom and staying with my aunt at the time. My saving grace during that rough patch was my favorite Outkast album, *Aquemini*. I played it every day in my 1991 Cadillac Brougham—white with burgundy interior. Yeah, I was flexin' on 'em.

But the *Aquemini* album resonated with me because it was so abstract but still so relatable. Every song was a self-contained story about Southern culture, Black women, and Black liberation. And just like the album before it, it showed incredible growth.

Outkast was introduced to us in the hood wearing jerseys, baseball caps, and playing pool. They left all that behind to go to outer space and become hip-hop astronauts. Their music stayed rooted in the Southern dirt from which they were born.

Even when they left planet Earth, they always came back home.

• • •

I'm a true son of Birmingham. Our city is a beautiful patchwork quilt of ninety-nine distinct neighborhoods, each one taking great pride in its identity. When people ask which neighborhood I'm from, I usually say "all over." And that's not just me trying to play all sides.

I resided in both the North Birmingham and Crestwood neighborhoods. But I had a great aunt who lived in Fountain Heights. An uncle in Central City and another in Vice Hill. An aunt in Kingston. Another aunt and grandmother in Southtown. More aunts in Collegeville and West End and Loveman Village. Family in Mason City, Harris Homes, and Woodlawn.

I fell in love with my city as a child, even before I knew what serving in city government was.

When I came home to Birmingham in 2003 after graduating from Morehouse College, I was distraught. A lot of the issues that had a stranglehold on my city during childhood were still as strong as ever. I saw blight. I saw gun violence. I saw drug and alcohol addiction. I saw families of color not getting the same opportunities as more privileged members of our community.

Morehouse had instilled in me the importance of giving back to your community. Your city is an extension of your family. So, I had to help my family.

I can't lie, I was discouraged. Coming home from college was one of the lowest points in my life. I didn't feel supported. I didn't feel like the older guard were doing enough to encourage the next generation to take action. So many of my friends were moving away to cities like Houston; Washington, DC; and Los Angeles. They saw opportunity in those places that they didn't see in Birmingham.

It hurt. So I told myself that I had to be the change I sought. I wasn't going to wait to become a gray-haired man to take risks. I was from Birmingham, where the children of the Civil Rights Foot Soldiers bravely took their lives into their own hands to fight for change.

I was born for this.

My former Morehouse roommate John and I decided to get to work. We started a breakfast club at Putnam Middle School, three days a week, pouring all the knowledge, support, and love into those kids that we could.

We ignored the naysayers, the loud noises, the Source Award boos that claimed we couldn't make change. That we couldn't do it. That it wasn't our time.

None of the negativity mattered. Even if we changed the lives of this handful of Putnam Middle School students, we'd sleep better.

Hip-hop fans might know one of those students. My homeboy Keshawn is currently blowing up the rap scene as Lil Bam, and I'm so proud of him. During the Morehouse Tuskegee Classic event that Birmingham hosted in October 2022, I had the pleasure of watching Lil Bam do his thing onstage right before another of my favorites, Young Jeezy, dropped some heat. It was an incredible moment that showed the power of hip-hop and the power of supporting your own.

This book will be a reflection of those experiences. I plan to show you the power of servant leadership, the fulfillment of lifting up your community—and the power that resides within hip-hop. I'm going to welcome you on my journey from bagging groceries at Western Supermarket to becoming the youngest mayor in my city's modern history.

And I plan to do much more than that.

I will be very open and honest with you about my life—the fears that froze my feet, causing me to make horrible decisions, and the hope that thawed them and set me on a better path.

Leadership is a calling, and it's not some award unattainable to all but the rich and powerful. It's a simple desire to want more for your community, taking the action to do it, and empowering others to join you on that mission.

I'm not special. I'm a kid from North Birmingham who loves Outkast.

When 3 Stacks and Big Boi talked about the hardship of Black women their songs "Jazzy Belle" and "Da Art of Storytellin'," I felt it. When they looked deep into their mortality on tracks like "13th Floor/Growing Old," it made me think about my future. When they hit us with the marching orders to make change on "Git Up, Git Out," I couldn't help but feel motivated. And when they branched out to mainstream radio with hits like "Rosa Parks" and "B.O.B," I understood the message—you have to expand your reach and connect with all audiences if you really want to make a difference.

Outkast taught me to be a better leader. I hope I can share some of that wisdom along the way.

Just remember: Comets can't hear those Source Awards boos from outer space. They're too busy moving.

TWO DOPE BOYZ
(IN A CADILLAC)

Déjà vu sucks.

Some people think it's a cool experience—that weird, ethereal feeling of briefly being transported back to a past life, even for a moment. But sometimes, even those fleeting movements of familiarity are wrapped in pain.

August 11, 2017, eleven days before I would appear on the ballot in my first bid to become the mayor of my hometown, I'm riding shotgun in a car headed to a fundraiser with my campaign manager, Ed Fields.

I get the call.

My eighteen-year-old nephew, Baby Ralph, has been shot.

Ed turned the car around and dropped me off at my car. I drove toward the scene, playing it cool while trying not to fall apart on the inside.

Only five years before, I'd had to make the same panicked drive to the scene of another shooting—Baby Ralph's father—and my brother—Ralph Jr. Déjà vu *really* sucks.

This is Birmingham, Alabama, a city whose history has been intrinsically tied to the liberation of Black people, yet sixty years removed from the Civil Rights Movement it remained wracked by so many shootings that I publicly stated that gun violence had become a public health crisis. I campaigned on promises of working to bring peace to our streets and stability to our homes.

I felt the pain of families ripped apart by gun violence because I lived it every day.

I wasn't the first to arrive at the scene of my nephew's shooting—his mother was already there—but I was the family member chosen to identify him. I never saw the body; instead, the officer came over and showed me a pic.

It was Baby Ralph. With a bullet hole in his head.

He was only ten days past his eighteenth birthday. He never had the opportunity to achieve his dreams. To start a family or career. To be happy and grow old.

That bullet snatched every bit of potential away from him.

Just like a bullet had done to his father. My brother.

And just like the death of his father, I didn't have time to grieve. I had to be the rock for my family. I had to be the mayoral candidate my city needed.

I could not weep. I could not mourn. I had to suppress it all. That's what I thought being a leader was. And that's why I can't *stand* déjà vu.

When I think back on it, I didn't have a lot of positive male influences in my life. That's not a shot at my father, whom I love and respect dearly to this day. But early in my life, our relationship wasn't the tightest. He divorced my mom when I was eight years old, and with that came a lot of distance. I looked forward to his visits, sitting on the couch, legs swinging, waiting patiently for him to roll by the crib to pick me up. Unfortunately, those moments were fleeting.

My uncles struggled with substance abuse, both drugs and alcohol (which is why the most you'll catch me with is a light beer or two these days). They also were caught up in the prison system. One uncle did twenty years, another did ten. One didn't get paroled until he was in his sixties. Another will never get out.

Male role models were few and far between. But the one guy I looked up to was my brother, Ralph. I knew Ralph wasn't living right, but he was just so damn cool, man. When he floated through the hood in his '64 Chevy Impala with the peanut butter–color interior blasting Do Or Die's "Still Po Pimpin'," you only had two options—stare or salute.

Ralph introduced me to a lot of hip-hop. While living in Birmingham's Kingston neighborhood, he'd let me come through and borrow his cars. That's when he put me on to Southern rap legends the Hot Boys. I was already into Master P's No Limit Soldiers, who had taken over the South and were planning world domination. But these Hot Boys were something special—flashy, but undeniably street and authentically Southern. Just like Ralph. Lil Wayne, Juvenile, B.G., Turk, Mannie Fresh, and Birdman had a track on the *Get It How U Live* album called "Neighborhood Superstar." That track will always remind me of my brother.

Whatever he was listening to, whatever he was wearing, I wanted all of that. I admired Ralph. But, deep down, I really didn't want to *be* like Ralph.

Ralph didn't finish high school. He was kicked out of Job Corps. He couldn't hold a real job, but he had a PhD in running the streets, hustling, and dealing dope.

Neighborhood Superstar.

Regardless, I was always loyal to my brother. Till the end.

Six hours before the shooting that would wreck my family, my brother and I spoke on the phone. I don't even remember what we talked about, but I do remember the last words we exchanged:

He said, "I love you, bruh."

I said, "I love you, too."

Those eight words rang through my ears hours later when I got the call that Ralph had been shot. The second I got on the scene and saw the flashing blue lights of the squad cars, my blood ran cold. I already knew what that meant. I just didn't want to admit it.

I jumped out of the car, ran to the scene, and was restrained by four cops. (One of the cops at the scene, coincidentally, was Lt. Scott Thurmond, who years later I'd appoint as Birmingham police chief.)

I didn't have the strength to call my mom and tell her that Ralph had been killed. I called my dad and had him tell her. Judge me all you want, but I just couldn't be the one to tell my mom that her baby was gone and her family was broken.

Let me tell y'all the three worst cries I've had in life. I'm talking ugliest, wettest, most guttural releases of emotion I've experienced:

1. When those four officers restrained me when I raced to the scene of Ralph's murder.
2. When I looked into his casket during the funeral.
3. At the trial of my brother's killer, when the foreman said, "Guilty."

In the years after that sequence of painful experiences, I often saw Ralph's face in my dreams, sometimes even heard his name. But I never really processed his death, never really grieved. How could I? I was more concerned with my mom's pain, the struggles of my sister-in-law who was now a single parent, and the void left in the lives of my nieces and nephews.

I didn't have time for grief. And all my tears? They were tears of anger.

That anger swirled inside me after the death of Baby Ralph. I was angry at Baby Ralph's obsession with guns and the fast life. Just like his dad. Another Neighborhood Superstar.

I was angry at how high-profile Baby Ralph's murder case became. The headlines read: Teen killed in Tarrant shooting was Birmingham mayoral candidate's nephew. I couldn't be Randall, the son and uncle my family needed. I had to be Candidate Woodfin, putting on a brave face for the press *and* for my family. It wasn't fair to anyone.

I was angry that the alleged killer of my nephew went on trial, had a hung jury, and eventually was found not guilty. (He'd eventually get convicted on another charge.) As a lawyer, I understand the court system—burden of proof, reasonable doubt, all that.

But as Randall Woodfin, Ralph's brother, Baby Ralph's uncle, I was angry.

Angry and hurt.

It's only been in recent years that I've realized how prevalent fear has been in my life.

My parents' marital issues fostered a fear of commitment. The lack of a father figure in the early years of my life triggered a fear of abandonment. And when I hit thirty-eight years old, seven years after my brother passed and two years into my role as Birmingham mayor, I reached a midlife crisis.

"Will I make it past my thirty-ninth birthday? Because Ralph wasn't with us much longer after his."

The fear of being taken away from my family—and now the city I had been elected to lead—shook me to my core.

The line between fear and hope is razor thin. I was tired of just straddling that line. As a son, as an uncle, as a brother, as the leader of my hometown, I was ready to embrace hope.

That fear became motivation.

First things first—I got a counselor. Here in the South, especially in the Black community, I know we were taught to pray our troubles away, and I do believe in the power of prayer. But I also believe in getting some good therapy. Trust me, it works. Do it.

I got a physical trainer. I got a financial advisor. I got over my fears of starting long-term romantic relationships.

Most important, I got over the fear of making peace with my brother's death.

See, during the graveside service at my brother's funeral, I refused to see him buried. But a couple days before my thirty-ninth birthday—more than eight years after his murder—I finally went to his gravesite to give him a proper goodbye.

I don't remember exactly what I said—I don't want to just make up some random stuff for this book. I'd rather keep it real with y'all. I do remember saying I miss him and I love him.

I wish every day that he could have partied with me as we celebrated my election and re-election as mayor of the city that raised us. I wish he could have stood by my side as I raised my hand on inauguration day and pledged to serve my city, vowing to fight back against the gun violence that took his life and the life of his son.

I wish he were here to read this book.

But at that gravesite I came to terms with my brother's death. I made peace with the fears that weighed me down so heavily. I know my brother loves me and is proud of me.

I've experienced a lot of death in my life, probably because I come from such a large family. Ralph's death affected me the most, but the truth gets clearer every day. Being vulnerable is not a curse. It simply makes us human.

I was already a man, but that day at that gravesite, I became an adult.

And maybe one day I'll be a different kind of Neighborhood Superstar for my city.

CHAPTER 3

LIFE IS LIKE A MUSICAL

My mom is never at a loss for words. So when you stun her into silence, you know one of two things has happened—either things have gone really well, or things have gone really wrong.

In this case, it was the former.

The kid she drove to Sixth Avenue Baptist Church that morning wasn't the same one standing now before the congregation. Until that moment, I had been shy, reserved Randall.

But this brother before them right now? He was built different.

I stood at the front of the congregation, flanked by a few of my homies. I wore big black boots and a belt that circled my skinny waist about eight times.

I stood there, motionless. Enveloped by silence.

That is, until I bellowed at the top of my lungs:

CHRISTIAN SOLDIERS!

My friends snapped to attention. And then it was on.

Stepping Ohhh ohhh
Stepping for the Lord

Stepping
Stepping
Stepping for the Lord

That chant was accompanied by the most furious step routine Sixth Avenue Baptist had ever seen. Actually, it was the *first* step routine Sixth Avenue Baptist had ever seen.

There were only a handful of us performing at the front of the church, but we rumbled through that sanctuary like an entire platoon. The vibration of our feet hitting the floorboards and our voices ringing in unison was exhilarating.

We turned Sunday morning service into *Stomp the Yard*.

My fellow church members—including my mom—had never seen me so animated. With every bead of sweat that flew from my brow, every syllable that scratched my throat as it left my mouth, I knew this was where I was supposed to be.

Sixth Avenue Baptist Church's InStep Ministry was one of three major turning points in my life, moments that put me on the path of servant leadership.

From grocery bagger to band kid to Christian soldier, my life as a leader began by serving others.

I'm a No Limit soldier. I thought I told ya.

To understand my story, you have to understand my city.

Birmingham is a city divided into twenty-three vibrant communities and, more distinctly among its residents, ninety-nine separate neighborhoods. Each one of those neighborhoods has its own name, its own elected association leaders, and, most importantly, its own identity.

I'm the product of a large family, so I was blessed to have relatives from all over the city. The benefit of that was being able to experience life from several branches of Birmingham's expansive tree. Kingston, Collegeville, West End, Southtown, Loveman's Village, Fountain Heights, Metropolitan Gardens, Pratt City, Mason City—I spent a significant amount of time in all those areas.

But my very first home was in North Birmingham.

I was born in 1981; my mom called me her Biscuit Baby.

Before you come with the jokes, I wasn't named that because I resembled the pasty Pillsbury guy who hangs out on biscuit cans.

At least I hope not.

According to my mom, she decided to make biscuits out of the blue one morning, something she had never done a day in her life prior. She knew something was baking in her oven.

It was me. Not the Pillsbury guy.

My parents, Ralph and Cynthia, married, divorced, and remarried in 1980. I popped up a year later like a fresh batch of biscuits. I didn't get to be the baby long—my youngest sister, Candace, was born a year later, joining my older siblings, Ralph and Cindy. My parents divorced for the final time when I was eight years old.

Being the middle kid wasn't easy, especially in a big family. I was sandwiched between two strong-willed sisters. Also, with my mother's seven siblings and my father's five siblings, I was never at a shortage of aunts, uncles, and cousins (more than thirty first cousins), who had my back.

As a child, I was very quiet. And I despised confrontation. Watching arguments between my parents (and later, when my parents found new spouses) rattled me. It made me want to be a peacemaker.

As I think back on it, those ideals of compromise were also instilled in me by my grandmothers—three guiding lights in my life:

My dad's mother, Rosa Lee, was from Southtown projects. We spent a lot of time at her place on weekends. She taught us to appreciate everything you had, no matter how little it was worth in dollars and cents. Like every sophisticated woman in the '80s, her living room furniture was essentially Ziploc'd in plastic covering. If you sat on it in the summertime, you'd literally have to peel yourself off of it.

At least that's what I observed because we were not allowed to get on that Saran-wrapped furniture. Rosa Lee was not here for games—the only playing that took place was outside. We knew better than to cross her.

My mom's grandmother Elnora Sullivan was our holiday hostess. Christmas Eve, Christmas Day, Fourth of July—we spent so many holidays at her home, a home she unfortunately lost in a 1998 storm. Still, her spirit never wavered. She had a tenacity that was unmatched.

And finally, there was my great-grandmother Mary McGhee. She lived to be a hundred years old, despite being blind from diabetes. She was a native of Stonewall, Mississippi, and I do not miss those trips. Sweltering heat, mosquitoes the size of the rapper Bow Wow, no kids my age to play with—not a lot of fun.

Check this out: My love of Cadillacs—something that you just might notice from time to time in this book—owes something to her and Grandaddy Cecil. My grandfather would drive me all over Birmingham in that white Caddy with its sleek, black interior. My grandmother was right there, riding shotgun. It felt like I was inside a NASA rocket. My feet would dangle from the seats, my legs not even long enough to reach the floorboards. We'd swing by Church's Chicken or head downtown to pay bills, but always without music playing. It was just the roar of the engine, the rumble of the tires over streets, and a view of the city.

There's an unspeakable power possessed by women. Femininity is often painted as "soft and demure" at best, and "weak" at worst. But there's absolutely nothing weak about a woman—especially a Black woman. They are our caretakers, our comforters, and our moral compasses.

They are our leaders. Women like my Spelman sister Carol Smitherman, a leader with an indomitable spirit who has served in all three branches of government: city council president, interim mayor, and Jefferson County civil judge. Faith leaders like Dorothy Porter, wife of the Reverend Porter, who led with compassion and grace as first lady and children's choir director at Sixth Avenue Baptist Church. Trailblazers like Vice President Kamala Harris, who are currently inspiring a new generation of Black girls and women to bring change to their communities.

They bear the brunt of a male-dominated society, enduring every struggle and setback with strength and solidarity.

They are the faces you never want to disappoint, nor do you want to cross them. You better stay off that plastic sofa.

They are the best of us.

How beautiful it is to be loved by a Black woman.

When I say I grew up around my whole family, I mean just that. When my mom remarried and we relocated to a neighborhood called Crestwood, our home became Big Momma's House. Shout-out to Martin Lawrence.

We never had fewer than eight people in our house, and we often had more. At one point, for several years, we housed four generations of our family under our roof.

Our doors were always open. If you were just released from prison, you had a home with us. If you were a recovering alcoholic or rebounding from drugs, we let you in. And that's not even counting the seemingly endless stream of friends and family who would pop in after work or on the weekends just to visit.

It's what I love about the Black family structure. Doesn't matter the label—brother, sister, stepdad, stepmom, second cousin, play cousin, friend—the only word that truly mattered was family. If you were in that house, you were family.

That environment taught me two key things. First, the art of compromise. With so many personalities in my life, I realized that I couldn't have it my way all the time. Problem-solving and meeting people in the middle became a key trait. It was essential for survival.

It also taught me perspective. So many generations under one roof comes with a plethora of different outlooks on life. Dismissing a view because it differed from my own seemed ridiculous to me. Instead, I opened my eyes and ears to experiences that differed from my own. I may not have always agreed with those perspectives, but it led to greater understanding and respect.

Simply put, I'm the living example of "It takes a village to raise a child," with each generation instilling morals, lessons, and discipline in me. Those individual pieces connected like a jigsaw puzzle, creating my full character. It made for a rewarding childhood.

Although I witnessed poverty firsthand, we were never crippled by it. Yes, many of my family members lived in public housing, but at its heart, it was still a community. Our days were filled with visits to the neighborhood candy lady to buy a twenty-five-cent bag of chips, a pickle, and a Cool Cup (basically a frozen cup of Kool-Aid—an '80s hood staple). We watched the adults play card games like tonk and bid whist until the sun went down and the lightning bugs came out, with new jack swing hits from Keith Sweat blasting over the radio. We watched movies, lots of movies.

This was life for me. Splitting chores with my sister, learning to wash and fold my own clothes—because my mom certainly wasn't doing the laundry of able-bodied kids. I sat at the kitchen table and ate every gross vegetable on my plate, no matter how slick I thought I was by smashing them up or hiding them.

I wouldn't trade those days for anything.

• • •

I loved movies as a kid.

I'm telling y'all, I loved them so very much. But if I could only watch five movies on repeat for eternity, they would be the Black kung-fu extravaganza *The Last Dragon*, classic action flicks *Lethal Weapon*, *Top Gun*, and *Die Hard*, and the ultimate treasure hunt that was *The Goonies*.

But I can't forget the hilarity of *Risky Business*. Or the incredible dance moves of *Breakin' 2: Electric Boogaloo*, which always makes me think fondly of my brother, Ralph.

Told y'all I loved movies.

By the '90s, *The Sandlot* was my go-to, but I also had an affinity for films that featured the government and their alphabets—CIA, FBI, etc. That included *The Hunt for Red October, Crimson Tide, Clear and Present Danger*, and *The Abyss*. Subconsciously, these films probably fed into my interest in government.

Looking back, I hated reading things like Homer's *Odyssey* and *The Great Gatsby*, but as an adult I can appreciate the storytelling much more. Love is always embedded in the themes—loss of love, desire for love, consequences for bad decisions. These themes flew over my head as a kid, but I respect them today.

And in terms of music, I grew up listening to what the adults in my life loved. It gave me an old soul. The Commodores, The Isley Brothers, The Temptations, The Jackson 5, and more were part of my experience. When sampling began to take hold in the '90s, like Ice Cube using the Isleys' "Footsteps in the Dark" for the foundation of his hit "It Was a Good Day," it gave me greater appreciation for both tracks and strengthened my musical education.

• • •

While in elementary and middle school, I often accompanied family members to visit my three incarcerated uncles—getting a different kind of education.

Let's be honest—I was a young, impressionable kid. And part of me wanted to be like my uncles. The life they lived was enticing, but also terrifying. I saw the drugs, the alcohol, the women, and the street life that led them to prison. And to their credit, they never encouraged me to follow their path.

Plus, I took my whoopings and punishment too seriously to try anything crazy.

So, I lived life as they said, not as they did. I didn't want to disrespect my mother, nor let them down. I focused on making good grades and working hard.

In sixth grade, all the pieces came together, thanks to an array of incredible educators from Putnam Middle School.

Mr. Washington—my homeroom and science teacher.

Ms. Flowers—My English teacher.

Ms. Snow—My reading teacher.

Ms. Archie—My math teacher, the only woman I know who would call you her "sugar lump" in one breath and throw you right out of the class in the next.

These educators laid the foundation for my academic career. I can't really pinpoint select lessons that each one gave me; their overarching love and support is what stuck with me. A great educator provides much more than one memorable lesson—it's that collection of wisdom over a school year that truly changes young lives. When I ran for re-election in 2021, it was important to me that their voices be part of that story, which is why they were part of my ad campaign.

Along with learning, I had another great love around this time.

I wanted to be the next Nick Cannon.

Let me clarify that. No, I didn't want to father enough kids to fill up the Alabama football defensive line. I wanted to be Nick Cannon's character from the movie *Drumline*—Devon Miles, the ultimate band kid.

I started playing drums in the fourth grade and it instantly became an obsession. I would drum on the back of the car seat. I'd beat on our cabinets. No surface was safe from my percussive prowess.

I was always a fan of music, but there's something special about the tactile feel of a drum, the vibrations that reverberate from it, the power and energy it produces.

I fell in love with the snare drum, and nobody could tell me I wasn't a beast on it. Until . . . someone told me exactly that.

When I made my way to Shades Valley High School, I thought my destiny was to be on that snare drum. That is, until the band director told me he was taking me off the drums and putting me on, get this, the cymbals.

The cymbals. The snare drum's boring little cousin.

Look, no shots to the cymbal players out there—y'all are great. But that wasn't for me and it certainly wasn't my passion.

Snare DrumGate was a big blow to my young, fragile, high-school ego and started me on a downward spiral.

I felt like I was in the slums of the band. It completely messed with my head, and my passion plummeted. Things got so bad that I rebelled during one game at halftime, threw down the cymbals, and picked up the drum again.

That wasn't well received.

Even worse was a later confrontation I had with the head drummer that ended in an actual fight. The result? I got kicked out of the band, got a bad grade, and eventually quit the percussion game.

Seriously, who gets a bad grade in band?

In hindsight, I know this seems like the most petty story ever. Clearly my ego was out of control and there was no reason for things to go so far left. But the band fiasco was my first confrontation with failure and, trust me, it wouldn't be the last.

It was one of the first times in my life I grappled with fear. See, what most folks saw that night was frustration manifesting itself as teenage rage. But there's more to the story—the root of the issue was fear, in all its harmful forms.

The fear of failure. The fear of being replaced. The fear of change.

Left unchecked, fear will twist your character into an ugly façade, one that makes you unrecognizable to your loved ones. Even the face staring at you in the mirror will look like a stranger's.

It was during Snare DrumGate that I gave into the fear. I succumbed to the things my incarcerated uncles warned me to avoid.

Fear feeds on our regrets, silently strangling us and stunting our growth. That's why I'm so thankful for the foundation that my family and trusted educators built in me.

If not for their love—both tender and tough—the specter of fear that manifested into band rage could have redirected my entire trajectory. I would be writing a very different book if they were not in my life.

So, yeah, band didn't quite work out, but years later, I gave it one more go. In 2010, I bought a drum set, hoping to rekindle that magic, maybe even following in the footsteps of iconic hip-hop producers like Pharrell Williams and Mannie Fresh. They're titans in the world of beatmaking.

Well, they say you can't go home again, and trying to reconnect with my inner Nick Cannon didn't work out. I just didn't have the same love for drumming I had years ago.

Still sounded better than those raggedy cymbals, though.

Yeah, I've got the music bug, but I'm a low-key movie buff as well.

I spent much of the '80s and early '90s watching my cinematic heroes on repeat. I've watched Tom Cruise whip that fighter jet through the skies countless times during my *Top Gun* rewatches.

And to this day, I'll hit you with a quote from Ms. Celie out of the blue as a nod to my endless rewatches of *The Color Purple*.

Hell, I even reenacted Bruce Willis's infamous ventilator shaft scene from *Die Hard* as part of my mayoral "12 Days of Christmas" holiday series. You can check it out on the City of Birmingham's YouTube page right now.

And yes, *Die Hard* is a Christmas movie. Argue with your auntie, not me.

But from all my favorite '80s flicks, there's one character I could relate to more than any other:

My boy Bruce Leeroy.

Bruce Leeroy, a.k.a. Leroy Green, was the lead character in the 1985 cult classic *The Last Dragon*. On the surface it was simply an '80s take on the martial arts films that took the world by storm in the '70s—I mean, if the name "Bruce Leeroy" didn't tip you off to that, I can't help you.

But there's so much more to the film than choreographed violence and cheesy dialogue. At its core, this was a movie about a regular kid, my guy Leroy, achieving great things from humble beginnings.

Watching Bruce Leeroy evolve from meek karate kid to martial arts master who unlocks his full potential was *everything*. We may not have had the Marvel Cinematic Universe in the '80s but the moment Bruce Leeroy achieves "the glow"—backed by an unforgettable song from soul specialist Willie Hutch—and puts the paws on his arch-enemy Sho'nuff, let me tell you, *that* was our *Endgame*.

We all wanted to be Bruce Leeroy. That didn't necessarily mean that we wanted to become master martial artists, but we all wanted to unlock our potential. We wanted that glow, that inner spirit to defeat the Sho'nuffs that loomed in our lives.

Sho'nuff personified the fear that we weren't good enough, not strong enough, not from the right environment.

In the wise words of Willie Hutch, "You need the glow to grow."

I found my glow at the end of the checkout line at Western Supermarket.

. . .

I've always been a people pleaser. I had to be the best.

If I was cleaning up the kitchen at home, I wanted that kitchen to be the cleanest it had ever been. Not a utensil out of place, not a speck of dust on the floor. I swept and mopped every square tile to perfection.

Wax on, wax off. But Bruce Leeroy style.

Some time around junior year of high school, I was ready for the next challenge, the next time to prove myself to be the best.

It hit me one day while shopping at Western Supermarket, our local grocery store. I wanted to work there, and I wanted to be the best employee they ever had.

Shout-out to store manager Dale Smith, whom I pestered for weeks. I'm grateful that he took a chance on an overly enthusiastic fifteen-year-old. And because he stuck his neck out for me, I had to put my best foot forward.

Remember back during middle school when we'd vote to give our peers accolades? There's one vote that always stuck with me. I didn't win best dressed. Or best looking. Or most likely to succeed. I won three others:

Most courteous

Friendliest

Best personality

Those designations might not be as high-profile as others—Best Looking, for example, is like winning Album of the Year at the Grammys. It doesn't get better than that to a needy middle schooler.

But they still resonate because they aren't labels I gave myself. It's how others saw me. Three decades later, I still try to live up to those titles every day of my life.

I kept those three character traits in the back of my mind as I started my job at Western Supermarket. Marrying a desire to be the most courteous, friendliest, and endearing person to customers and coworkers—along with my drive to be the best at my job—became the foundation for my work ethic.

That was the secret to unlocking the glow.

When I started the job, I noticed how baggers just threw groceries any type of way. They'd be looking down at the purchase, not at where they were placing the goods. Tossing eggs around, setting heavy objects on top of bread.

Bruh. What. Are. You. Doin'???

I went in the opposite direction. I'd engage the customers in conversation. I'd pay careful attention to the placement of items.

Instead of hanging out at the back of the aisle, I'd go into the aisle, pull their buggy down to my end, and place the bags inside for the customer.

These seem like little things, but they meant a lot to our customers.

After two or three visits, I'd know the customers' names, I'd know their children, even details about their lives. I knew which customers wanted paper or plastic before they even asked. By the time I was sixteen and seventeen years old, the tips were crazy. I was getting $100 tips during Thanksgiving or Christmas. I soon became the go-to bagger—people only wanted Randall Leeroy Woodfin handling their groceries.

And that wasn't all. I also represented our store during grocery stacking competitions.

Yes, there are actual competitions where baggers stack the most product most efficiently in the quickest time. I'm not making this up. The Alabama Grocer Association held an event at the downtown civic center, and I came out on top in the local competition. I placed regionally, as well.

Eventually, I was moved up from bagger to cashier, to building displays. Not long after, I served as acting assistant manager, where I was allowed to guide our team—lessons that still serve me well as the CEO of the City of Birmingham today.

Putting People First is more than a motto; it's the way we conduct business here in Birmingham. And that started at Western. People don't want a "bagger" in name only. They want someone to treat their property with care. They want to be respected. They want to be heard.

It's not about a tip or winning a competition. It's about good service.

That said, if anyone wants to go toe-to-toe with me in a bagging competition, pull up. I'll meet you at Publix. You'll know it's me—just look for the glow.

When I stop to think about it, I can tell you honestly that bagging groceries is a whole lot like running a city.

I'm dead serious. Hear me out.

The best strategy for bagging groceries is knowing your customer. When I worked as a bagger, I never hung out at the end of the conveyor belt, waiting for the items to trickle down slowly to me. I walked halfway up the aisle, greeted the customer personally, offered to take their cart, and went to work.

That might seem like idle small talk, but it means a lot on several levels.

It allows you to acknowledge the customer directly. You immediately establish a connection, which will help you with the task at hand.

It proves to the customer that you're an active participant in this experience. You're not a houseplant staring off in the distance while cans of green beans roll down the conveyor belt.

It shows you're approachable. If the customer has a specific request, they're now comfortable making it to you because, in that brief interaction, they know you better.

I've found that there's an invisible wall that divides government officials and the people they serve—a barricade that blocks City Hall from its communities. It's unseen to the naked eye of city leaders but best believe, our residents feel it. It's intimidating. The best way for leaders to break down those blockades is to walk over that imaginary line and meet residents where they are.

They want to be seen. They want to know you're approachable. And they certainly want you to be there for them.

Now, back to bagging. The most important key is to start with the end in mind. Ask yourself, when this person gets home, how will they unload their goods? Most folks want to get perishables in the house first, so if I'm helping to pack a customer's car, I make a note to put those goods close to hand.

When it's time to bag, it's a big game of *Tetris*. Heavy items on the bottom, similar items grouped together, light items on top.

And if you've already made a verbal connection with the customer, it's even easier. They're more likely to share what best works for them. Service should always be 80 percent listening, 20 percent responding.

I carry those lessons with me every day. For every big community initiative we propose, we never move without first reaching out to residents. We go into neighborhoods, knock on doors, and put ourselves in a position to listen.

Those visits aren't meant to hammer home our points or browbeat those who may oppose us.

We walk up that aisle to meet residents where they are. We hear their concerns and propose the best way to organize resources for our game plan. We walk with them every step of the way—whether that's to their car or through their questions about needs in their community. And when the door closes and they're in their homes, hopefully we've given those shoppers/residents the tools to properly unpack those items that will nourish their families.

It starts with a connection. We build bonds through service. And our community is healthier and happier.

Not bad for a day's worth of bagging.

I was always a church kid.

My dad was Sunday school superintendent. My mom was a Sunday school teacher, who was often in charge of youth plays and events.

But here's the thing about faith—it's not a spectator sport. No matter how many times you attend church or half pay attention to a sermon, faith doesn't make its mark on you until you become an active participant.

Soldiers, it's time to mount up.

I grew up in Fourth Avenue Baptist Church, but after my parents' divorce, we began attending Sixth Avenue Baptist Church.

I credit the beginning of my faith walk to the Reverend John T. Porter, who baptized me at a young age. I soon became an active participant—singing in the children's choir, attending Vacation Bible School, essentially the usual events for kids in this era.

The Reverend Porter had higher aspirations.

Looking back, Sixth Avenue was a pretty progressive church, comprised of several generations of worshippers, which often included a lot of young people. To better connect with them, the Rev. Porter decided to launch a youth dance team.

Now that might not seem like a big ask today. Liturgical dance squads are pretty commonplace today. But back then? Not so much.

I love the church but my frustration with it has long been its unwillingness to evolve with the times. There was a time when liturgical dance was seen as controversial and "too worldly" to take place in the hallowed halls of a sanctuary.

If only people read the Bibles they so often thump.

In the sixth chapter of 2 Samuel, there's a famous story of David literally dancing out of his clothes in celebration of the Lord. He was throwing holy hands in the air like he just didn't care. Michal—clearly one of those crotchety church members—scolded David for running around half naked, embarrassing her in front of other folks.

My man David kept it real, essentially saying—I'm celebrating everything God has done for me; if you don't like it, watch me go harder.

Michal couldn't see the vision. She was making David's praise about her, when in fact it was solely between David and God. What was a public expression of faith was simultaneously an intimate reflection of David's desire to be closer to God.

Bet y'all didn't expect that mini-sermon, did you?

Again, that's credit to the Rev. Porter, who saw this dance team as a way to recruit a new army of Christian soldiers.

Enter Jacqueline Lockhart. The InStep Ministry was her brainchild. The concept was very similar to the step teams strolls that frequent Historically Black Colleges and Universities, but instead of Greek chants, it was more spiritually based.

My mom would drive me to practice but was too busy chatting with other adults to notice what we were actually doing.

What was happening was my metamorphosis.

I was a shy kid with a light voice. When it was decided that I would be the leader of InStep, I couldn't be the same shy kid.

When it was time to stand in front of that congregation, I had to be different. I had to be bigger. I had to be bolder.

So, during that very first performance, I put on my army fatigues, black boots, and that oversized belt. Y'all know the rest.

This wasn't the time to be shy. I was a Christian soldier. I had to put on for the Lord.

CHRISTIAN SOLDIERS!
Stepping Ohhh ohhh

We shook the pews that day. And I shook away every fear and doubt that clouded my mind.

I never asked to be the leader of InStep. Honestly, I'm still not sure how it was decided. All I knew is that I couldn't let my team down. I couldn't worry about what others thought of me or dwell on supposed secondhand embarrassment.

I had to be David—unapologetic in my faith.

We took InStep on the road, performing at other church programs, parks, and even local events like the Heritage Festival. Heritage Fest was a huge deal, by the way. Seeing artists like Beyoncé perform there with her group Destiny's Child—*long* before she was the biggest star on the planet and every Black woman's aspiration—proved that it was a showcase for future superstars.

That's why we went so hard at Heritage Fest. We were blessed with this opportunity: We weren't going to let down our parents, our church leaders, and especially not God.

What I love most about InStep is the community it created. Members of the group are still close—we even have a group chat called Old School ISM. Those boys are now men—shout-out to Wanya n' dem—and we've created a space to talk about life, jobs, kids, and Alabama football.

I mean, it's mostly talking about Alabama football.

But still, InStep was special. It's where I found my voice—a louder, stronger voice. It taught me to be unashamed of my faith. It taught me leadership.

It taught me to be like David. Watch us step on those haters.

· · ·

My administration has five core values that have been drilled into our team since the day I walked into City Hall:

1. Customer Service.
2. Efficiency
3. Effectiveness
4. Transparency
5. Accountability

Customer service leads that effort because it was drilled into me from birth.

The three biggest turning points in my young life—my days in the band, my time with InStep Ministry, and bagging groceries at Western supermarket, shaped that journey.

InStep taught me to step outside of my comfort zone, giving me the leadership skills to build a team for a greater good.

Western taught me to serve, to listen to our customers and treat them as I'd want to be treated. Kindness and attentiveness go much further than careless speed and an impenetrable attitude.

And the band, well, that taught me how to rebound from failure. No matter how well-researched and well-executed your plans may seem, there will be hurdles. You can lash out, drowning in your fear of failure, or you can reset and find a new path.

I'm far from perfect. I've made many mistakes—and best believe I'll make a few more before the Lord calls me home. But one thing that will never change is my dedication to service.

From cleaning up a messy kitchen that served meals to a dozen family members on any given night, to listening to a customer share her day while I stack her groceries carefully in her cart, to lifting my voice and slamming my feet in praise of the God who brought me this far on my path . . . I'm only here to serve. Like every good soldier should.

Cool story about delivering the commencement at Tuskegee University in 2019: Weeks before I gathered my thoughts to address those graduates, I took a transformative trip to Washington, DC, to visit the National Museum of African American History and Culture.

It wasn't just any trip, though. I brought my dad.

Bonding with him while being immersed in our rich culture brought one word to mind—legacy. I wanted those graduates to know that they're building their legacy on the foundation of giants.

Good afternoon, graduates! Y'all good?

On behalf of my administration, and my hometown of Birmingham, Alabama, I'm so honored and privileged to share this moment in time with you today.

About a month ago, my dad and I took a trip up to Washington, DC, to tour the National Museum of African American History and Culture.

It was an incredible experience, y'all. Being immersed in our culture, our triumphs, our history, while sharing that moment with one of the guiding forces of my life, was incredible.

That museum is a monument to our legacy.

And today, you stand at another point, one that will define your future. Like me, many of you are joined by your family.

And, also like me, your journey here at Tuskegee will stand as a monument to your legacy.

Like you, I'm a graduate of a Historically Black College. I'm sure you'll agree that there is no experience like an HBCU experience.

You're surrounded by Black excellence on the daily.

I don't care if it's algebra or accounting, every single class you take is basically a Black history class.

And dealing with the financial aid office? Look, if you can survive that, you might as well sign up for the Avengers. Thanos is light work after that struggle.

But what happens when you leave the comfort zone of this campus? When those friends who are with you daily are now miles, sometimes even states, away? When family is nowhere to be seen and those trusted teachers and mentors are absent?

It goes without saying—when you leave these walls, you will be hit with adversity.

Adversity always waits until our expectations reach their peak, only to smash us down to earth. Adversity comes in the form of heartbreak. Disappointment. Setbacks.

That job that fell through. That medical exam that didn't turn out right. Those friends you expected to ride with you forever but wound up just being a season in your life.

I'm speaking from experience.

The first time I took the bar, I failed.

The first time I ran for the Birmingham school board, I failed.

Even during the midst of my mayoral campaign, I lost my nephew to gun violence. At the time, my family was still attempting to heal from the loss of my brother, who also died tragically.

I had to look my mother in the face, a woman whose heart was still torn, and watch her wrestle with even more grief.

More often than not, adversity is part of the Black experience.

Our people know setbacks. Our people know devastation. Our people know pain like few others on this planet.

But last month when I toured the museum of African American History in DC, I was reminded that our story is greater than the struggle.

Our story is that of survival.

And it's a story that I relived with my father, my family, walking by my side that day.

Tuskegee, you are the continuation of a grand legacy.
A legacy that boasts names like:

George Washington Carver

Betty Shabazz

Ralph Ellison

Lionel Richie

Keenen Ivory Wayans

Giants in their fields who reshaped our country through science, literature, music, politics, and entertainment.

That's the impact they made on this land.

That's the way they kept Tuskegee's grand tradition strong.

That's their legacy.

But what will yours be?

I challenge you to unlock your potential using the keys that you've acquired over the past few years here at Tuskegee.

Maybe it's time to unleash your inner Nipsey Hussle by digging deep into your communities to bring change on a fundamental level, reminding us all of the meanings of *hustle* and *motivate*.

Perhaps you need to tap into your inner Lizzo, being unapologetic about who you are and teaching your community the importance of self-love.

Or maybe you embrace your inner Solange—being unconventional in your thought and free-spirited in your approach to life. Paving a way for new voices to have A Seat at the Table, When You Get Home.

I won't stand here and tell you that your degree equals guaranteed success. That's not how this world is set up.

But what I will tell you is that you have been built to face adversity head-on and knock down any obstacle that's in your way.

That's the HBCU way. We mold champions.

Challenges will come, but those challenges won't last because you're built of sterner stuff. The very fact that you're sitting here proves it. And your families, your communities, your world need your fortitude.

Healing starts with you.

Activism starts with you.

Reform starts with you.

Restoration starts with you.

Empowerment starts with you.

Compassion starts with you.

Martin Luther King said, "You don't have to see the whole staircase, just take the first step."

That first step begins when you walk across this stage.

And the path you leave behind you will clear the way for the next generation. Just as the forefathers and foremothers of Tuskegee have done for you.

You are all monuments to greatness, as tall as that big ol' building in DC.

And Whether It's Sunny or Gray

We Gon Ball and Parlay

Keep It Crunk Every Day

It's the Tuskegee Way.

Thank You, Tuskegee.

Randall L. Woodfin, Mayor
Tuskegee University Commencement Address
July 2019

CHAPTER 4

ATLIENS

I t blows my mind that we're having this conversation, but I think this book is the perfect place to address it.

There have been louder and louder assertions that Historically Black Colleges and Universities are outdated relics.

HBCUs were created during a time when Black students were barred from attending white institutions of higher learning.

The solution was simple: Y'all won't let us in your spaces? Bet. We'll create our own.

From Cheyney University of Pennsylvania opening its doors as the nation's first HBCU in 1837, to more than a hundred that would follow—including fourteen in my home state of Alabama, the most of any state in the nation—HBCUs have become an incubator for Black excellence.

But we're more than a hundred years removed from HBCUs' origins, and minority students are no longer banned from attending PWIs, or Predominately White Institutions. The playing field is now even, they say. Opportunities are now equal across the board, they say.

Yeah, they say a lot of things. But here's what I know.

In a time where so many Black families lack the means to send their children to expensive, high-profile PWIs, when students are eager to embrace their culture among like minds, and where lawmakers are actively trying to erase the truth of trauma inflicted against Black Americans by eliminating critical race theory from classrooms . . .

Scratch that. Don't call it critical race theory. It's American history, plain and simple. And it's not multiple choice—you can't cherry-pick which parts of our story to tell and what you can ignore. Stop short-changing our struggle.

As I was saying, now, more than ever, we need HBCUs.

I won't deny the fact that HBCUs have faced major hurdles in recent years. Though great organizations like the United Negro College Fund raise money for these institutions, many have struggled due to a lack of federal funding.

Recruitment has also been an issue. PWIs have beefed up their attempts to lure the best and brightest minority students, offering large financial aid packages to improve their enrollment diversity.

But that's just half the story.

You see, while HBCUs make up just 3 percent of American colleges and universities, the results are mighty, producing 20 percent of Black grads, as well as 25 percent of Black graduates in STEM—science, technology, education, and mathematics.

Black students also are more likely to feel the squeeze of the racial wealth gap in higher education. Roughly 54 percent of Black students between the ages of twenty-five and forty have student loans, compared with 39 percent of white Americans in that age group. HBCUs are here to ease financial burdens with a more affordable tuition—HBCU rates run about 30 percent less than at comparable institutions.

And let's not overlook the obvious—no other institutions celebrate the Black experience as strongly as HBCUs. These schools are for us, by us, rooted in the same values and traditions as our homes, which makes for a much more comfortable environment for first-generation college students.

An HBCU is one of the few places in this country where a stranger can step foot in an environment and instantly feel at home.

Knowing that you can achieve your full potential in a warm, uplifting environment shared not just by familiar faces, but Black leaders who shaped our country—hell, that can mean so much to a young student.

Oprah Winfrey earned her degree from Tennessee State University. Vice President and 2024 Democratic nominee Kamala Harris is a proud graduate of Howard University. Jesse Jackson attended North Carolina A&T. And the Rev. Dr. Martin Luther King Jr. was a Morehouse man, just like me.

I would not be the man I am today—let alone the leader I became—if not for the lessons of Morehouse College. If you don't believe me, track down the September 2002 edition of *Ebony* magazine. R&B star Usher is on the cover. Inside, there's an article featuring young leaders from HBCUs. In that very article, I made my goals clear:

I hoped to one day be the mayor of my hometown.

That dream became a reality thanks to my HBCU.

Anyone who dares question the relevance, the impact, and the power of HBCUs can go sit in a corner. Better yet, go to an HBCU.

They'll show you how to make leaders.

As I neared high school graduation, I didn't have a clear view of my future yet. I strongly considered the Marines, and had multiple conversations with a recruiter.

Ultimately my path would lead me straight to Atlanta.

I didn't know much about Morehouse College prior to high school graduation, only that the Rev. John T. Porter had studied for his master of divinity there and spoke highly of it. In 1999, I attended a Morehouse prospective student seminar, to get the feel of the school during spring break. I stayed in a hotel off campus but got the full Morehouse experience once we stepped on-site. I visited classrooms and sat in on seminars. We stopped by local malls and just got a feel for Atlanta life.

They were five of the most transformative days of my life. I knew Morehouse was where I wanted to be. My mom needed a little more convincing.

It's not that she was anti-Morehouse, not by any means. Morehouse was just very pricey for our lean budget, and she was already putting my sister through four years at the University of Alabama at Birmingham.

We stopped by McDonald's on the ride back from Morehouse and my mom laid down the law as all moms do. She told me that she could only afford one year at Morehouse. After that, it was up to me to fill in the gap.

I wasn't sweating it. I knew I'd make it happen. Morehouse was where I needed to be.

To this day, my mom says, "In 1999, I sent a boy to Morehouse College; four years later, Morehouse sent a man back."

She's not wrong.

Morehouse is the intersection of academic rigor, community service, and leadership. I've never been more pushed and inspired to excel. I've also never been around such a diverse display of Black excellence. Intellectuals. Orators. Problem-solvers. Hustlers. We were all there, trying to be better.

But the pressure was on. The first day of orientation, the presenter stood before us and said, with near menace in their voice: "Look to your left. Now look to your right. Every brother you see next to you now won't be there at the end. Will you be here?"

Hell, yeah, Imma be here. And I had friends who had my back.

My boy John Cox from middle school joined me at Morehouse. Our dorm room was, coincidentally, 205, the same as Birmingham's area code. We became the 205 Boys. It was great having John in my corner, a brother I had known since I was eleven.

As first-year students we had to wear a shirt and tie twice a week. I see a lot of y'all giving me props for my suits today on social media, but I have to give credit to Morehouse for teaching me how to dress. Of course, it was the late '90s, so all our suits were big and baggy—I'm talking about those Steve Harvey specials. We kept K&G Fashion Superstore in business in those days.

I served as a Morehouse ambassador in those early days. I'd throw on my finest *Kings of Comedy* suit, pick up prospects from the airport, and usher them around campus, introducing them to organizations like the Student Government Association and the Alpha Phi Alpha Fraternity—two groups I'd be closely linked to later in my college career.

Down the line I'd connect with Joe Carlos, who would become my roommate junior year. We were both political science majors and we bonded quickly. Joe knew everybody—all the coolest guys, all the girls, plus he was nice with photography and one of the best writers I've ever met.

The great thing about attending Morehouse at that time is that it felt like we lived in the golden age of rap club bangers. Every year was defined by a different hit. True to the prophetic words of Juvenile, Cash Money Records and Mannie Fresh's pavement-cracking production took over the clubs for '99 and the year 2000. Sophomore year, Outkast's *Stankonia*—my favorite group's mainstream breakthrough album—dominated my speakers. By 2002, Lil Jon was the King of Crunk, screaming at us to turn up on the dance floor—and we obliged. In 2003, Pharrell Williams and Chad Hugo, the Virginia production duo known as the Neptunes, were everywhere. Rap, R&B, alternative rock, no one was safe from their *Space Invaders*–inspired production.

During freshman year, I also met a girl from our sister school, Spelman, and we dated for quite a while. Spelman was like the pearly gates, filled with strong, smart, and beautiful women. Whew, God is an awesome God.

I was having so much fun. But there's a time and place for everything. Pretty soon, it was time for me to lead.

One of the earliest lessons I learned about leadership is that opposition can come from those you believed were in your corner all along. Standing for justice in the face of hypocrisy is the truest test of leadership.

During my senior year at Morehouse, while serving as president of the SGA, an incident went down between two men. Allegedly, one young man looked at another man while he was showering. Things escalated quickly, and violently. The man who was showering later attacked the other brother with a bat.

It was called a hate crime on campus, and the administration wanted to keep everything quiet.

But we couldn't. To remain silent in the wake of this horrific attack went against everything we were taught—everything Morehouse represented. How could we turn our backs on the plight of another brother at the very same school Dr. King called home?

Like it or not, Morehouse breeds activists.

The conversations about the situation got loud—very loud. As tensions rose, the SGA sought healing. Our goal was to create a safe space for brothers to talk about what happened and seek viable solutions. We planned a forum and distributed flyers, but the school removed them.

Well, we held the forum anyway.

In retaliation, the school suspended the SGA charter, rendering us a nonentity as an organization. It wasn't just unfair, it was hypocritical. These weren't the ideals Morehouse taught us.

Thankfully, we'd have an unlikely ally in our corner, one who spent years using thought-provoking storytelling to fuel his activism and change our world.

Spike Lee had our back. A Morehouse man who would do the right thing.

For some schools, it may be the football field or the basketball court where leaders are born and bred. At Morehouse, student government is a varsity sport.

One of the young leaders whose words always stuck with me was our SGA president my freshman year. His words commanded such attention. If there were 2,800 students in a room, there were 5,600 eyes fixated on him. Not only that, but his words left us inspired.

Leadership is all about planting seeds. Truly great leaders don't try to hoard power for themselves or scorch the earth for those who may come behind them. Instead, they pave the path for the next set of leaders, sowing seeds in that fertile ground. When those seeds of leadership begin to sprout, there's room for growth.

Leadership isn't always what you've done, it's whom you inspire.

Those SGA leaders inspired me.

During my sophomore year—call it the Year of *Stankonia*—I ran for SGA corresponding secretary. I was running against more established students, so I was the underdog from the start.

I felt that the best way to establish connections with students was to meet them where they were. So I started a door-knocking campaign, knocking on every dorm door to introduce myself.

Eventually, I was in a runoff with a very popular junior. My strategy didn't change—I went back and knocked on every dorm room door I could, again. When the last votes were counted, I pulled it off, defeating the more-established candidate in a big upset.

I wouldn't know it at the time, but my SGA corresponding secretary race would be the blueprint for my mayoral race and victory sixteen years later.

I'm sorry, Ms. Jackson, but imagine fixing your lips to say that HBCUs are irrelevant. There would be a lot of blank pages in this book if not for my HBCU. I am for real.

By junior year I set my sights higher. First, I pledged Alpha Phi Alpha Fraternity, Inc., joining a prestigious brotherhood that included W. E. B. DuBois, Thurgood Marshall, Mayor Richard Arrington, Donny Hathaway, Jesse Owens, and Michael Jackson—

No, not the Jackson you're thinking about. I'm talking about Michael Jackson, the Birmingham brother and member of the Seattle Seahawks, not the guy who tried to steal Iman from Pharoah Eddie Murphy in the "Remember the Time" video. My Alpha Phi Alpha brother MJ was the original Mr. Steal Your Girl.

The Alphas are the first intercollegiate Greek-letter fraternity established for Black men, and for more than a century they have dedicated themselves to brotherhood and advocacy. First of All, Servants of All, We Shall Transcend All. That's the motto. And living a life of service has defined my existence ever since I pledged to stand beside my brothers.

After pledging Alpha, I decided to go for the big one. I ran for SGA president.

My sophomore secretary strategy worked so well that I ran it back for the presidential campaign.

You guessed it, I knocked on every door again. This time I already had cache around campus but, as I mentioned earlier, there's a power in meeting voters face-to-face, looking them in their eyes, hearing their concerns, and, most important, helping them to make a personal connection with you.

Door knocking: check. And for this campaign, I added a twist: My brother Joe created a newspaper specifically for the campaign. Called the *Common Sense*, we named it in tribute to the pamphlet by Thomas Paine that pushed for the colonies' independence from Great Britain.

The paper laid out my campaign strategy and, just as important, gave the reader a snapshot of my personality. I touched on everything from ways to improve freshmen orientations and beef up mentorship programs to the best ways to keep your Cadillac shining.

The section that still sticks with me today is "50 Reasons to Vote for Randall Woodfin for Prez":

No. 8: He's the only candidate who has a working relationship with Deans Gaffney, Nimes, Phifer, and Blackburn and Gloster Hall.

No. 21: He's the only candidate who has ever organized a successful Town Hall meeting.

No. 26: White Hall 1999–2000 Alumnus: Come on, you know who got it crunk.

No. 44: He has watched *Friday, Money Talk, Rush Hour,* and *Rush Hour II* 1,000 times.

Tangible results, the crunkest parties, and Chris Tucker movies. I had it locked.

My campaign theme was simple: Building community through servant leadership—sound familiar? It's the same theme I use today as mayor of Birmingham.

I won with 70 percent of the vote.

Being SGA president was like being quarterback of an SEC team. And though I wasn't the best orator, I knew how to connect with people, especially younger students. I did not give soul-stirring speeches, but I had no problem popping in on students while they played video games—dorm room smelling like feet and corn chips—to offer guidance and direction.

Leadership is also standing firm, ten toes down, even in the most challenging situations.

During my senior year, when our SGA charter was snatched for raising awareness around the attack on our fellow student, we did not wilt. Instead, we planned a protest at Kilgore Hall at the same time a meeting of Morehouse's Board of Trustees was taking place.

Scheduled to attend that trustee meeting were the president, the dean, and Morehouse board member and alum Spike Lee. Spike was cut from the same cloth as us—outspoken and unwavering in his beliefs.

The next morning, at 7:00 a.m., hours before our protest, the dean came to my dorm and made one last plea to stand down. We refused.

Spike stood with us.

He told leadership that we had every right to speak out and that the school was unjust in taking the charter.

If the dean thought we were going to stand down after getting the co-sign of one of the greatest filmmakers and activists in Black cinema, he better Get on the Bus. (My bad, I couldn't resist.)

Not only did we move forward with the protest, but we also got our charter back.

It was at Morehouse where I began to dedicate myself to servant leadership.

Let me break down the term.

The servant leadership movement was founded by Robert K. Greenleaf in the 1960s. Greenleaf believed that the usual power-centered authoritarian leadership structure was flawed and didn't do enough to empower the constituents under a leader's care.

Instead of traditional leadership, which positions one figure as the singular head that controls operations, servant leadership is truly power to the people.

Servant leaders work for the good of their team and constituents, hearing others' needs and helping them develop their skills so that they, too, may lead one day.

It's not about power. It's empowerment. Sowing seeds.

Servant leadership is what kept us united during the controversy over the SGA charter. I made very clear that this conflict wasn't Woodfin vs. Morehouse leadership. My goal was to use my position to elevate the voices of our student body so that justice could be heard.

Listening. Empathy. Empowering constituents. Building community.

I wanted our student body to have tools necessary to face adversity long after I was gone from the Morehouse campus.

I wasn't there to rule. I was there to serve.

And it's exactly how we run city government today.

I'm proud of my school for standing strong against a very powerful administration. And I hope Spike was proud of us, too.

Aside from the drama with the SGA charter, my junior and senior years were wild rides. I was one of the first SGA presidents who didn't use SGA funds to pay for my dorm—mainly because we'd exhausted our money before the year was out.

Prior administrations used a large chunk of those funds for SGA housing. Add in expenditures for big events like homecoming, and SGA's pockets would look like rabbit ears by spring. So I decided that our administration would not use SGA budget dollars for leadership housing on campus.

(Being a good steward of other people's money is yet another guiding principle of servant leadership.)

Even though there were some challenging days, I mainly remember the fun times. I met rappers, dignitaries, elected officials, and more. When the Cash Money Millionaires showed up for a concert, I snuck into their warm-up area and got all their autographs—Lil Wayne, Juvenile, Slim, Turk, Birdman, Mannie, the whole crew.

I was also a part of the Oprah Winfrey Endowed Scholars Program during senior year. I was one of more than three hundred grads who were invited to fly out and surprise her on her final show. It was an amazing experience—we met Tom Cruise, Tom Hanks, Jamie Foxx, Michael Jordan, and even got to see Beyoncé and Patti LaBelle perform. Getting to interact with so many artists who shaped my love of pop culture was exhilarating.

Sure, I met Oprah Winfrey—"Queen of All Media"—and a roster of stars while I was in college. But it was hard to keep up with TV shows and even movies while experiencing campus life. Never gave up on my music, though. Specifically, this was the era when the Neptunes captured my entire being. Pharrell Williams and Chad Hugo were sonic geniuses, lacing everyone from Britney Spears to Snoop Dogg with hit after hit. Futuristic and funky.

Jay-Z seemed to drop new music annually, so I usually devoured whatever he put on our plates. But you know I had to rep the South. Cash Money Records continued to take over for '99 and the 2000s. Juvenile's *400 Degreez*, Big Tymers' *How You Luv That*, all the Hot Boyz albums—producer Mannie Fresh was basically the DJ for my college experience.

I've gotta show love to those No Limit Soldiers, too. And I was obsessed with any chopped and screwed tracks—a Houston staple of hip-hop that slowed tracks down to a crawl, producing the most mind-bending remixes you could imagine. It was a great time to be a Southern hip-hop fan.

I can't front—with all the distractions, I began to lose my way academically. I rebounded at the eleventh hour, pulling my GPA above 3.0. But by this time, I realized I had fallen into the same trap as countless other upperclassmen—I poured so much of myself into Morehouse that I hadn't properly planned for life outside of Morehouse.

Some of my friends were heading to the military, others planning to conquer Wall Street, and others taking PCATs and MCATs ahead of medical school.

I didn't have any of those type of CATS in my future. I was so caught up in the Yard, student government, being a friend, being a leader, that I didn't know my next play.

I hadn't invested in my future.

So, I thought hard, and by the time I graduated in May 2003, I knew what I wanted my destination to be. I had already announced my intentions to the world eight months earlier in that *Ebony* magazine—I wanted to be the mayor of Birmingham.

I knew the destination, but the road I would travel was very unclear.

Still, I was confident about one thing—no matter how long it would take me to achieve that dream, Morehouse College had already equipped me with the tools to make it a reality.

Morehouse sent a man back to Birmingham.

———

I'm proud to be a member of Alpha Phi Alpha Fraternity. Those brothers made me who I am and they never left my side. Their overwhelming support during my two mayoral campaigns is a big reason why you're reading this book today.

I had the great honor to address them during the Chicago Constitutional Convention in the summer of 2024, just as the presidential election season was heating up, and divisive rhetoric began burning through social media feeds.

I used the opportunity to remind them of what they've instilled in me—that there is no more urgent time to lead than right now.

To the brothers of Alpha Phi Alpha.

To General President Willis L. Lonzer III and Immediate Past General President Everett B. Ward.

To all the past general presidents joining us today, along with friends and supporters.

I'm honored to be in your presence as your brother, as your peer, as a fellow leader.

And on that theme of leadership, today's luncheon couldn't be more timely.

This is a day where we celebrate the aspects of servant leadership. We thank the incredible work of our outgoing leadership team and we stand in encouragement of the incoming team leaders who are ready to serve and uphold the values that have guided our walk for the past 117 years.

First of All.

Servants of All.

We Shall Transcend All.

But to the incoming leaders, to those outgoing leaders, and to the brothers who will soon lead us one day, I bring a very important message to you today:

Beyond our chapters, beyond these four walls, even beyond our individual communities,

Our nation is in dire need of your leadership.

Right here. And right now.

I proudly serve as mayor of my hometown, Birmingham, Alabama. As you all know, it's a city with a deeply complicated past. But it's a past we own. We don't run from it.

Because with every black-and-white photo you see of Black bodies being drenched by fire hoses . . .

of well-dressed brothers and sisters being assaulted by corrupt law enforcement . . .

of children being called unspeakable names while simply walking down the street . . .

There's a more vibrant picture that is too often missed.

A portrait of men and women rising up in the face of oppression. Standing firm in their faith. Refusing to bend to the intimidation of cowards.

From the seasoned Civil Rights icons who led marches across Birmingham's streets, to the children who skipped school to participate in rallies so that their future kids might one day know freedom.

Birmingham is not a city of victims. It's a city of victors.

Singing. Marching. Praying. Voting.

A fierce, defiant people.

A city of leaders.

Here's why that lesson is so important today.

Sixty years after the landmark change brought about by the Civil Rights Movement in Birmingham, our country is reaching another crossroads.

Now, I know you've heard people say during the last few presidential election cycles, "This is the most important election of our lifetime."

You hear it so much that it goes in one ear and out the other.

And since I have your attention, let me say it louder for the people in the back.

My brothers, "this is the most important election of our lifetime."

Just look at what we're facing as a nation.

States attempting to pass voter ID and absentee ballot limits, raising disenfranchisement especially in underserved communities. We're seeing the blatant and disgusting policing of women's bodies.

And just a few weeks ago, we saw an unprecedented Supreme Court ruling that could give the president of the United States immunity from prosecution, putting the presidency itself above the law.

It's funny because I thought one of the reasons America was founded was to get away from kings, not create our own.

The rights that so many in Birmingham bravely risked their lives for just sixty years ago are quickly and blatantly being stripped away.

Leaders of Alpha Phi Alpha:

The portrait of progress that is Birmingham's true legacy . . .

You are cut from that same cloth, painted by that same brush.

The same vibrancy that defined the legacy of our brothers Martin Luther King Jr., NAACP founder W. E. B. Du Bois, Justice Thurgood Marshall, and so many others.

So hear me when I say this: Our nation needs your leadership. Right here. And right now.

Our nation needs a refresher on its past, and how victory for our people began with the vote.

We cannot forget that lesson.

The opps know it's the most important weapon in our arsenal—and that's why they're working so hard to take it away.

We must remind our people of that critical fact.

As this election looms, we must push back against the threat of disenfranchisement, especially among our elderly community. We must work to silence the rampant misinformation that floods our social media feeds by uplifting factual stories about the realities of our communities.

Some call it critical race theory. I just call it history. Regardless, it must be remembered and upheld. The whitewashing and erasure of the Black experience must not stand. To do so is an utter form of disrespect to the men and women who sacrificed so much so that we could stand here today.

Hear me when I say this: Apathy is the enemy of our democracy.

But the vote? The vote is the gateway to equality. To justice. To representation.

To freedom.

Our brother Dr. King once said: "Give us the ballot and we will no longer have to worry the federal government about our basic rights.

"Give us the ballot and we will fill our legislative halls with men of good will.

"Give us the ballot and we will place judges on the benches of the South who will do justly and love mercy."

To simplify Dr. King's poetic words, the ballot is our deliverance.

But to bring it 2024, my good brother Kendrick Lamar also said: "Sometimes you gotta pop out and show 'em."

He actually said more than that, but we'll leave it right there for now. If you know, you know.

My brothers of Alpha Phi Alpha, we can no longer have a DoorDash mentality for government, where we sit on our couch and expect justice to be hand-delivered to our doorstep.

Nah, it's time to pop out and show 'em.

We must be an army, boots on the ground—a sea of black and gold soldiers marching with the same fire and passion as those foot soldiers on the streets of Birmingham six decades ago.

In a few weeks we'll be welcoming my first child into this world.

And I refuse to allow our child to enter a world that stands in defiance of the freedom and liberties our forefathers and foremothers fought for.

Alpha Phi Alpha taught me better. Birmingham taught me better.

So, for the sake of our present, and for the sake our future:

We must lead.

Alpha Phi Alpha, this is our legacy. Leading from the front. Being advocates for the underserved. Reminding our communities that change starts at home but takes root at the polls.

My brothers, answer the call. Let's lead.

Thank you.

Randall L. Woodfin, Mayor
Alpha Phi Alpha Fraternity, Inc.
Chicago Constitutional Convention
July 2024

CHAPTER 5

RETURN OF THE "G"

Ride with me on this one.

Kid leaves his hometown to attend the college of his dreams, with nothing with him but a few clothes and wide-eyed ambition.

Four years later, when he crosses back into Birmingham's city limits, he's a young man, wiser, a diploma in hand, and a bit more swagger. He's one step closer to accomplishing his dream—to one day become mayor of his hometown.

So what's his game plan?

Well, as that young man sat in his friend Kelli's downtown Birmingham living room, pondering the strategy to achieve his career goal, only four words came to mind:

Hell if I know.

I wish I could tell you about my grand master plan to come back to Birmingham and insert myself into the political arena, to infiltrate the system, inject it with fresh blood, and position myself as a rising leader.

But y'all are reading this book for the real story, right?

Here's the real—I spent so much time living in the present at Morehouse College that I didn't think to plan for the future—for life on the other side of campus.

So, as I packed my Morehouse life into my Cadillac and rolled down I-20, I knew I was headed straight into my wilderness experience.

First, allow me to take you to church real quick. Church in the wild, so to speak.

In the Bible, there are various examples of wilderness experiences. The one I relate to the most is the story of Moses. After he freed the Israelites from slavery—parting the Red Sea in the process—he planned to take his crew to God's promised land.

Thing is, it took forty years for them to get there.

Imagine thinking you were finally getting a breakthrough moment in life, the freedom you always wanted, the new start God promised you, only to spend four decades wandering directionless in a sweltering desert.

My friend Kelli's place was definitely no desert—shout-out to both her and her mom for some great meals; they get down in the kitchen—but I still felt just as lost as the Israelites.

However, I found inspiration in another scripture—Ezekiel 25:17. But this message came from a completely different spiritual leader, the Rev. Dr. Samuel L. Jackson.

My Morehouse brother may be known as one of the biggest actors in the world today, but his road was much bumpier than you probably realize.

While at Morehouse, Jackson switched majors from marine biology to architecture before falling in love with drama. He'd spend the next few years post-college honing his craft in stage plays before being hindered by drug and alcohol addiction, which ultimately cost him two Broadway plays.

Those kinds of wilderness experiences aren't just demoralizing. They can be lethal.

But you can't keep Morehouse men down. Jackson would connect with fellow alum Spike Lee, who found small roles for him in classic films like 1988's *School Daze* and *Do the Right Thing* the following year.

That was just a taste of what was to come. Jackson's true breakout moment was as the scripture-quoting madman Jules Winnfield in Quentin Tarantino's 1994 masterpiece, *Pulp Fiction*. His Ezekiel 25:17 monologue—which takes quite a bit of creative license with the true scripture—is the stuff of cinematic legend.

Pulp Fiction became the oasis in Jackson's long-journeyed desert. Mace Windu in the Star Wars franchise, Nick Fury in the Marvel Cinematic Universe, the FBI agent who was yelling about snakes on a plane in, um, *Snakes on a Plane*—Jackson went from his own personal hell to a legit Black superhero, one of the highest-paid actors in the game today.

I was no Nick Fury—there were no Avengers set to fight my battles for me.

I had political experience, yes. I'd spent the year 2000 interning on Capitol Hill, and the following summer, I interned for the Seventh Congressional District office. I spent the following years sharpening my political skills as SGA president.

But I still didn't have a clear path.

There were only two options—sit in the wilderness or find my oasis.

And, lucky me, I didn't just find one oasis, but two.

Oasis No. 1: Birmingham's Division of Youth Services.

Back in 1992, a Youth Advisory Commission was formed in Birmingham to address some of the biggest challenges youth faced at the time, including education, gang violence, substance abuse, and unemployment.

The Division of Youth Services, or DYS, was born out of that effort. Not only did DYS develop support and enrichment programs for youth, it also became known for its Kids & Jobs program.

If you were a kid looking for summer employment, DYS was your hookup. And since I had a heart for both children and education—going way back to my days volunteering at Atlanta schools while at Morehouse—I figured it might be a good fit for me.

At that time, DYS was led by Cedric Sparks. I didn't know Cedric personally, but I was familiar with his work—he was known around town as an incredibly engaging speaker. Also, I knew Cedric was an Alpha, like me, so I decided to shoot my shot.

I rolled up to DYS in my trusty Cadillac, introduced myself to Cedric and his team, and, soon after, I was part of the team, as a member of the executive-level internship program.

Remember the *Ebony* magazine with Usher on the cover? Cedric had read the article inside that featured me during my days as SGA president, so he was already familiar with me. Because of that article, he was familiar with my ultimate goal of one day becoming mayor of Birmingham.

Cedric would later admit that he took it upon himself to protect my dream. My brother Cedric had foresight—he knew that a young man announcing that he was returning to his hometown to someday run for mayor might upset the political apple cart. Some might seek to squash a potential political adversary out of the gate; others might try to use me as a tool for their own political gains. I had unwittingly put a target on my back, but Cedric was wise enough to protect me, long before I knew I needed it.

It certainly wouldn't be the last time Cedric would have my back.

For the next year, DYS would be my home away from home. I wasn't making a ton of money, but I loved working with youth, whether it was setting up interviews for the Kids & Jobs program or just doing odd jobs around the office. The dreams of these kids—and the roadblocks that were stopping them from achieving them—would become major agenda items in my political career years later.

Long after I moved on from DYS, I always stopped by to show love. I even continued to volunteer there while serving on the school board. And after becoming mayor, I gave DYS a long-overdue upgrade.

No longer was it the Division of Youth Services. I approved making it, officially, the Department of Youth Services. It might seem like semantics on the surface, but words matter. DYS put in just as much work and made just as much change in our city as other departments linked to the mayor's office, so it, too, deserved to be a department.

DYS gave me a glow-up. It was only right to return the favor.

Oasis No. 2: Birmingham City Council.

I knew I wanted to make City Hall my base of operations one day. Why not get a head start?

One day in the summer of 2003, I took the elevator up to the third floor of City Hall and knocked on the door of Lee Loder, president of the Birmingham city council. He was a Birmingham Municipal Court judge as well as founder of the Loder Law Firm. And most importantly, he was a fellow Morehouse brother.

My ask of Judge Loder was pretty direct—I wanted to learn more about city government, and I hoped to do that under his wing. He obliged, and the timing couldn't have been more perfect.

It was an election year, and Judge Loder was one of more than a dozen candidates challenging incumbent mayor Bernard Kincaid. I had a front-row seat to just how raw Birmingham politics could be.

The campaign was arduous. I learned that there were fine lines in campaigning—you couldn't be too timid (which is perceived as weak) but you also couldn't be too abrasive (which looks like bullying).

I wasn't anti-Kincaid. Honestly, I was pretty agnostic toward his administration—I didn't have strong feelings for or against him. It was more important that I support the home team. I was riding with my Morehouse brother. I stood by his side, even when he went down in defeat.

All of the drama of that race was popcorn-worthy, but I looked beyond the foolishness and soaked up every bit of knowledge I could. A decade later, I'd be on a ballot myself. That on-the-job training paid off.

Working at DYS and on the city council were an encouraging start for my political aspirations, but a brother had to eat—I needed to bring in more money. Plus, I still had that service bug in me from my days working at Western Supermarket.

The solution?

Meet the new bellman at the Sheraton Birmingham hotel downtown.

Most days, I was scheduled to work at DYS from eight to four but I'd get the OK to leave a little early to spend my evenings at the Sheraton from four to ten.

I approached that job the same way I did at my grocery gig. Meet people where they are. Be kind. Be observant to their needs. Actually listen when they talk.

And, oh yeah, in case you forgot, be kind.

I had my lil' name tag, my tight lil' vest straight from a 1993 Jodeci video, and a big smile on my face.

It wasn't a front. I really did enjoy serving.

Y'all know how it is when you're checking into a hotel. If you've spent the day traveling, most likely you're tired. My job was to make sure the little things were handled so our guests could focus on settling in and relaxing. I made sure that valeted vehicles were taken care of. I tried to take their bags up to their room as quickly as possible.

And that service paid off. The tips were nice.

My best tip came from a bunch of musicians who were checking in just before a big show. Not only did they break me off with $100, but they were so impressed with my service that they invited me to their show at the BJCC Arena.

That show? Prince. Rogers. Nelson.

Unfortunately, I had to decline—I was still on the clock, after all. But I called my mom and basically said, "Get down here. You're going to see Prince."

She made her way downtown faster than a little red Corvette.

At some point, I did sneak away from work and into the show. I don't remember what song Prince was playing, but I do remember those high heels he was wearing.

The moral of the story—treat everyone you come across well. Your mom might get to see a music icon for free. (Also because it's the right thing to do n' stuff.)

By the fall of 2003, I knew I needed more. DYS and City Hall were keeping my ear to the political streets and the Sheraton kept the 'Lac gassed up, but I still felt like I was too far away from my goals.

My political science degree from Morehouse didn't seem like it was enough to advance my career. Although I had no desire to be a lawyer, I looked into the juris doctor program at the Cumberland School of Law at Samford University in Homewood, Alabama. I considered going for a master's in public policy or public administration, but the JD program was more appealing due to its flexibility. I hoped it would give me a deeper understanding of law—specifically how it directly affects communities—which could help me down the line in the political arena.

I took the LSAT and by 2004, a year removed from undergrad, I was at Cumberland, a student once again.

Too bad I was a subpar student.

Of 170 law students, only 19 were Black. And man, I was probably near the bottom of that bunch.

I had a clear understanding of criminal law. But everything else? I was lucky to get Cs and Ds. I could have had Matlock, Perry Mason, and Maxine Shaw, Attorney at Law, as my tutors and I would still be riding in the back of the struggle bus.

And I knew exactly what the problem was—I didn't have a passion for law. I just wanted a degree. And while I loved engaging with other students, I didn't have the same community I had at Morehouse. Everything felt off, and I felt like I made the wrong decision.

I went to the dean and asked him to sign papers so I could withdraw from school. He did, but I never submitted them. And it's all thanks to the Fulton County district attorney's office.

That was God's grace in action. My breakthrough was just around the corner.

In the summer of 2005, I went back to Atlanta to intern at the Fulton County DA's office in the appellate division. Here's where I really started to see doors opening in my favor.

While working at the office, law was no longer just a means to an end for me. I saw the importance of Black prosecutors.

Prosecutors in general get a bad rap. I get it; it comes with the territory. But having Black faces on that side of the law is essential. We can better converse and connect with faces that look like our own. By learning the law and understanding the use of discretionary power, we can make a difference in the lives of Black people—my people—who are so often devoured by the system.

In essence, that's what I wanted to do with my political career—be an advocate for those who were unable to fight for themselves. The system has its fair share of innocent people who wind up in unfair circumstances, as well as guilty parties who receive sentences that are much harsher than they deserve. As a prosecutor, I was guided by the word *discretion*—it allowed me to not see defendants as criminals, but as people. My goal wasn't vengeance, it was to set people back on the right path.

Finally, this law thing clicked.

I took that energy back to Cumberland for my second year. Honestly, I still didn't want to be a full-time lawyer, but if that was destined to be my path, criminal law was where I needed to be. By the summer of 2006, I was working as an intern for the City of Birmingham's law department. I got exposed to courtroom and jury trials while there.

Legal street wasn't the road I expected to be on, but I knew I was there for a reason. Why not enjoy the ride?

That ride's soundtrack was a bit of a sonic detour, taking me down previously unexplored roads. Post Morehouse I was in a bit of an emotional funk as I tried to figure out life, and my musical tastes reflected that. Maroon 5, John Mayer, Linkin Park—I was turning emo.

But I always kept it hip-hop. This era coincided with the rise of Jeezy—his music was everywhere, and I soaked it up, raspy ad-libs and all. Same for T.I., as he was staking his claim as king of the South. However, they all paled in comparison to N.E.R.D., the rock band formed by production gurus the Neptunes. I loved them so much that I got a car tag that read NSRCHOF, after their *In Search Of* debut album.

. . .

OK, I've confessed to my Emo phase, but I have another confession to make. I've been holding back a little bit of truth from y'all. You bought this book, so I have to keep it 100 with you.

I didn't attend law school only because of my political aspirations, or because of my growing interest in criminal law. Part of the reason was for a girl.

I grew up with a girl named Natalie; we were close since childhood. She'd be in church with her pigtails and white stockings; I'd have on my slacks with the crease down the leg with the matching church shoes.

Our friendship blossomed into something more while we were in college, and we began dating during my junior year. I was excited—I could really see a future with her. But things were tough right out of the gate. I was attending Morehouse in Atlanta; she was at Georgetown in DC. Two college kids attempting to make a long-distance relationship work—yeah, that's really, really tough. It didn't help that our parents weren't very supportive of our relationship.

Her decision to attend law school at Emory was a big influence on me, especially since I was still wandering in that wilderness at the time, trying to find a path to my own Promised Land. At that point, my focus wasn't on political or professional aspirations—my only dream was for us to be together. If that meant mimicking her law school aspirations, so be it.

After I finished law school, I didn't feel like I was any closer to that Promised Land than before. Once again, everyone was patting me on the back for completing an educational milestone, but, once again, I didn't have a job or clear direction. And I didn't have my girl by my side either.

Natalie and I briefly split—I casually dated for a bit—but I eventually went back to her. She was one of the few constants I had in this sea of uncertainty.

Desperate men do desperate things, so I turned to the CIA.

Not for help, for employment.

The application said I'd be out of the country for at least three years.

I said, "Aight, cool."

I was also told that, afterward, I'd be outside of the US 80 percent of the year.

I said, "Aight, cool."

Then I learned that I would not be able to choose the country I would be stationed in.

I said, "*Nope.*"

So the CIA was out.

I tried to find comfort in the arms of Natalie, but this time she wasn't having it. We cut things off and my heart was shattered.

In the aftermath of that heartbreak, I took and failed the Georgia bar.

That forty years in the wilderness was starting to feel like four hundred years.

By 2007—four years out of Morehouse and four months after law school—I was still looking for the next step in my political career. With nothing to lose, I packed up and headed to Washington, DC, to work with an organization called SEG Strategic Consulting Group. Essentially, they provided professional campaign training for emerging candidates.

Despite the setbacks with law school, Natalie, and every other roadblock I ran into headfirst since leaving Morehouse, my ultimate goal of becoming mayor was still just out of arm's reach. I felt like this training could be a stepping stone to get me just a bit closer.

Around the same time, an upstart candidate in Chicago by the name of Barack Obama—maybe you've heard of him a time or two—was making waves in the realm of field organizing. I had taken a similar path, learning the basics of financing, management, and fundraising. I quickly learned that campaigning is the cross section of art and math—connecting with people creatively and crunching numbers.

I was thrust into an existing congressional campaign in Prince George's County, Maryland, for candidate Donna Edwards. That December of '07 felt like the coldest winter—and not just because my man Pimp C of the legendary rap duo UGK died, leaving a hole in the soul of every Southern rap fan. It was also because Maryland winter weather was absolutely frigid. I stayed warm by staying busy—setting up events, planning fieldwork for the campaign, analyzing data. It was a crash course in campaigning.

But I didn't stay on the campaign long. My heart was back in Birmingham, and home was calling.

I returned in January 2008 with the clearest focus I'd ever had.

I moved to a loft downtown (with zero idea of how I'd be able to keep up with the rent) and launched the Veritas Group to serve as a consultant and professional campaigner.

The first race I worked on was in the spring of 2008 for Shanta Owens—for free. Shanta ran for district criminal court judge in Jefferson County, Alabama. She went on to win her race and still serves as a criminal court judge in Alabama. Her twin sister, Shera, would later win a seat as a civil court judge in the same county. Now, it wasn't about making money at this point. It was about proving myself. I knew there was a path for victory if we effectively studied and applied the lessons we learned from analyzing campaign data. It was a numbers game, and we leaned on a combination of data-driven research and boots-on-the-ground campaigning to find success.

I then worked with Clyde Jones, who ran for the statewide Court of Criminal Appeals, which is one level below the Alabama state supreme court. We won his primary race.

Things finally started coming together. Based on those two wins, I became the go-to guy to support judges who ran for criminal law seats. I even branched outside of Birmingham, supporting candidates in areas like rural South Carolina.

Around this time, I decided to take the bar again—this time failing by two pitiful points. I was devastated once again but I was beginning to learn a very valuable lesson—good things will come in time.

I took the bar one last time and, honestly, didn't even look at the results. A friend and law school classmate, Jennifer Reid, somehow got the news, called me, and said, "You weren't going to tell me you passed?" I replied, "I didn't even know I had!" Going to Montgomery to be sworn in as a lawyer, with my mom, dad, sisters, and brother-in-law by my side, was one of the happiest moments I'd had in a very long time.

Now that I was officially a lawyer, I split my time between working on campaigns and serving as a city attorney. I became a contract lawyer for Birmingham, working with folks who couldn't make bond or bail.

Even today, I run into people who say "you were my lawyer when I had a situation going on, thank you." It means a lot. I've always wanted to serve my city, to be a voice for its residents and an advocate for change. But I never thought law would be one of the paths that would help me achieve that.

Hindsight always provides us with clearer vision, and that's why I embrace my wilderness experience.

When you're in the middle of the desert, you're often so busy searching for an escape route that you don't realize you're attaining survival skills to guide you on the next stage of your journey.

- Gaining a better understanding of Birmingham youth's needs at DYS

- Getting a front-row seat for Birmingham politics at city council

- Sharpening my customer service skills at the Sheraton

- Gaining an understanding of criminal law at Cumberland, my internships, and City Hall work

- Learning the art of field organizing and campaigning both in Birmingham and beyond

- And overcoming personal setbacks and heartbreak along the way

That's why I never judge a graduate who is uncertain about their future following graduation. Hell, I *was* that student. It just makes me that much more dedicated to finding a path for them.

Speaking of paths, I found my next journey while attending a Birmingham school board meeting. If you've seen the 1995 movie *Braveheart* (another of my favorites, by the way), just picture the Battle of Stirling every week.

Grown folks were at each other's throats while Birmingham City Schools were losing accreditation.

I couldn't just watch. I had to step in and help build a better school board, for the sake of those kids I served at DYS.

It was a long shot, but life in the wilderness makes you feel bulletproof. Challenge accepted.

It's always good to go home again. In May 2022, I returned to Cumberland School of Law to speak to graduates. But I wanted to be very real, very transparent to those students. While at Cumberland, it took me a long time to find my purpose. I walked through those doors looking for direction, and I struggled when those answers didn't come easily.

Here was my challenge to them—in all things in your life, find your why. Achieve that, and you will achieve clarity.

Good afternoon, graduates.

It's so good to be here with you today and, I'm happy to say, it's also so good to be back home.

Stepping back here on campus took me back to my days as a student here. Back when I was blasting songs from my favorite artists like Linkin Park, Maroon 5, and John Legend. I know I'm dating myself, but those songs were hot.

One of those artists, in fact, had a song that in an indirect way made me realign my focus when I was floundering as a student. Because it was that great musical philosopher Clifford T.I. Harris, who asked listeners at that time:

"Why you wanna do that, love huh? Why You Wanna Do that?"

Today, that's what I'm here to ask you, graduates.

What *is* your why?

Let me state the obvious.

Lawyers make a difference. Whether you're a defense attorney or prosecutor, whether you represent a victim of crime or represent an organization, you are the shield. You are the protector. You were made to defend.

Despite that fundamental truth, sometimes we are so consumed with the when and where and the how that we miss that important question—the why.

That's a lesson I had to learn.

I took a year off from school to figure out my why. Truth is, y'all, after I finished undergrad with a political science degree, I was lost. I didn't know what I wanted to do.

I had not yet come to terms with my why.

I came here to Cumberland for answers, and truthfully, those answers did not come easily. I struggled, mainly because I wasn't sure if I really wanted to *be* a lawyer. I even went to the dean and asked to withdraw.

That is, until I took a summer internship in Atlanta. And it was there I found answers.

That's where I learned my why.

It was there that I was reminded that, as a son of Birmingham, I had a heart for social justice. It was in my DNA. I knew the importance of truth, of being a voice for those who can't speak. For being a sword and shield for those needing protection.

I was inspired by men like the Rev. Fred Shuttlesworth, a freedom fighter from the very streets of the Magic City who endured beatings and home bombings while saying loudly and proudly:

"We will no longer stand back while the future beckons us on."

It was through years of challenges and misdirection that I finally found my why.

I was destined to be a servant leader. I was destined to protect my community—those who live in it and for generations to come.

My why became my truth.

So, today, I ask you, graduates. What is your why?

Here's the beauty of it, though—if you haven't determined your why yet, it's not too late.

Some of you are here because you were encouraged by your parents. For others, maybe you wanted to make money. Still others might just want the prestige of being called esquire.

But that's not enough.

That's not enough when you're sworn to serve a community that is hurting. When communities of color are being afflicted daily by unjust laws. When internal strife is tearing families apart. When our neighbors are being denied their constitutional rights. When innocents are victimized by abuse and crime.

It's not enough to be a lawyer because of fame or obligation.

Your why has to be stronger. It has to run deeper.

I can't tell you your why. Each journey is different. But I can tell you how to achieve it.

You achieve it by connecting with the communities you serve. You cannot expect to be a voice for the unheard when you aren't listening to what *they* are saying.

You achieve it by finding your passion. Like I did in Atlanta, realize what it is that motivates you to make change every day. When you live out your why, people can't say lawyers are jerks who only care about cash and billable hours. Learn what motivates you and let that drive you forward.

You achieve it by being real with yourself. Each of you has a story, a journey, a path that brought you to this moment. Use those experiences to build upon the next steps of your career. What injustices have you seen? What flaws have you seen or experienced in our system that need change? Don't turn a blind eye to your past; use those experiences as a road map to guide your journey ahead.

You achieve your why by embracing your truth.

Dr. King once shared this:

I believe that unarmed truth and unconditional love will have the final word in reality. THIS IS WHY RIGHT TEM-PORARILY DEFEATED IS STRONGER THAN EVIL TRIUMPHANT.

No matter if it's delayed by evil legislation, political interests, unjust laws, or systemic racism, I firmly believe that unarmed truth will never be denied. Eventually, no matter how slow, no matter what attempts to derail it, truth always wins.

I'm confident in that because I know my why. I know that my time here at Cumberland put me on the path to open doors.

To protect.

To lead.

To serve my community.

And I'm confident in all of you graduates as well. Because all of us have walked this same path, on this same campus . . .

. . . probably had the same meal plan . . .

. . . and I *know* paying those same student loans . . . whew . . .

Let your why be the catalyst for change.

Listen to your clients and community. Hear their cries. Build bridges and kick down the barriers of injustice and intolerance.

Be more than a well-paid employee. Be the difference our world so desperately needs.

Have no doubt that your community is behind you every step of the way. Because you are born leaders.

You are born changemakers.

You are born defenders of truth and protectors of the law.

That's your why.

Congratulations, graduates, let's get to work.

Randall L. Woodfin, Mayor
Cumberland School of Law Commencement Address
May 2022

CHAPTER 6

KNOWING

One of my greatest joys as president of Birmingham's Board of Education was to stand onstage with high school graduates as they walked into the next chapter of their lives.

It was also one of my greatest frustrations.

As the students lined up to walk the stage and receive their hard-earned diplomas, I'd often ask, "So, what's next for you?"

They'd stare. They'd stammer. And in most cases, they'd just make something up—all to please an adult they didn't really know.

This wasn't about me; it was about their future. And I wanted better for our students.

As you read, I was in their shoes not too long before them. When I received my degree from Morehouse College, my future was about as clear as a bowling ball.

I've spoken a lot in this book about my own wilderness journey and, sure, there are many lessons that can be learned while navigating uncertainty. However, there's an even greater chance to be discouraged, derailed, and possibly broken by it. We never want our kids to stumble down the same jagged roads that hindered us. We want better for them.

As a leader, I refuse to let another young graduate's potential be clouded by life's uncertainties. Not on my watch.

Birmingham's graduates deserved clear, well-defined options, whether that was in the workforce or seeking higher education. Likewise, Birmingham's employers deserved a direct pipeline for fresh, bright, energetic, homegrown talent.

Those graduates deserved more than a handshake and a piece of paper, only to send them on their merry way directionless. We helped guide those young minds for twelve years—why stop now? I wasn't going to let them roam in the wilderness like I had to do.

We had to give these kids a future. That was my promise to them.

Educators are the unsung heroes of this country.

It's easy to say that teachers mold young minds, but that's like saying Pharrell Williams makes beats sometimes. There's a lot more to the process than that.

Teachers are surrogate parents. They're family therapists. They're mediators and conflict-resolution experts, diffusing all sorts of drama inside and outside of classrooms. They're often on-call nurses when accidents occur. Many became tech experts when the 2020 pandemic suddenly forced education to be virtual. They're the gentle hand when a delicate touch is required, and they're the tough love when it's time to keep it real.

And they certainly don't do it for the money. The pay is disrespectful. They do it because they love their students.

I was grateful to be surrounded by educators. My stepmom was a high school math teacher for thirty-three years. And my mom, who worked at AT&T for nearly three decades, left her job to pursue a career in education at age fifty. She went on to serve as a second-grade teacher for eleven years.

Here's a lesson from Mama Woodfin: Never be afraid to walk away from something you've done for something you want to do. Age be damned.

People said I was too young and inexperienced to be mayor. Glad I listened to my mom and not other people.

Besides my connection to the educators in my life, my stint at the Division of Youth Services also made me keenly aware—and hypersensitive—to the issues facing our young people.

I could see the cracks in Birmingham's education system, specifically how it seemed like our kids weren't being put on a path for success. They were just being funneled through a system. It was a bare bones approach to academics that wasn't nurturing our students. It was more or less "get in, get your degree, and get out."

I could complain about it, or I could be the change.

So I ran for the school board in 2009. And I caught the biggest L.

I got my butt handed to me in that race.

Looking back, my inexperience got the better of me. I didn't have enough money to campaign districtwide for the empty seat, so I focused all my energy on one precinct. The approach I used was the same one I had used at Morehouse while running for SGA president, and later in my mayoral campaign. I knocked on doors. I stood on dozens of porches. I shut my mouth and opened my ears to the concerns of residents.

I won that precinct. I lost everywhere else.

Fear, and its little homeboy doubt, love to run rampant when we're at our lowest. I had every reason to believe that this campaign was a waste of time. That I was too young or out of my league.

I thought back to performers like 2Pac and the Fugees—artists whose first albums didn't make much of a mark, but by the second and third go-rounds, they were megastars.

As much as we love and rightfully celebrate Michael and Janet Jackson, they did not start off with *Off the Wall* and *Control*. Their first albums were *Got to Be There* in 1972 and Janet's self-titled album in '82. MJ's first album was solid but far from a classic. Janet's debut, well, not even that. Sorry, Ms. Janet.

Regardless, my point still stands—music's biggest legends, even with their well-established names and family pedigree—had to grind before they reached their potential.

Nothing worth having comes easy.

So, to rebound from that loss, I had to Start Anew, Workin' Day and Night. The OG Jacksons fans will feel me on that one.

Yeah, I took an L, and I owned it. But you can't spell *landslide* without an L. That's what I was aiming for next time.

If at first you don't succeed, dust yourself off and try again.

Aaliyah taught us that in 2000.

And this time, I'm comin' out hard.

8Ball & MJG taught us that back in 1993.

Although I lost my first chance at the school board, I never lost my hunger to bring change to Birmingham schools. I stayed involved in all things education, becoming a member of the Birmingham Change Fund, the Birmingham Education Foundation, and STAIR, a child-hood literacy nonprofit that encourages a love of reading in first- and second-graders.

As a voracious reader myself, STAIR's mission hit home.

I attended school board meetings twice a month. I raised my voice about issues plaguing our youth.

And I was patient. I knew my time was coming.

When the calendar flipped to 2012 and it was time for another school board race, I took an honest assessment of all that went wrong in the previous campaign, and what I could now do to reestablish myself.

It came down to three big flaws I'd have to rectify:

1. I didn't have enough money.
2. Besides the neighborhood of Gate City, the one precinct I won, few people knew my name.

3. I didn't have a team.

I figured out a way to address all those flaws at once—build a coalition of like-minded candidates. By this point, I was much more visible in the education space and knew the major players. I knew who had a heart for our students, and I also knew who was in it for personal glory. I made connections with the former and sidestepped the latter. Individually, we were great, but united? We could be a force.

We were like the Dungeon Family of Birmingham education, an eclectic, soulful, hip-hop collective like the classic rap union of Outkast and Goodie Mob in the '90s.

This union also meant a sharing of resources while we simultaneously built an army of volunteers and campaign organizers.

When the smoke cleared, we all won our races. And it was a key lesson that would define my career going forward: Individuality is cool, but if you want to succeed, build a strong team.

Now that I was on the school board, my career moved very quickly—and unexpectedly. Just a few months after being elected, my colleagues elected me as school board president.

I could use this book to flex and pretend that going from defeated school board candidate to board president was all part of my grand master plan, but it wasn't. I wanted to be a voice for academic change in our city and, in the blink of an eye, I became the leader.

It was unexpected, but I was ready. I knew that there was a very tough road ahead for all of us.

By 2013, Birmingham City Schools were in dire straits. Over the past couple of years, public infighting had caused several board members to be removed. Audit reports showed that some schools didn't have accurate accounting for their cash accounts. Poor test scores and chronic absenteeism infested the system. There was so much drama that our schools lost accreditation, and the State of Alabama had to step in to run things.

Our children were suffering because adults couldn't put their egos aside.

My first edict as leader: We were going to make school board meetings boring again. Our school board meetings had become notorious for ridiculous outbursts and chaos. Meetings were now going to be productive and, most importantly, civil. Sure, we might disagree, but we could work through that without throwing insults and throwing hands. And the days of putting board members on the spot or airing grievances publicly were immediately over. We might have inherited a circus, but there would be no more clowns on my watch.

Next, we had to stabilize our finances. Our schools were cash-strapped, and the first thing that suffered were the arts.

As a band kid and music junkie, I couldn't let that happen.

To bring in more funds, we passed a property tax increase—the first in more than twenty-five years. As you can imagine, there was community pushback, and that led to our next goal—actually *listening* to the community we served. We held community listening tours that encouraged civil discourse and healthy debate. While everyone didn't agree with our plans, we moved forward with a citywide referendum, which voters passed. That brought $8 million a year to support music, arts, and extracurricular activities.

By that point, we had finally moved the needle enough on student achievement that the state withdrew and Birmingham City Schools was back on its feet.

What I learned during my time on the school board is that our schools are too adult-driven, meaning we make decisions based on the wants and needs of adults, not our children. The result is a roster of antiquated and outdated programs and initiatives. Mismanagement of funds. Egos run amok.

My favorite thing to do as school board president was to go out and connect with young people. How can you understand their strengths and assess their weaknesses if you're barking orders from a far-off island?

Second favorite? Connect the pieces of the machine: Parents. School board members. Teachers. Mayors and city council. Community leaders. Principals. Superintendents. We are cogs in the education system, and each of us has a specific role to play. And there's beauty in every cog interlocking to power this machine.

Prior to 2013, we had a bunch of cogs spinning independently. All I did was reconnect the system.

I said it before, and I'll say it again—if you want to succeed, build a strong team. When it comes to the education of our greatest resources, our children, we're all in this together.

I have to take a moment to acknowledge Birmingham Board of Education member Mary Boehm. She was the very first person to support me and hold a fundraiser when I ran for school board (unsuccessfully) in 2009. When I told her in 2017 that my time at the school board was up and I was planning to move on, she wasn't happy. She said there was too much work left to do for our students.

And, as usual, she was right. But I truly believed that I could make an even bigger difference in the lives of our students if I could become mayor.

I had a promise to fulfill, after all.

But first, a little bit about personal fulfillment. You see, a lot of my entertainment options changed when I served on the Birmingham City School Board, and not due to that position itself. Much of what was on my screen was simply unfulfilling.

I was really, really sick of reality TV. I was into the Kerry Washington–led *Scandal* for a minute but I fell off. Same goes for cable news. The constant barrage of negativity, especially during President Obama's second term, was so off-putting that I turned that crap off.

But that was a good thing because it helped me embrace my love of reading, channeling the mission of the STAIR literacy nonprofit I'd done work for. I became a huge Malcolm Gladwell fan. *The Outliers*, *Blink*, and *The Tipping Point* were all staples that I read multiple times. Geoffrey Canada's *Whatever It Takes* and Thomas Friedman's *The World Is Flat* also were required reading, helping to expand my worldview. Basically, anything nonfiction, self-development, or dealing with geopolitics made its way into my hands. It gave me perspective about why humans behave the way we do and the best ways to address our needs.

I know we haven't gotten to my election as mayor on the timeline just yet—hold tight, we'll be there soon enough—but I'm in the mood to speed up the timeline a bit. Since we're talking education, I want to steer the conversation toward two huge issues that were on my plate when I walked into City Hall after being sworn into office:

1. Providing direction for our graduating high school seniors. As I mentioned earlier, I've never been able to shake the awkwardness of standing on a stage with a graduate, nodding my head while they make up plans about their future on the spot, just to appease me.
2. Keeping homegrown talent in Birmingham to bolster our workforce. When you grow up in our city, there's always the allure of "getting out" and going off to make it big.

Most of the time, for both of those issues, that destination was Atlanta.

Every other Black Birminghamian treats Atlanta like it's the US branch of Wakanda. And that's no shade to Atlanta—I spent four great years there myself, after all—but I always knew I wanted to come home and make my city better.

In order for the current generation to feel that love, businesses have to extend the olive branch. Those young grads need to know they're wanted here—and our business community needs to know that they can't let talent continue to flee across state lines.

I found inspiration in Kalamazoo.

The Kalamazoo, Michigan, school system had an intriguing solution to the problems Birmingham faced. The program, known as the Kalamazoo Promise, offered a scholarship—funded by anonymous donors—that would pay 100 percent of the in-state college tuition of graduates of the Kalamazoo Public Schools school district. There were also options for apprenticeships and trade school programs.

Kalamazoo was getting results.

The number of Kalamazoo high school graduates ballooned from about 450 students to 700 each year. Thanks to those incentives, 95 percent of Kalamazoo graduates now pursue higher education after college.

Making higher education affordable, increasing graduation rates, and stimulating the local workforce? Bet.

Remember in the mid-2000s when Lil Wayne would hop on the beat of an already-hot song, add a dash of his wild New Orleans flavor, and make it even doper?

The Birmingham Promise would be the Kalamazoo remix.

Of course, the number one question was, "Where is all this money coming from?"

That's where relationships come in.

I'm a huge proponent of public–private partnerships. It takes a village to raise a child, and a whole lot of philanthropists and businesses to raise the funds needed to make the promises to our children a reality. The city would make the initial investment, of course, to the tune of $2 million. The rest would come from our partners. Josh Carpenter, director of the Department of Innovation and Economic Opportunity; Rachel Harmon, who was named executive director of the Promise; and Birmingham City Schools Superintendent Dr. Lisa Herring all pitched in to make the case to our partners.

It wasn't an easy sell, and you can blame fear for that. Fear of the unknown, fear of failure, hell, fear of not getting credit if the program was a success. We faced it all.

In fact, some members of our school board pushed back hard, claiming that no one was going to tell them what to do with "their money."

"Their money?" Really?

I thought *we* were working together for *our* students.

In time, we got the support we needed, about $3 million in private donations, as well as commitments from local employers to set up apprenticeship programs.

It was very important to me that the apprenticeship programs provided a livable wage. That "working for the exposure" stuff ain't gonna fly when you have real bills to pay. We set things up so that students would make $15 an hour—$7.50 provided by the employer, $7.50 from the city. That was more than what some of the adults in their lives were making per hour. Essentially, the setup provided on-the-job training for students, in addition to possible hires for employers looking to fill their ranks. In our pilot year of 2019, twenty students received internships.

And we can't forget about the scholarships. Thanks to the Promise, to this day any graduate of the Birmingham City Schools system who attends an in-state public college or university will have their tuition fully covered. As long as I'm in office, I'll fight to make sure that promise will always be fulfilled.

Now, the Birmingham Promise is a last-dollar scholarship, meaning that it covers any remaining costs not covered by other grants or scholarships. Put it this way—if your child has enough grants and scholarships to cover two-thirds of their tuition, the Promise takes care of that last third. If your child has no grants or scholarships, it's all good, the Promise takes care of everything.

Regardless of circumstance, the Promise has you covered.

In our first full year, backed by $1 million pledges from businesses like Alabama Power, Regions Bank, and the Altec/Styslinger Foundation nearly three hundred students benefited from the Promise.

After that first year proved the Promise to be a successful, sustainable concept, the support came rolling in. Major businesses like Blue Cross Blue Shield of Alabama, Protective Life, and Alabama Power dropped $1 million each.

It's one thing to say you're committed to our students. It's another to put your money where your mouth is. I was proud to see our community come together.

As of this writing, the Promise has distributed roughly a thousand scholarships, to the tune of $5.5 million. There have also been two hundred internship placements at eighty local businesses.

That's a lot of lives changed, especially Black, brown, and underserved students.

When my boy John Cox and I attended Putnam Middle School, we called ourselves NTO, Nerds Taking Over. After graduating college, we returned to Putnam to serve as volunteers, helping a new generation of students find a passion for learning. We were just two guys making the most change we could with the limited resources we had. We didn't have much, only a passion to uplift children from our hometown.

If only those NTO kids knew what the future would bring.

Of all the things I've accomplished as mayor, nothing gives me more pride that the Birmingham Promise.

From NTO, to the school board, to the Promise, the game remained the same—Birmingham deserved better.

Oh, and the haters? They still look silly.

During my re-election campaign, I was ambushed during a debate by fellow candidates who took the opportunity to disparage the Promise.

The accusations were outlandish—that students were being denied scholarships if they didn't meet GPA requirements (there is no GPA requirement), that money was being stripped from Birmingham City Schools to fund the project (nope—funding comes from public–private partnerships and donations), and that it was a stunt to buy votes (man, the only thing we were paying for was tuition, have several seats).

I can't lie, the attacks really fired me up. If you want to criticize my administration, cool. But to tear down a program that only exists to support our students—without any of those critics providing any alternative options to fund their education, by the way—got me hot.

It doesn't matter what they said. I only care about the Birmingham City Schools students who now have a guaranteed path to college. I'm only here for that graduate who now has a job lined up at a local agency after a successful internship. I'm only listening to the mothers and grandmothers who were unable to pay for their child's education but now rest easy.

The next time I'm on a graduation stage, I'm only hearing that grad who can now confidently say, "I know what I'm doing with my life."

A promise kept.

———

Truth can be a really bitter pill to swallow. But as a leader, when an elephant is rampaging through a room, you can't ignore it.

During a December 2023 news conference, I had a very frank conversation with our community. The yearly assessment of our school system—its report card—showed that we were underperforming.

In my eyes, that meant we were failing our kids.

Now, we could sit back and accept mediocrity, or we could push for change. One of the changes I instituted was very outside the box—an incentive program that would reward families if their child achieved perfect attendance for that month. Those families would be entered in a raffle to receive a free month of rent. And guess what? Absentee rates decreased.

I also had a very clear message for teachers who weren't committed to excellence—please retire. I received some blowback for those words, but I stand by them.

I come from a family of educators. I know what it takes to be a great teacher. And I respect every one of those unsung heroes who give so much to our kids. But my message is clear—if you aren't giving, get gone.

If you're a caring, giving educator, we stand with you. If you're not, well, as the Southern saying goes, "a hit dog will holler." That December day, in front of my colleagues at city council and the residents of the city I love, I had to speak up.

This is something that I'm very passionate about. . . . I want to read a couple things.

You all know that the Alabama State Department of Education unveiled the annual Alabama State Report Card. They revealed it last week, and it covered all schools statewide, those included in our city. Birmingham City Schools received an overall letter grade of C. To be exact, the score was a seventy-two. Each of the forty-three schools also received a letter grade reflecting varied progress toward state goals.

Now, Birmingham City Schools has forty-three schools that received a grade. Twenty-five out of the forty-three schools, which, if you do the math real quick, is almost 60 percent—58 percent, to be exact—received a D or an F grade, categorizing them as priority schools, according to state standards.

The grade letter summarizes a school's overall performance, considering achievement, graduation rates, readiness for post–high school life, and chronic absenteeism. . . . There were three elementary schools and one high school that received a letter grade A, and I think it's important that we say the good, the OK, and the bad out loud, because we need to own our data. No, I'm not the superintendent. No, I am not the school board, but I am the mayor of the city where I think everything we are attempting to do is directly attached to education, and so we all collectively own this data.

The three elementary schools that received the letter grade A, middle schools, as well, were Epic Alternative School, Phillips Academy, and W. J. Christian. One high school received a letter grade A, and that's Ramsay High School. There was one school that received a B; that elementary school was Princeton.

Eleven schools received a letter grade C. This combined elementary schools, middle schools, K–8 schools, and two high schools, and I will read them again . . . Avondale Elementary, Central Park, Charles Brown, Glen Iris, Norwood, Oxmoor Valley, Robinson, South Hampton, Sun Valley, Washington, and Wilkerson. And the two high schools were Huffman High and Carver High.

The schools receiving Ds and Fs. There were twenty-one elementary middle schools—Arrington, Barrett, Bush Hills, Green Acres, Hayes, Hemphill, Hudson, Huffman Academy, Huffman Middle, Inglenook, Jones Valley, Martha Gaskins, Minor, Oliver, Ossie Ware, Putnam, Smith, Tuggle, the Virtual Academy, West End Academy, and Wylam. And the four high schools—Jackson-Olin, Parker, Wenonah, and Woodlawn.

And so BCS has a total of sixteen schools improve. Actually, let me say that again, BCS had a total of sixteen schools improve. So I never want to talk about the challenges first; I want to talk about the improvements. This is good to have sixteen schools improve, nine improving an entire letter grade. And so those schools are Brown, Central Park, Epic Alternative, Glen Iris, Hemphill, Norwood, Phillips, Robertson, Sun Valley, Washington, Wilkerson, W. J. Christian. And the high schools that received that improvement—Carver and Huffman and Ramsey.

As you know, parents are allowed to visit statereportcard.alsde .edu and they can learn more information about the individual school that their child attends.

That is from a statistical standpoint. . . . What I want to do is break down the importance of this information. . . .

I attended Birmingham City Schools, K through eighth. So, this is personal. My mother was a teacher for eleven years in the county schools, and my stepmother was a teacher for thirty-three years in Birmingham City Schools. This is personal. Galvin [Billups] leads the Division of Youth Services for the City of Birmingham . . . and he's equally passionate. And a lot of the things up here in my head, I give to him, and he runs with it. So I'm proud of him and his team for what they do in support of our schools.

I met Galvin when I was eleven years old. We walked to the bus stop together. He was a year ahead of me, and I always looked up to him, and we both attended Putnam Middle School. And some years later, when I finished high school and I finished college, and I came back and moved to Birmingham, I started a breakfast club with my college roommate, who also went to Putnam Middle School, and his name is John Cox. . . . And we used to go to the school early in the morning a few days a week. We started with the sixth-grade boys. We would bring in breakfast. They'd come off the bus, and instead of going into the cafeteria, they would come into the library, and we would teach them all kinds of life skills.

One of the things we talked about often was work ethic. And I would tell those boys that, with a few exceptions, because there are some subjects that are hard, there's teachers that are really hard . . . I told them that getting Cs and being comfortable with Cs meant the following—that you were either lazy, didn't care, or doing the bare minimum.

And so often I would ask them, "Hey, be honest with me, are you okay with the C?" And they would raise their hands, and I would just drill into them.

"OK, so tell me, which one are you? Are you lazy? You don't care? Are you doing the bare minimum?"

"Which one? Lazy? Don't care? Or doing the bare minimum?"

And I would do it over and over and say, "Hey, be honest, which one are you?" And they would say out loud, "I'm lazy." "I don't care." "I'm doing a bare minimum."

What does that have to do with anything I've just mentioned to you? It has a lot to do with it, because the same thing I would say to those sixth-grade boys when they got into seventh grade, when they got in the eighth grade, I would tell that to every adult that is employed with the Birmingham City Schools system.

I would say it to the school board, I would say it to the superintendent, I would say it to the superintendent's cabinet, I would say it to those people who are responsible for the principals. I would say it to the principals, the assistant principals, the teachers, the custodians, the bus drivers, cafeteria workers, and every single employee group that I missed.

[Former Alabama football coach] Nick Saban liked to say, "We got about twenty-four hours to celebrate, then we got to get back to work." So, while I applaud Birmingham City Schools that from the time this state test was first administered, they've gone from a D to a C, that twenty-four hours is over. Cs, in my humble opinion, are unacceptable, and I do not accept that as a system, and I'm pretty sure they would agree with me. . . . Although a seventy-two is passing, that doesn't cut it. Because if I drill down, our children deserve As and Bs—not just the actual school, not just the district.

And I pose the question to the district: Which one are we doing? Which one are we? Are we being lazy? As adults? Are we doing the bare minimum as adults, or do we not care as adults? I would definitely say that for the individual schools with Ds and Fs.

Now I want to be very clear. This is not a matter of the Spider-Man meme where everybody points at somebody else. So I'm not blaming any one particular adult group. There's no time to blame teachers. There's no time to blame students or parents or any adult group—that includes the school board or the superintendent. We're all accountable. If you are adults in this community, we are all responsible for educating our children, and we should be doing everything necessary to educate our children, and we should not accept Ds and Fs, and we should not be comfortable with Cs, because these are our children.

And as far as I'm concerned, if a current school is at a D or an F, we should move with a sense of urgency . . . and do whatever is necessary legally—because cheating is not cool. Don't do that. That's dumb and stupid. That gets you fired. Don't do that.

But everything that's legal, we should be moving with a sense of urgency, because I find this unacceptable. If you are a parent, this should not be acceptable. If you are a teacher, this should not be acceptable. If you are a principal, a superintendent, a school board member, this is not acceptable.

Ever since I was elected mayor, I feel I've been a great partner with the school system and with leadership, and I will continue to communicate with them, but there is no world where I'm just going to be quiet about what exists. Our twenty-four hours are over. So, I would say this: Because my parents, my mother and stepmother, are retired teachers, I have an affinity to our teachers, so I never pick on teachers. I actually feel bad for them, and I know their job is extremely hard.

And so kudos to the teachers that are busting their butt every single day and giving everything, everything for the love of their children, that they're passionate about presenting and being in front of their children, and what they do goes well beyond 8:00 a.m. to 3:00 p.m.

However, if you are a teacher in the Birmingham City Schools and you are lazy and you're doing the bare minimum, or you don't care anymore about the children that come to your class. Please resign. Please retire. Please leave. We don't want you.

That's pretty direct. Some people may get mad at me for saying that, but it needs to be said, because our children already have a lot going on at home. I'm going to get to *home* in a minute, by the way, but our children already have a lot going on at home. And so there's a higher expectation in an urban school system like Birmingham that our teachers go well beyond just being responsible for their curriculum. That it takes some extra pouring on, some extra leaning in, of loving that child, of caring for that child, of doing everything you can for that child of that school [such as] having a washer and dryer, because at home, they may not have a washer and dryer, and a kid may be too embarrassed, so they act out when they come to school when their shirt is dirty.

And so what am I talking about? In this, what I just read to you, the best example I can give, the school that I am most proud of, the leadership I am most proud of, is Central Park Elementary School, because they went from an F to a C. Y'all know how hard it is to do that in one year? This principal has only been in the district three semesters, all last year, and the completion of this one semester that just was completed last Friday. So, in one school year, he moved his school from an F to a C. That is hard.

I want to be clear: That principal, those teachers, that school has the same demographics as all the other schools in the City of Birmingham. So if he can move his school from an F to a C, then all the schools can move, all the principals can move, all the teachers can move.

There's a fair question you'll ask: "Mr. Principal, how did you do it?" And then you listen to him. . . . His words, not mine: "I made more deposits into my human capital than withdrawals."

He invested more into his teachers. Washed their cars, stayed at the school late with them, arrived early as they did, figured out their needs. What are their wants, so they can maximize their time in front of their children. Ladies and gentlemen, we call that culture and climate. He focused on the morale of his teachers.

He did everything in his power to empower his teachers, for them to give their best for their children. That's an intangible. But I'm gonna tell you, if you don't have it, if you don't have a school or a principal who is focused on culture and climate, you cannot teach. I'm not an educator. Don't take my word for it. Take this: Go interview him. Go talk to him. Go embed yourself in his school.

Some of these schools, I'm gonna pull the information up here: I got a school that went from a D to an F. I got another school that went from a C to a D. I got another school that went from a D to an F. I got too many schools that went down.

We have too many schools that went down.

I want to be very clear. I respect Dr. Sullivan. I do not envy his job. The job is extremely hard. I found that when we talk and we collaborate, we get things done. So I respect him as the superintendent, the CEO of our system.

But, like you, I desire more of this district. Not just him, not just the board, but of this district. Our students, at this moment, require us, as adults, to be bold and we should be making recommendations. The superintendent should be making recommendations to his board that are outside the box. We should be trying things differently to move the needle for our children.

So, parents, you don't get to escape from this conversation, because I told y'all months ago, we had an absentee problem. And I told you these state grades are not just predicated on testing, but absentees and high absentees and chronic absentees are factored into these scores. I got schools that have north of 20 and 30 percent chronic absentees, and I'm not just talking to high schools where it's possible that—oh, come on, we know high school children skip school. That's not what I'm talking about. Because as I go through this data, and I encourage every person to go through it, I got elementary schools, y'all, where people as adults are too comfortable with six-year-olds, seven-year-olds, eight-year-olds, and nine-year-olds missing school. Unexcused absence, chronic absentees. That's not on the child, it's only on the adults.

If there was one thing that as adults in this community we could get right, it's just the ability for children to go to school. Parent, if you're uneducated yourself; parent, if you're working too much; parent, if you don't understand; that's fine. One request—please make sure your child comes to school. And if they have to be out, please provide a valid excuse. I don't think that is a tall request.

And yeah, I got hammered because people thought I was only approaching it from a "stick" standpoint a few months ago when I talked about it and I brought up the district attorney's office. So here's a "carrot."

I go through this data and I see schools like Hayes, Hudson, Putnam, and a few others. Majority of students are zoned from public housing. So I'm going to get with the CEO of the housing authority. And we're going to come up with the carrot, and we're gonna say, hey, if your child has perfect attendance for this month, you have the ability to get in a raffle, and you're renting free for that month.

I shouldn't have to incentivize attendance, but I will. . . .

This is an important conversation, and all adults have equal culpability, and all adults should be held accountable for what exists at the state of our schools. I'm grateful to every adult who gives their max to every teacher, to every employee in the school system who goes above and beyond the call of duty for our children. Thank you. I admire you. I appreciate you. I love you, and I will bust my butt to continue to support you.

But if you are one of those employees in front of our children and you are lazy, don't care, doing the bare minimum, please, please step aside.

Randall L. Woodfin, Mayor
City Hall News Conference
December 2023

CHAPTER 7

DA ART OF STORYTELLIN' (PT. 1)

I t was 2016 and I stopped by my mom's house to share some pretty big news I'd been sitting on for a while.

I tore my mom away from reruns of *Wyatt Earp* and asked her and my stepdad to have a seat. I needed their undivided attention for this.

It was time to speak my dream into existence.

"I wanna talk to y'all," I said.

My mom hesitantly said, ". . . OK."

I knew she was expecting the worst. So I got straight to the point. "I'm running for mayor of Birmingham."

"You're running against Mayor Bell?" my mom replied. Her words were wrapped in astonishment and a hint of unease.

"No, ma'am," I replied. "I'm running *for* Birmingham."

My mom's reaction was echoed by so many established voters in my city. William Bell, Birmingham's then-current mayor, was an institution. He had started his political career on Birmingham's city council in 1979, two years before I was even born. He eventually served as council president.

Bell was a city council mainstay throughout the '80s and '90s, even serving as interim mayor after the retirement of Richard Arrington in 1999. Though he'd lose in a runoff to Bernard Kincaid later that year, Bell returned to the council in the new millennium. By 2008, he would transition to the Jefferson County Commission and, after the conviction of then-mayor Larry Langford, he won a special election in 2010 to serve the final two years of Mayor Langford's term.

From that point on, William Bell had been the face of leadership in Birmingham.

I didn't have a grudge against William Bell. There was no long-standing vendetta to oust him. Like I told my mom, this wasn't about him. It was about the people of Birmingham.

I felt that our leadership had become complacent. Kind of like when a once-dominant sports franchise starts to lose its hunger. Yes, the name is celebrated and the big wins of the past are constantly acknowledged, but, eventually, that current program begins to suffer.

Janet Jackson asked some guy in 1986, "What have you done for me lately?" And Birmingham was starting to ask those same questions.

As I've mentioned before, Birmingham takes incredible pride in its ninety-nine neighborhoods. Bell's development strategy seemed to focus primarily on downtown, with the mindset that bringing development to the city's core would benefit the city at large.

But there's a bit of a problem with that strategy—focusing on just one neighborhood, Central City in this case, meant that ninety-eight others were being ignored. Areas like Ensley, a once-thriving business district, were left with rotting buildings and promises of development that never came. You had spots like Titusville and Wahouma, once thriving middle-class communities, now blighted with burned-out homes, overgrown lots, and pothole-littered streets.

It was hard for residents to celebrate downtown ribbon cuttings when they stepped out on their porches and saw nothing but piles of trash ignored for weeks and abandoned homes with shattered windows.

Birmingham was in dire need of a makeover. Smooth streets. Grocery stores in underserved communities. Job opportunities. Abandoned buildings torn down. New homes built up. Hope.

I had two options: I could sit back and complain about the conditions on social media—drag a few council people in a Facebook post that gets a few likes and is forgotten in six hours—or I could be the change I wanted to see.

Social media slander ain't really my thing. It was time to get to work.

Whenever I made my intentions clear about running for mayoral office, I was met with the same responses:

It's not my time.

It's not smart to run.

I *better* not run—my political career would be over before it began.

And yeah, if I had one of those Magic 8 Ball toys from the '80s, I'm sure it would have told me "outlook not so good."

I was going up against an incumbent with nearly forty years of political experience, next to my barely three years on the Birmingham Board of Education. He had a seemingly endless stream of financial supporters, community leaders backing him, and name recognition. And he had been in the Birmingham political arena for a very long time. He knew all the tricks of the trade.

Outlook not so good.

However, despite all the times in my life that I've been paralyzed by fear, this wasn't one of those. This wasn't sixth-grade Randall who stayed home from school for two days because I was being bullied by eighth-graders. This wasn't the Randall who was insecure about his place on the school band with those stupid cymbals.

This was grown man Randall, and I was ready to do right by my city.

This wasn't about Bell. This was about Birmingham.

Once my mom and stepdad gave me their blessing, I knew it was time to get to work.

Step one—I needed a team.

It can amaze you to look back and reminisce on the people God puts in your life.

The casual acquaintance you give a head nod to, that familiar face you might dap up in the hall but can barely recall their name—when those faces become integral to your story, it's something special.

Ed Fields went from a guy I sorta knew to a true brother.

Ed was born and raised in Milwaukee, Wisconsin, and found his way to Alabama as a student at Alabama State University. It took him seven years to make it through undergrad, but whether you're *summa cum laude* or just Thank You Lawd-y, finishing is the important part.

It might be hard for friends and acquaintances to picture it today, but back then, Ed was more Mos Def than Jesse Jackson. Though he's been a political force in Birmingham for nearly a decade now, Ed "Version 1.0" was as apolitical as they came. He found his voice in poetry, not policy, building a name for himself in Birmingham's spoken word scene.

Whether he knew it or not, the brother always had a heart for service, and always relished being a voice for the voiceless.

Ed established his career at the Birmingham Regional Chamber of Commerce, eventually working his way up to vice president of business development. He later cofounded Relax, It's Handled, an event management company that worked closely with area nonprofits and executives.

Slowly but surely, Ed was building a base and making the connections that would serve as the foundation for loftier career aspirations.

He's proof that there are never wasted steps in your life's journey.

I'd run into Ed at the Chamber (the Birmingham Business Alliance's chamber of commerce). I was interning for a law firm on one floor, he was handling business—rocking his suits and locks—on another. We'd pass each other in the hall, say what up, nothing major.

But Ed and I didn't truly cross paths until the creation of the Birmingham Change Fund.

BCF was an incredible concept built on the strength and power of philanthropy. In 2003, a group of young professionals saw areas of great need in Birmingham—specifically in the realms of education, economics, and healthcare in Black communities. Instead of approaching these issues individually, they wisely found strength in numbers.

Those twenty-one founding members—both Ed and I included— would form like Voltron to pool our resources in support of the city we loved. Those first investments included four grants for a total of $10,000.

These were young Black professionals pooling their time, talents, and treasure together to make change. Their ingenuity inspired me.

By 2009, BCF began to steer its focus toward education—and not a moment too soon, as Birmingham City Schools were beginning to struggle due to limited resources and ridiculous infighting between leaders.

Ed's Relax, It's Handled business was based in Innovation Depot, a coworking space and business incubator nestled in the heart of downtown, which became an impromptu war room for the betterment of Birmingham education. It was during those meetings that a BCF member decided to run for school board.

Concurrently, I was out doing my own thing, attempting to run for the Birmingham Board of Education myself, and failing.

You see, I was still learning the lessons of the BCF—the strength in numbers. The Voltron Force of change.

During my second bid for school board, I built a coalition, which included partnering with BCF members to share ideas and resources and to present a united front for change.

It's around that time that I reached out to Ed. I needed a data expert who could help extract data from voter files. I'm a bit of a numbers nerd, sure, but I needed help not to let this opportunity slide by again. I thought it best to bring in experts. Ed hooked me up with Dwain Golston, a data science major and numbers guru. Ed even stopped by the campaign quarters on 18th Street. Maps adorned every inch of the walls, high school volunteers running throughout—it was a high-energy atmosphere. My team and I felt like we were on the verge of something big.

Now I wouldn't say Ed was skeptical . . . but he was skeptical.

He didn't see me as a politician; he only saw me as a baby-faced attorney, the nice guy, not the take-no-prisoners candidate. Besides, I was running against an established candidate.

Outlook not so good.

But due to our hard work—and some luck with district lines changing—we beat the odds and won.

Ed may not have been a big believer in politics, but what he did believe in was the power of people. His heart for philanthropy, his gift of being a connector and convener of brilliant minds, and his willingness to push for a more progressive Birmingham thrust him into the political sphere, whether he wanted it or not.

By that time, our relationship was more than professional. I remember Ed calling to check on me when my older brother, Ralph, passed away. The weeks following Ralph's death were tough; I immediately went back to work, so there wasn't time to process the grief.

Although he wasn't physically there, Ed's presence was strongly felt. Ed and Ralph are just a year apart in age, so I guess it's natural that he'd slide into that big brother role.

It's a role he's held for more than a decade now.

So, in September 2015, I had to call my brother. "I'm calling to let you know that I want to run for mayor and I'd be honored if you'd be my campaign manager."

His response?

"Let me get back to you."

I told y'all he wasn't political.

When I called Ed to offer him the position of campaign manager, he was in a time of personal transition himself.

When I hit him up, he was on the road driving back from Charlotte, meeting up with his ex for the last time. Just a day earlier, his ex had asked him if he would consider a career in politics.

His response to her question was pretty prophetic: "I couldn't see myself doing it, unless Randall ran for mayor or something."

Then a few hours later he gets my call. No wonder he was so freaked out.

Ed asked me to give him until Thanksgiving to make his decision, which was a little more than two months away from the initial conversation. In the meantime, he still put in work, agreeing to serve as volunteer campaign manager.

Ed tried to recruit several other people for the role, including my friend DeJuana Thompson, a political strategist and founder of Woke Vote, one of the South's most important political organizing groups of the past decade. She declined, as she was in the midst of building a business at the time. Several more names came and went. Most just didn't want that smoke.

It's not that Ed was avoiding the role, but he knew it would be an uphill fight. Incumbent Mayor Bell was one of the most noted orators in our city at the time. Just a few months earlier, he was hanging out with the Dalai Lama on a tour of our city. Meanwhile, Ed was just getting accustomed to life as a single guy and figuring out the next stage of his life.

But you can't outrun your destiny.

Ed finally committed to the campaign in early 2017, about six months after I declared my candidacy.

And not a moment too soon. I was pretty uncomfortable operating without an official campaign manager. I had a team of students who were volunteering, but much of the heavy lifting was on my shoulders. I needed someone to prop me up.

Ed was always that guy.

By the time Ed joined, I had a loose campaign strategy, but we were long overdue for refinement.

The first thing Ed wanted to talk about was which churches and neighborhood associations we'd hit up for support.

I said none.

Yes, none.

No shade to those group meetings and churches, but we had to look at reality. Bell already had a foothold in many of the established neighborhood meetings and the largest churches. So, we needed a different approach.

Let's break it down by the numbers.

How long does a neighborhood association meeting last? Let's say one, maybe two hours. How many people are at those meetings? Let's be generous and say twenty people, max.

So let's take that knowledge and apply it to my most successful political endeavors—from my days campaigning at Morehouse for SGA presidency, to my successful school board run, it was knocking on doors that led to my biggest wins.

How many doors can you knock on in two hours? I'd guess about fifty, max.

Fifty doors for two hours, where we can have deep, meaningful one-on-one conversations with residents versus two hours with twenty people who probably are chatting among themselves and distracted by other things going on in the meeting?

Yeah, man, we're knocking on doors.

Churches have long been an important way to reach voters, as well, but they come with their own challenges. Many of the largest churches aren't just filled with voters from inside the city; they're filled by residents of suburbs outside of our districts.

They vote, but they don't vote in Birmingham. That's an important distinction. We couldn't cast our net too wide in search of *all* Black voters; we had to be hyper-focused on where those voters were, and specifically, those who were active voters—those who had cast ballots in the last three to five voting cycles.

Established churches were not going to defy Bell. He was too familiar, too established. I was a risk. Folks with money were not going to defy Bell and possibly lose their connections. Neighborhood leaders likely were not defying Bell either—he was the pipeline to the resources they sought. Even if they weren't happy with the support they were receiving from City Hall, they weren't going to totally sever ties with Bell.

If I wanted to find support, I had to go straight to the streets.

I wasn't running *against* Bell, I was running *for* Birmingham, after all. It only made sense.

We had a plan. But we needed a way to examine data to chart our success. We needed funding. A lot of funding. And if we were going to knock on countless doors, we needed an army of volunteers.

. . .

When you think of a campaign office, you probably picture a fancy office space crammed with hyperactive volunteers running through the aisles waving polling results over their heads, like rapper Petey Pablo twisting his shirt like a helicopter; data gurus clad in white dress shirts stare at laptops while their eyeglasses slide over the bridges of their noses, eyes bulging as their brains calculate figures. Meanwhile, the campaign manager stands at the front of the office, lording over the frantic staff like a vengeful taskmaster.

Campaign offices are nothing like that. Certainly not mine.

First off, our campaign was not based in a swanky office building. Our space was shared by a downtown furniture-making company. The floor was concrete, the air-conditioning didn't exist, and we were serenaded by the constant buzz of saws from the workshops adjacent to us.

Oh, and there was sawdust. Everywhere.

Our staff was eclectic. From the devout, middle-aged Christian women to vape-smoking, La Croix–drinking, twenty-something atheists, there didn't seem to be much in common between many folks on staff. And as you'd imagine, there were often differences in opinions—a byproduct of uniting so many varying walks of life.

Take, for instance, the Great Yard Sign Debate.

My staff ordered round, black yard signs that looked snazzy, but there was a big problem—you couldn't really see my name very well against the background. Plus, they were a lot smaller than I had envisioned.

Y'all know me—if I see a problem, I'm not going to wait around on other people. I'm going to fix it myself. So I ordered different signs that were much larger. These were burgundy and rectangular.

Some members of my team were hot. The new signs didn't match our original branding. But my point was, if you can't even read the original signs, what's the point.

After a ton of back-and-forth, I had to make it plain: "Forget them yard signs; yard signs don't vote!"

(Disclaimer, the previous quote may or may not be edited for the sake of this book. Y'all use your imaginations.)

Looking back, every frustrating moment was worth it. There was a team of volunteers all fighting for a singular goal. We wanted a better Birmingham. We deserved better—which became our campaign slogan.

Emotions were high, but we were all on the same team.

Those black signs were still wack, though.

I knew early on that I wanted my campaign to be data-driven. Going back to my days as a field organizer, I knew it was the most effective way to gauge results and refine tactics.

That's why when Daniel Deriso knocked at my door, we quickly found him a seat at the table.

Daniel was a local kid who had served as a field organizer for Bernie Sanders's 2016 presidential campaign. According to Daniel, one day he was scrolling Facebook and came across an article that detailed the mayoral race. My campaign caught his eye, he found my website, and he emailed me a three-paragraph summary of his campaign experience. Ed and I invited him over to chat the next day.

Daniel came in with roughly four thousand ideas, everything from software and organizing strategies to data and analytics. It was exactly what we needed—a modern, data-driven campaign.

Alabama sorely lacked (and still lacks) an organized Democratic Party. Most races are rooted in name recognition—you pay a few folks to work the streets, hit up the major churches to show your face, and that's about it. The most visible candidates get the win. It turns elections into popularity contests.

There hadn't been a large-scale, grassroots, door-to-door campaigning strategy in years, possibly even generations. And there certainly weren't data-driven techniques to target specific voters and address their needs where they lived.

We wanted to change that.

With Daniel's help, we were the first in the state to use NGP VAN, also known as the voter activation network, a voter database and webhosting service provider that has become the leading tool for Democratic campaigns. It found prominence during President Obama's 2008 campaign and picked up steam in 2016 for both the Bernie Sanders and Hillary Rodham Clinton campaigns. NGP VAN allows candidates to access voter files and target voters down to the smallest details—age, race, sex, and more.

(Coincidentally, I served as the state chair for Clinton's campaign during that same 2016 race. It was my first glimpse of campaigning at the presidential level and gave me invaluable understanding of how policy and national politics play out in Alabama.)

During one of our first canvassing efforts in District 2, we all met in the parking lot of W. J. Christian School, armed with lists created from the voter database. We used those lists to knock on the doors of residents who were already supporters or were undecided and wanted more info. We used that effort to recruit volunteers.

It was a more effective way of directly reaching prospective supporters than just blanketing the community with mailers.

My original strategy was to target seasoned voters—the aunties and Big Mamas who were very active in their communities and sought something new. Daniel suggested going in the opposite direction—building a coalition of young, progressive residents, especially those returning to Birmingham after graduation. Bell wasn't speaking to that generation, and it could be a difference-maker in a tight race.

Thanks to NGP VAN, we knew exactly who they were and where to find them.

• • •

During campaign season, I turned to the greats for motivation.

Jay-Z's *Reasonable Doubt*: I loved Jay's grit on this album, but his delivery was so smooth, so thoughtful. His focus was laser-like and my team brought that precision to our campaign planning.

Nas's *It Was Written*: Specifically, his hit single "If I Ruled the World" with Lauryn Hill. Nah, we weren't out for world domination, but if I could make my hometown a better place, it was mission accomplished.

Outkast's *ATLiens*: "Me and you, your momma and your cousin too"—that was the movement we were attempting to create. We wanted total buy-in from our community, from Big Mommas to Lil' Junior n' dem. We wanted every corner of Birmingham to feel included, and to be a voice for them.

Also, Tee Grizzley's "First Day Out," Lil Wayne's "Swag Surfin'," Future's "Mask Off," and 21 Savage's "Bank Account" kept the speakers jumpin'.

When I say our campaign touched all of Birmingham, I mean we hit every corner. By the end, we had knocked on fifty thousand doors, many of them repeat visits.

But it was the kind of grassroots campaigning that our city desperately needed.

Our initial polls showed that only four out of ten voters knew my name at the start of the campaign. Meanwhile, Bell had a negative rating in the polls, so we knew he was vulnerable. We just had to get out and plead our case.

The gameplan was simple. Our volunteers, me included, would knock on a hundred doors a day, five days a week. We'd meet at 10:00 a.m., head out at 11:00, and get to work.

Did I mention that it was also summer in Birmingham? That heat was oppressive.

Once residents opened those doors, our team operated like sales-people: "Hello, I'm [so and so] from the Woodfin campaign. Are you familiar with Randall? Well, let me tell you about him."

Polls are cool, but speaking directly to residents gives you a different perspective of the needs of your community. No matter the neighborhoods we canvassed—from Collegeville to Norwood, to Pratt City to Smithfield—the concerns were the same. Residents were fed up with abandoned, burned-out structures marring their neighborhoods. And they were even more fed up with an administration that they believe ignored their cries for help.

Now, covering so much ground meant we had to have a large collection of volunteers. Our staff was pretty lean in the early days, and it caused a rift within our team.

During those initial stages of campaigning, we had our white volunteers focus on white areas of town, with Black volunteers focusing on Black areas. Obviously Black volunteers will be able to better connect with Black voters, and vice versa. But here's where things got tricky—we had more white volunteers on our staff than Black. And since our city is nearly 70 percent Black, that meant our Black teams had to cover way more ground with much less support.

Thankfully, things turned around after classes ended and students of all racial and ethnic backgrounds flocked to join canvassing efforts. Daniel reached out to a bunch of graduates of the nearby University of Montevallo, many of whom were political science majors filled with restless energy—fired up due to the Bernie Sanders campaign but directionless after Trump's victory. We put that energy to good use.

It became quite clear that our campaign would be a youth movement. In the spirit of the Civil Rights Foot Soldiers that came before them, these young men and women were hungry for change and their age wasn't a detriment. It was our secret weapon.

To supplement those long, hot summers on the streets, my friend Lindsey McAdory helped us put out direct mail pieces while Daniel set up a remote team who made calls on my behalf. A woman based in Hawaii would make calls ninety minutes a day to drum up support. A young man from San Diego would do the same, but for three hours.

Daniel also brought in Griff Gray as our get out the vote (GOTV) director. Griff had hired Daniel for the Bernie campaign in 2016 and Daniel was happy to return the favor. Those two guys were cut from the same cloth and helped keep our data-driven strategies flowing.

We were gaining momentum, but where was the money coming from?

Financing would be one of our biggest campaign weaknesses. We didn't have decades of connections like the incumbent.

So, once again, we had to go grassroots with it.

We devised an $18.71 monthly donation campaign for supporters, which played off the year Birmingham was founded, 1871. Naturally, we called it the 1871 Campaign, and it brought in roughly $12,000 during the first seven months of our campaign.

But the true key was making it a social media–driven campaign. Donations came in from across the country: Philly, California, Boston, and all points in between. I think out-of-state residents empathized with our message—a fresh-faced, progressive candidate looking to revitalize forgotten neighborhoods. It was a theme anyone could get behind.

Still, it wasn't enough money. Birmingham businesses weren't supporting us; they knew their bread was buttered with Bell.

I turned to my family, my Morehouse brothers.

Several of my former classmates already had been fundraising on my behalf, including former South Carolina state representative Bakari Sellers. I was greatly appreciative of that outpouring of support. But things didn't really take off until we obtained a list of 757 Morehouse alums.

Chris Barrineau saw the vision. I didn't know Chris, but he was a well-established political finance guy. I met him through friends. He came on board as finance director after learning that we had already raised $40,000 from small donors. He knew we were serious. Chris lived on a farm outside of Prattville, Alabama, eighty-something miles away, but in the digital age, working remotely wasn't an issue. With his help, we reached out to hundreds of other Morehouse brothers from across the nation to enlist their help.

I spent hours on the phone collectively with each of them, sharing stories and outlining my vision for Birmingham. And they came through big. In total, we raised more than a half-million dollars with about 30 percent of that coming from Morehouse and Spelman contributions.

My Morehouse family has always had my back, and I'm forever grateful for their continued support.

Even though we were closing the gap, my opponents weren't taking us seriously.

I was one of twelve candidates, which included community activists, seasoned politicians, and blue-collar residents.

During the first debate, I leaned hard into the incumbent. I had already laid out my plan to build a better Birmingham on my website, randallwoodfin.com. Prioritizing neighborhood revitalization, stimulating economic development and small business growth, targeting long-standing issues of pollution in North Birmingham, highlighting social justice and LGBTQ+ issues, reducing crime—no other candidate, including our incumbent, had a bullet-pointed plan to attack issues in our city.

Once the polls said I won the debate, there was an immediate target on my back. The opps were coming for me.

First, there were questions about my fundraising. Most of Bell's funding came from within the state. So he built upon the "outside agitator" narrative that was first flaunted during the Civil Rights Movement, when protesters from outside Alabama's borders joined in the fight for change.

Bell painted himself as the victim, saying he was running a local race while I was being funded by outsiders, including the dreaded "over the mountain" money.

Over the mountain is a Birmingham colloquialism for the affluent community that surrounds our city.

Basically, Bell was saying I was the tool of white outsiders. In a city of nearly 70 percent Black folk, many of whom are very wary of meddling by white interests, it was a nasty low blow.

But the opps would go even lower.

If you ever heard a rumor that I once secretly ran off to Atlanta or DC or New York to marry a white man, blame the opps.

I can't place the blame on one specific candidate, but it was around this time that a whisper campaign circulated that I was secretly a gay man living a double life.

Look, bruh, I have nothing but love for the LGBTQ+ community. In 2018, I named Josh Coleman as the city's first LGBTQ liaison. And under his leadership, Birmingham has received a perfect score on the Human Rights Campaign's Municipal Quality Index, which measures the inclusiveness of our LGBTQ+ policies, every year since 2019.

I'm a proud ally of the gay community. But I'm not gay.

What angered me wasn't being called gay; it was that candidates were weaponizing homophobia as a scare tactic. A young, single, soft-spoken brother who wears nice suits? Oh, he *must* be gay—and we can't have him leading our city.

What does a candidate's sexuality have to do with addressing those burned-out homes that our residents have begged for years to be addressed? What does someone's life partner have to do with working to build new grocery stores to alleviate food deserts or provide scholarships for graduating seniors with eyes on higher education?

How dare we make sexual preference a barrier in a city where no less than sixty years ago, men and women bled on our streets for the equality of all people.

It infuriated me, not because of my pride, but because it was a reminder that we still had so far to go—and grow—as a city.

A former colleague at the Birmingham Board of Education even claimed that I threatened to hit her after a school board meeting. She went on a livestream and—get this—claimed that after an argument I put up my fists and was like "come at me!"

Like I was Scrappy Doo trying to fight somebody in a ghost costume, or something.

If you've made it this far into this book, I'm pretty sure you can tell I'm not the "come at me, bro" type. I don't talk like a drunken frat kid.

The mudslinging upset my sisters. And my mom was ready to go upside somebody's head. But I told them that this is the price of politics in Birmingham.

Misinformation, manipulation, and outright lies seem to be the standard in today's world, especially on social media, where anything with enough "likes" attached is all but guaranteed to be seen as true.

I'm just asking y'all, think beyond the moment. Rely on trusted news sources, not random tweets from strangers. Do your own research. And trust your gut. If something feels suspicious, it probably is.

Turbulence was expected on this journey, but I was determined to land the plane.

Social media was another huge component of our campaign. Not only was it a big driver for fundraising, but it showed us in action, in real time.

Using social media might seem like a no-brainer today, but even in 2017, most of my opponents were ignoring its power in favor of traditional tactics. Thanks to social media, we could livestream the concerns of residents. It was an easy way to document our daily door-knocking, too. Our campaigning wasn't just idle cheerleading; you saw us making plays.

And that helped to energize our base further.

One of my favorite social media blitzes was the "If" video. We brought in Daniel Roth, a super dope videographer who would go on to be a cornerstone of my future administration's video team, to edit a profound thirty-second post that showed the real side of Birmingham.

This wasn't the eye-catching downtown development that's plastered on postcards.

The video showed me knocking on doors, speaking directly to residents. I stopped by a classroom to spend time with students. But I also walked through blighted neighborhoods, with stop signs riddled with bullet holes. And it ended with me literally at the drawing board—dry erase marker in hand, headed toward a giant whiteboard, to plot a new course for the city.

Roth suggested that the video be narrated by my reading of Rudyard Kipling's poem "If." I loved that idea. "If" just happens to be my favorite poem. And it was such a powerful depiction of the road we were traveling.

If you can keep your head when all about you . . .

If you can trust yourself when all men doubt you . . .

If you can wait and not be tired by waiting . . .

If you can talk with crowds and keep your virtue . . .

Yours is the Earth and everything that's in it.

So many times on the campaign trail, I was asked the same question: Do you really think you can win? I answered the same every time: I wouldn't be running if I didn't think I could win.

For every doubt that entered our minds, every blatant lie thrown our way or obstacle placed before us, we received confirmation that we were on the right path. It came from all corners of my support systems.

It came from Our Revolution, the progressive political action organization birthed from Bernie Sanders's campaign that not only endorsed us but provided financial and volunteer support.

It came from Washington, DC–based Pine Street Strategies, which spread our message on the national stage when local media still doubted our impact.

It came from donations and support from Morehouse brothers who fought on my behalf, and the scores of volunteers who knocked on those fifty thousand doors in blistering heat and soaking rain.

The irony of hope is that it invokes fear—fear of the unknown. Fear of new leadership. Fear of a shaking of the status quo.

But the unpredictability of hope is what makes it so beautiful. It represents a fresh slate, a new start. Hope is the sharp left turn away from the tired, stagnant present.

We were on the precipice of change.

Music—yeah, I've given this book a musical refrain. And music was a big part of my campaign.

Tee Grizzley's "First Day Out" was a song of redemption. While he was celebrating his future after walking away from incarceration, we were also embracing our new destinies. 21 Savage's minimalistic trap banger "Bank Account" was simplistic in its approach but brilliant in its catchy execution.

Jay Z's "Story of O.J." took a different approach, sampling Nina Simone's "Four Women" to craft a commentary around the Black community's relationship with wealth. O. J. Simpson, the song's namesake, once said, "I'm not Black, I'm O. J.," as if his success had transcended his race. Jay's dismissive response to that mindset—". . . OK"—is a reminder that no matter the success we achieve, we have to stay grounded.

N.E.R.D.'s *In Search Of. . .* album never left my rotation. In the early 2000s, Virginia-based superproducers Chad Hugo and Pharrell Williams were dominating the R&B and hip-hop scene with their hyperactive, space-age production. But as the collective known as N.E.R.D., they expanded their near-limitless creativity, embracing rock elements to transform into an alternative rock/hip-hop/funk band that felt like an intergalactic mosh pit on Pluto.

As The Neptunes, Chad and Skateboard P were already on top of the world. But they had more to give, and they knew complacency was the gateway to apathy. As N.E.R.D., they kept experimenting, kept pushing the needle, kept moving music forward.

The lessons of all these songs, and more, motivated me in the most stressful of moments. My campaign even released a mixtape to residents, a tradition that continues today with my Mayoral Mixtape series.

Check them out on Spotify. You won't regret it.

But my greatest musical life coach during the campaign may have been the big homie Jeezy.

By 2017, Jeezy (back when he was still considered Young) had already been an established rap star for nearly a decade, helping to establish Atlanta as the capital city of rap. His 2008 album, *The Recession*, was the third of four consecutive platinum releases. The Snowman was on fire.

Don't misunderstand me, I by no means condone Jeezy's criminal past (he's even condemned aspects of it in recent years) but I've always respected the frank authenticity in his raps. Due to a broken home life, he found solace in the streets. Gang members became his family, and the drug trade became his occupation—that is, until music became his new hustle.

True to their names, Jeezy's previous albums—*Thug Motivation 101* and *102*—used triumphant trap tracks to glorify the fast life. But *The Recession* was a little different. Released during the height of America's Great Recession, Jeezy's motivational speaker message evolved. Instead of a celebration of rags to riches through ill-gotten gains, it was a much more grounded look at the price of fame.

The *Motivation* albums were about overcoming by any means necessary. *The Recession* was about surviving when your world begins to crumble.

If you can stop bopping your heads to the majestic production of "Vacation" and "Crazy World" for a second (and I won't blame you if you can't) and absorb Jeezy's messages, there's a lot of sorrow in his words. "Crazy World" begins with a plea for listeners to vote for Barack Obama, a blatant cry for change for a community where job options are few. "Vacation" showcases Jeezy in search of peace of mind, outright saying that the only thing he fears is the Feds.

That's not hyperbole—Jeezy's name was attached to the Black Mafia Family, a drug trafficking organization that's probably best known today for being depicted in the *BMF* TV series. The FBI was investigating the group around this time, so Jeezy was having some sleepless nights.

The fear of past sins catching up to you will humble even the bravest of men.

Again, I don't glorify or even relate to Jeezy's past indiscretions, but I definitely could relate to the frustration of wanting more from your community, and its leaders.

The Recession featured one of his most notable songs to date—"My President." Jeezy made amends with former rival Nas to record the track on the very day Barack Obama claimed the Democratic nomination for the presidency. It may have seemed presumptuous to claim that Obama was the new president four or five months before the election took place, but Jeezy's enthusiasm embodied the hope of a nation hungry for change.

No matter the outcome of the election, Obama was the face of hope. His community was in dire need of that hope so, as the church folks say, he named and claimed his victory.

"My President" proved to be prophetic. Why wait for change when you can speak it into existence?

As we neared Election Day, I only had one request from my team. If the people of Birmingham saw enough faith in me to elect me as their mayor, I wanted to enter the victory party to Jeezy's "Put On," my favorite song on the album.

The concept of the song is simple—in everything I say, in every step I take, in every action I make, I represent my city to the fullest.

When Jeezy shouts out the Eastside, he might as well have been saying East Lake. When he yells Southside, I'm yelling South Titusville. Westside? I see you West Goldmire. Jeezy didn't mention the North, but what's good, North Birmingham?

Every quadrant of our city deserves that love. And I was going to fight for every corner, every one of those ninety-nine neighborhoods, if I received the honor of leading.

The days before Election Day were tense. We were confident, but we knew a runoff likely was in the cards. We didn't have it in the bag. Not yet.

The biggest X-factor was well-known family man Chris Woods.

Woods had the double whammy of being a recognizable name in both the civil rights and sports arenas. He's the son of the Rev. Calvin Woods, who was a big figure in the Birmingham movement for civil and human rights. But he had also made a name for himself on the gridiron, playing football at Auburn University and later with the Los Angeles Raiders and Denver Broncos in the NFL.

Birmingham reveres its civil rights heroes and obsesses over football. On paper, he was formidable. He was also motivated—Bell wasn't knocking on doors, but Woods was. He seemed like he could be a good alternative for voters seeking change. The Christian family man with a known name and decorated sports background might be a safer bet than the skinny kid from around the way.

But we didn't have time for hypotheticals. We pressed hard in those last days.

A big turning point came from Bernie Sanders himself. Our campaign had been reaching out to Sanders's team for an endorsement, which came two days before the election. Bernie recorded 12,000 direct-to-voicemail drops to people who likely voted for Sanders in 2016. Instead of calling voters directly, this message went straight to voicemail boxes.

"I'm Bernie, vote for Randall, it's important"—that's the condensed version of the message, and it hit home. Someone ripped the audio, posted it online, and it went viral across social media. The face of the progressive movement had my back, and I was very grateful. Due to Bernie's endorsement, 1,200 of those 12,000 people we targeted with that call—all first-time municipal voters—came out to the polls in support of this movement.

We were empowering a new base of voters.

The final days of the campaign were all about turnout. Once again, shout-out to my Morehouse brothers—so many of them came to town to voice support and get folks to the polls.

But it all came down to Election Night.

Ed's downtown loft once again became the war room. Lindsay was posted up poring over numbers, and my homegirl Kelli was there at like 5:00 a.m. ready to work.

As the numbers came in, I was calm on the outside but stressing on the inside.

Would this work? Do the people of Birmingham really want me? Can we do this?

I retreated back to my days with InStep Ministry, the little kid who no one believed had a commanding enough presence to lead a gospel step troupe.

But I believed it.

I flashed back to hitting the campaign trail for the school board. I was just a law student with no background in education; no one believed I could represent a district, let alone lead the entire board.

But I believed it.

Leadership isn't just having the capacity to lead; it's having the ability to prove to others that you can lead.

I believed, but did Birmingham?

It turns out they did.

I won 40.8 percent of the vote that night, with incumbent Bell gaining 36.6 percent. Woods came in at 18.1 percent.

That election night, in my opinion, was the real turning point in my career. Everything prior to that was hypothetical—the incumbent likely was vulnerable, I might be able to tap into a new set of voters, I possibly could shake the status quo . . . but it all reeked of speculation, of false hope.

Nah, bruh, this was real. We were here.

And there was no time to rest, no big celebration for the win.

There was a runoff looming, and we had to gameplan.

We took Wednesday off, held a meeting to strategize on Thursday, and got back on the streets Friday.

We were in the endgame now.

• • •

When I think about the moment I'm most proud of in my campaign, I think of two names—Phyllis Green and Carol Hatcher. When Phyllis and Carol volunteered for my campaign, they were strangers. But they quickly became not just partners, but best friends.

Phyllis Green is better known as Ma Phyllis, a stalwart in the Gate City public housing community. Almost every close-knit Black community has a "Big Momma"—the elder stateswoman who brings equal parts joy and tough talk to her neighborhood. You never want to cross Big Momma; you have too much respect for her to let her down. But seeing her smile means everything. It turns out this is true, even when that Big Momma is white.

Along with being Gate City's surrogate mom, she was also a very active volunteer. She wanted to make change in her neighborhood and was more than willing to be at the forefront.

Phyllis didn't know me but she believed in me. She visited our campaign website and signed up as a volunteer for our canvassing efforts, knocking on doors and hearing from residents.

Carol Hatcher didn't know me either, but it only took one meeting to make a connection. When she entered our campaign office with hopes of volunteering, we had no idea that she carried decades of campaigning expertise. Carol had volunteered in every Birmingham mayoral campaign since Mayor Richard Arrington's historic first run in 1979.

She had been volunteering in races longer than some of our staff had been alive on this planet. Including me.

Though she had no prior knowledge of me, Carol knew my name, thanks to months of our daily door-knocking and meeting with residents. We were gaining buzz, and she wanted to help spread it.

Historically, Birmingham has been an incredibly divided town—and not just in the ways you're probably thinking. Yes, the days of segregated water fountains and lunch counters are gone, but the gaps remain. There are divides in ideologies, in access to basic services like healthy foods. There are inequities in infrastructure between affluent neighborhoods and underserved areas. And these disparities often boil down to color lines. They're the cost of segregation, the sins of our grandfathers' past still crippling our communities.

Carol and Phyllis represent two different walks of life in Birmingham—they're from different parts of town, two different backgrounds, two different races, two different cultures but with one core belief: They knew things could be better. And they were willing to roll up their sleeves and do it. Together.

It takes bravery to knock on the doors of hundreds of strangers, but Carol and Phyllis had backbones of steel. During one day of canvassing, Phyllis was paired with an older Black gentleman. He was happy to canvass but he was a bit nervous about knocking on doors after dark in Gate City.

Oh, but he'd never met anybody like Ma Phyllis. She didn't bat an eyelash—she chuckled and told that brother to press on and keep knocking. There was a job to do.

Those ladies were fearless. And they found a bond with each other.

The duo teamed up and were a force of political nature. They hit the streets so much and so often that they began to exceed the designated homes they were assigned to visit.

We could barely rein them in. Our canvassing strategy was very targeted, and we often discouraged volunteers from branching out on their own. Carol and Phyllis were too motivated for that, however. Forget what a run sheet of that day's canvassing instructions told them, their plan was to engage as many people as they could for as long as it took. If that meant starting at 6:30 a.m. and walking until nightfall, so be it.

Here's what's most beautiful about their relationship: Their bond lasted well beyond that first campaign. They continued to work diligently in Gate City, meeting with residents, hearing their concerns, and serving as their advocates.

Their commitment to service has made them inseparable friends. That's powerful.

If not for the campaign, those two beautiful women might never have met. You see, there's something special about walking the streets for a cause you believe in. It fosters camaraderie, and in their case, friendship.

When I embarked on this journey, my goal was to unite Birmingham. Phyllis and Carol were the personification of that unity, looking beyond themselves for a greater goal, and building new coalitions along the way.

If nothing else came of my mayoral run, I'd rest easier knowing that I helped bring people together.

Phyllis and Carol were the superstars of our team. They shined brighter together than individually.

Gate City has two Big Mommas now.

As the runoff kicked into high gear, so did a new round of support. We had a massive volunteer event at Rogue Tavern, a beloved community gathering spot that sadly closed in 2019. The place was packed with hundreds of folks who believed in our mission. We received an endorsement from Chris Woods, and his team was absorbed into ours.

And, of course, we knocked on doors. Our original goal was to knock on the door of every municipal voter in the city—hopefully three times over. Sometimes we spoke to residents face-to-face, sometimes we left campaign material on doors.

By now, people knew my name.

I can't say that we didn't have our struggles, though. We brought in a new team to assist with the runoff, which caused a few clashes with the original staff. The approach was more old school—honking horns, waving signs, etc. It was a far cry from the more data-driven, grassroots approach we had been using months earlier.

I also blew a debate against Bell in those final days. Bell is a powerful, bombastic presence. My approach was much more soft-spoken back then. Plus my energy was off and my nerves were rattled. Fortunately for me, folks seemed more preoccupied with Bell's poor makeup job than with my shaky delivery. Whatever makeup they used on him didn't blend well and man, the memes were ruthless. I got lucky with that one.

But there would be no luck involved on the day of the runoff, October 3, 2017, and it all focused on historic Legion Field.

Legion Field, a.k.a. the Old Gray Lady, is a proud Birmingham landmark. Its biggest claim to fame currently is as the home of the annual Magic City Classic, the largest HBCU football game in the country. When Alabama A&M University and Alabama State University come to town every October, it's an event.

We were ready to make more history on that night.

The voting box at Legion Field represents the largest precinct in the city. More often than not, that Old Gray Lady dictates the fate of elections in Birmingham.

Around 7:00 p.m. I went to the box, surrounded by friends, supporters, Morehouse brothers, volunteers, and family. They stood around me and prayed that God's will be done.

It was out of my hands at that point. God would have His way.

I went home, took a shower, and while getting dressed got a text from Daniel saying "you're the next mayor of Birmingham."

We beat Bell at Legion Field, hands down. I knew it was going to be a good night. Daniel's data had predicted that turnout would be even larger for the runoff, and things were looking up for us.

I headed over to Haven, the event venue where my team was hosting a watch party, to see the results come in. My mom was there, as was Daniel, Ed, my Morehouse brothers, the whole crew.

I was calm. Confident. Happy.

And when the final numbers came in, I was overjoyed.

Randall Lee Woodfin, the bagger from Western Supermarket, defeated longtime political mainstay William Bell, with 59 percent of the vote to his 41 percent.

The atmosphere was electric. Don't ask me what I said during my victory speech, I barely remember a thing. I do know that, just as I had requested, I approached the stage to Jeezy's "Put On." From that night forward it became the theme song of my administration. I remember hugging my mom. I remember bringing my family and Morehouse brothers onstage. I remember shouting out the volunteers who worked countless hours and walked countless miles in support of my vision.

I also remember Bell calling me after the win. He was gracious in defeat and continues to be so today.

But I also remember thinking that this night proved that Birmingham can be more than a city of perpetual promise.

Birmingham's incredible Civil Rights achievements have made it a beacon of hope for generations. Many of those achievements were driven forward by its youth, those fearless Civil Rights Movement Foot Soldiers.

And no offense to the gains made in our city in the decades that followed, but for so long we rested on our laurels, as buildings literally crumbled around us and weeds grew tall in their wake. We talked more about our potential than we spent time achieving it.

In that one special night, though, hope began to peer from behind the clouds again.

My victory was far from a one-man show. Volunteers ranging from teenagers to eighty-five-year-olds fueled it. It was Ed's unconventional management style and Daniel and Griff's mastery of data that were the foundation. It was the scores of volunteers—unsung heroes like Arnee Odoms, Rashad Grimes, Emily Poole, EJ Turner, and so many more who were our arms and legs.

It was the Morehouse brothers who were by my side all the way back in the early 2000s and still stand shoulder to shoulder with me today. It was the love of my mother and father, my sisters, and my brother who still looks down on me from above as I write this.

It was every young person who wanted to be part of change, and every longtime resident who deserved more in their community.

It was Phyllis and Carol, the representation of a city united.

It was as Birmingham as you can get. Scrappy underdogs who changed the course of history.

We beat the odds.

We put on for our city.

———

October 3, 2017. It was the night I defeated a seemingly unstoppable political giant, becoming Birmingham's youngest mayor. It was the night countless campaign workers, supporters, and volunteers felt validation.

It was a night that changed Birmingham. And my life.

Here are my prepared remarks for that night—although I'll admit, the adrenaline was flowing so rapidly, I didn't always stick to the script. But y'all can see what I intended to share with Birmingham: a message of hope.

Thank you, everyone. Thank you all for coming out tonight!

I've said it once and I'll say it again, the resistance to President Donald Trump starts in Birmingham tonight.

It's been one year, one month, and twenty-one days since I declared my candidacy for mayor at the North Birmingham Recreation Center. Since that humid summer day, it has been a glorious challenge. From the very beginning, the pollsters and political insiders thought our campaign didn't have a chance. We heard it all. That "I was too young," my opponent was "too formidable to overcome," and my personal favorite—"it wasn't my time."

To the early and late skeptics, tell that to the volunteers who knocked on 50,000 doors and made 45,000 phone calls. To those who dedicated many long nights and early mornings and created a grassroots enthusiasm that helped spread our message across this great city and beyond, tonight belongs to you. You believed. And so did the people of Birmingham.

I want to congratulate the newly elected and re-elected officials tonight. Rest assured, you have a partner in the mayor's office who is eager and willing to work with you to make this city better and improve the lives of all Birmingham residents.

To William Bell, this was a long, hard-fought campaign, and though we may have had our differences, I have the utmost respect for the forty years of service that you have given Birmingham throughout your career. You are a true son of Birmingham, and I thank you for your service.

And to those who did not support my campaign, I want to let you know one thing. I might not have earned your vote today, but I promise I will work, and continue working, to earn your support. Because, the reality is that we love and deeply care about the future of Birmingham. And moving this city forward requires a genuine all-hands-on-deck approach.

Accordingly, I also want to thank Chris Woods, Patricia Bell, Fernandez Simms, and the other candidates in the August 22 election for your persistence in elevating the many issues challenging our city and holding our current administration accountable. I thank you dearly for your service to our city.

To my family. Growing up in North Birmingham, you made me resilient. You brought so much joy and purpose to my life. I love you dearly. Thank you.

And my mother:

Your example of selflessness and generosity over the years has shaped my outlook on public service. As a public school teacher, you opened your heart and classroom to countless children. You often bought school supplies with money you did not have simply because you believed that every child had a calling in life. You believed that every young person should have the opportunity to reach their God-given potential. And today, I share this same belief with families across the city.

My mother's experience from the front lines of our public school classrooms fueled my passion for education and ultimately shaped my life's purpose. Mother, thank you.

And my campaign staff—wow, you guys are amazing! I'm humbled by the countless hours you put in. Volunteers of all ages, from various corners of Birmingham—knocking on doors and making calls. Often operating on just a couple hours of sleep, stale bagels, and a slice of cold pizza. But driven by the belief that Birmingham won't change unless we change the people we send to City Hall. I look forward to bringing your passion and work ethic to City Hall.

I'd also like to thank the good people across our great city. As a true son of Birmingham, it was a privilege meeting so many families over the course of this campaign. You opened your homes to me, and you shared your stories wherever I went—from local diners to community meetings and town halls. I listened as you shared your hopes and dreams with me. Great aspirations such as starting a small business. Or sending a child to college.

You also shared your anxieties with me. For instance, is my child safe walking home from school? Or is it possible to thrive when my family is part of the 30 percent of Birmingham's population living under the poverty line? These are real fears that kept my family, as well as countless others, up late at night thinking about a way forward.

To those I have met along this journey, I will not forget you. As your mayor, I will carry your heartfelt stories with me to City Hall. And I will be the voice and champion that you deserve.

Today's election did not take place in an environment of peace and prosperity. Our country is faced with real, urgent threats. Threats to our national security and global economy. Threats from growing inequality, climate change, and mounting federal debt.

Moreover, the Trump administration has been a nightmare for many Americans. Our healthcare is under constant threat of being repealed. Voting rights and various civil rights that many of our forefathers fought tirelessly to obtain are being taken away.

And just yesterday, over fifty innocent people were murdered and five hundred injured during a senseless act of violence in Nevada. Our country is hurting.

But people are also hurting right here in Birmingham.

Last year, 109 people were murdered on the streets of Birmingham. And sadly, we are on pace for 125 more murders in 2017. That is way too many lives lost, too many funerals for our young Black men and women. Too much potential lost. Those grieving mothers and fathers deserve better.

And because violence is a symptom of poverty—the real sin of society—it is no surprise that opportunities are scarce. Thirty percent of Birmingham residents live under the poverty line. How can families possibly thrive under these conditions?

Additionally, the American City Business Journals ranked Birmingham 102 among the nation's 106 largest metro areas in job growth between 2010 and 2016. As if starting a business wasn't tough enough, city licensing, taxes, and regulations force Birmingham entrepreneurs to spend more time navigating City Hall than running their own business.

These are real concerns that keep residents up at night, and they inspired me to run for mayor.

That is why strong progressive leadership at the local level is more important than ever.

Residents should expect basic services like street paving, sidewalks, curbs, and lighting to be implemented with a sense of urgency.

But what does progressive mean? Merriam-Webster defines it as "making use of or interested in new ideas, findings, or opportunities."

I know the campaign is over and folks want to celebrate tonight, but our work is not over. We are just getting started. If you want to change Birmingham, if you want to transform all ninety-nine neighborhoods, I can't do it alone. If we want to make Birmingham the best version of itself, you must stay engaged. You must hold my City Hall accountable. And I encourage you to hold me accountable.

Keep organizing. Keep volunteering. And together, we will build a system that works for everyone.

Thank you, good night, and God bless Birmingham, Alabama.

Randall L. Woodfin, Mayor
Acceptance Speech at Haven in Birmingham
October 2017

CHAPTER 8

Y'ALL SCARED

Before we reminisce together about my initial years as mayor, let's skip ahead to the most challenging times I faced in office.

The year 2020. I know, it sends shivers down my spine, too.

New Year's Eve 2020 was one of those nerve-wracking nights. It's usually a time of celebration, an ode to new beginnings.

But for me and my family, December 31 is a somber reminder of life's fragility. For two years, there were no bottles popping. The only things flowing were the tears.

On December 31, 2019, we lost my stepdad. As you can imagine, my mom was devastated. For the year that followed, she made a social media post about him almost every day. Her heart was torn, and it hurt me to see a woman who had experienced so much heartbreak in her life dealt another aching blow.

December 31, 2020, only brought more pain.

My mom had planned to visit her husband's grave on the anniversary of his death. But that wasn't to be. My great-grandmother was in the hospital, suffering from the COVID-19 virus. She was unconscious.

And I was bedridden at home, also suffering serious effects from the COVID-19 virus.

Although I could barely move my body, my mind was racing. I thought about my mother. Her husband? Gone. Her grandmother? Unconscious. Her son? Isolated. And, due to COVID protocols, my mother was unable to be at either of our sides. Knowing my mother was in pain hurt more than anything 'Rona could throw at me.

The next day, the beginning of the new year, my great-grandmother passed away. And my mom lost it. She went from Mama Woodfin to Mama Bear.

She went off on the hospital folks. And can you blame her? She had lost her husband a year ago, just lost her grandmother, and she was terrified I was next.

And she wasn't even allowed to see me.

My mother is also immuno-compromised; so, no matter how badly she wanted to be by my side, it was a risk none of us—not my doctor, not me—wanted to take.

I called my mom, told her that everything was going to be OK and to just follow the doctors' advice.

I had to be strong for her. But it just hurt so damn much.

I was close to my great-grandmother. She had driven me to work at Western Supermarket many times. I had sat by her side many summers as she watched *The Young and the Restless*. (That Victor Newman was a pimp.) She was our rock, my mom's best friend.

And now she was gone.

My body was wracked with COVID and my heart was drowning in fear. I couldn't save my great-grandmother. And I couldn't protect my mom.

Since the beginning of the COVID-19 pandemic in early 2020, at least 1 in 260 residents of Jefferson County, which houses my city, died of the disease. As of this writing, there have been more than 2,500 reported deaths here.

It rips me apart that my great-grandmother's name is part of that horrible statistic.

It's why I get so pissed off when COVID deniers try to write off a devastating pandemic as some sort of fairy tale made up by the government. Since 2020, COVID has ripped so many loved ones from our lives.

These aren't talking-point characters for Twitter debates or cable news banter. They are real people, with real lives, whom we loved immeasurably. They were moms and dads, aunts and uncles. Our children. Our church members. Our coworkers and friends. Our great-grandmothers.

How dare we politicize their deaths. It's a mockery of their memory.

I wasn't able to attend my great-grandmother's funeral. I had to watch it on video. And although I hope my words helped from afar, I was not able to comfort my mother personally.

COVID sucks. In so many ways.

My introduction to COVID-19, or the coronavirus, if we want to use its OG name, was sometime in January or February of 2020. Down the hall from my chambers in City Hall, there's a TV that's usually tuned into a cable news channel. While strolling by the television, I caught a glimpse of the mayor of New York speaking live about this virus and the lives affected.

There was an accompanying split screen that showed death tolls, along with makeshift morgues. Chilling stuff.

I thought to myself *this is crazy*, but naively thought that the issue would be isolated to New York.

A few weeks later, I'd be proven very, very wrong.

On March 10, I called my friend Josh Carpenter, who at the time served as director of the City of Birmingham's Department of Innovation and Economic Opportunity. He was on paternity leave from work—his first daughter had been born just seven days prior. I was his first visitor after the baby's birth, and I hated to bother him during this blissful time in his life.

But I had a feeling a storm was brewing. I wanted his input.

My question was simple: "How will COVID impact our city?" Josh went into data collection mode.

The very next day, the National Basketball Association suspended its season after a player tested positive for COVID. Everything changed.

Before that suspension, COVID was just a hypothetical bogeyman in the minds of most residents. Sure, it was sad that people were losing their lives, but this would barely be a blip on most of our radars. This wouldn't change our day-to-day.

Right?

Well, if you want to get America's attention, screw with their sports. Things got really real, really quick in that instant.

The World Health Organization had already declared the COVID-19 outbreak to be a worldwide pandemic earlier that day. But the shutdown of the NBA signified that the comforts of normality were being eradicated.

Terms like *global pandemic* and *quarantines* were no longer reserved for science fiction movies. This was our real life.

What started out simply as data gathering quickly became pandemic prep. And here in Alabama, we knew there would be a very difficult road ahead.

To understand the scope of what we were facing, you have to understand Alabama's history.

Simply put, our population is unhealthy.

According to data from the census bureau, one in ten Alabamians are without health insurance. Communities of color are disproportionally uncovered. Among white Alabamians, 91 percent have some form of health insurance, yet only 88 percent of Black Alabamians can say the same. That 3 percent difference may seem slight, but when you consider that Black residents face higher rates of death due to heart disease, diabetes, stroke, and cancer than white residents, according to the Jefferson County Health Action Partnership's Community Health Equity Report, it can be a large cause for concern for many families.

And let's not forget the infamous "Tuskegee Experiments."

Originally known as the Tuskegee Study of Untreated Syphilis in the Negro Male, the study began in 1932 and enrolled 600 poor Black sharecroppers from Macon County, Alabama, with promises of free medical care. Of those men, 399 had latent syphilis, 201 did not. The researchers callously did not tell the infected men of their illness, instead giving placebos and other ineffective attempts as care, even after antibiotics became available.

They used us as lab rats.

What was planned as a six-month study became a forty-year-nightmare. After funding was lost, the men were never treated.

The result: Eight patients died from syphilis, one hundred more died from complications related to syphilis, forty of the patients' wives were infected with syphilis, and nineteen children were born with congenital syphilis.

Over time, this horror story would be misunderstood, with the incorrect assumption that the men were intentionally infected with syphilis instead of being denied treatment (which became a big talking point for the anti-COVID vaccine crowd).

Regardless, this study continued all the way until 1972, just fifty years removed from the events of COVID. When you add the fact that this occurred in our own backyard, then yes, Black residents had every right to be fearful of public health initiatives.

To paraphrase the sobering words of Dr. Selwyn Vickers, one of the many medical partners we leaned on during these tough times, COVID-19 poured gasoline on the smoldering embers of health access and racial inequality.

It also became very clear to me that we'd have to shut down businesses to save lives—a fact that infuriated state representatives who said I didn't have the power to do so.

My response? I have a responsibility to save the lives of my residents. If you have a problem with that, you have my number; give me a call and pull up.

But more on that later.

Local businesses only have enough money to survive two to three weeks on hand. A closure—especially for an extended amount of time—would be devastating.

It was a no-win situation. But I had to save lives.

In collaboration with the Department of Innovation and Economic Opportunity, we had worked to put $1 billion in capital investments into our community. In an instant, that would all be gone. By August of 2020, 17 percent of Jefferson County's workforce would be out of work.

I knew the tax system would plummet. I knew that all the hard work we had done to rebuild Birmingham's economy would be lost. (We'll talk more about those efforts soon.) I knew small businesses would be the first to bear the brunt of the coming maelstrom.

Think of it this way: That small business owner has a family. If the business shuts down, it hurts that owner's family. Likewise, we're a city that derives its revenue from sales taxes. If that business isn't operating—isn't making sales—we as a city hurt, as well.

But I had to save lives.

One day I walked into Josh's office to see a clearly frazzled man. He had been consulting the dissertation of Ben Bernanke, former chair of the Federal Reserve of the United States, to get an understanding of what we were facing. The numbers didn't lie—from March to August 2020, we could be facing a crisis unseen since the Great Depression.

All these folks would be losing jobs, and so many of our uninsured, at-risk residents could be staring death in the face in the coming weeks. And Josh and I were taking it personally.

The weight of my city was on my shoulders. And here's what I said to Josh: "Hey, want to watch some *Chappelle*?"

It wasn't to make light of the moment. But when it comes to leadership, sometimes you have to take a step back, regroup, and recalibrate.

In this case, recalibrating came in the form of *Chappelle's Show*'s sketch called "The Racial Draft."

For just a few minutes, we could escape the grim realities of the coming battles and find a bit of joy in the world. In 2020, we spent so much time chasing "normality"—those fleeting moments reminded us of less frightening times.

I knew that we couldn't put our head in the sand. We had to confront and adapt to this new normal. But we couldn't lose ourselves in the process.

You laugh to keep from crying, I guess.

My admiration of hip-hop icons Outkast is well documented by now, but they aren't the only ATLiens who took Southern hip-hop to the stratosphere.

A year after Outkast's debut album—months after the 1995 Source Awards set hip-hop on a new trajectory—a new Atlanta-based collective hit the ground running.

Cameron "Big Gipp" Gipp, Willie "Khujo" Knighton Jr., Robert "T-Mo" Barne, and Thomas "CeeLo Green" Callaway were known as Goodie Mob and were cut from the same Southern cloth as 'Kast. In fact, Goodie Mob members popped up on two different tracks on Outkast's debut album and both groups were part of the infamous Dungeon Family collective I mentioned earlier.

Some of you are probably familiar with CeeLo, who became a high-profile star away from his Dungeon siblings thanks to his appearances on TV shows like *The Voice* and hit singles like "Crazy" and, um, let's call it "Forget You."

CeeLo's solo aspirations are cool, but I'll always know him best as one-fourth of one of hip-hop's most underrated acts. While I personally prefer Goodie's sophomore album (their single "Black Ice," ironically, is pure fire), their debut, 1995's *Soul Food*, is what broke ground.

Due to their affiliation with Outkast, most fans and critics expected Goodie's debut to be in the same vein as 'Kast's, but what we got was a much more bleak depiction of Southern life.

Bleak, but absolutely accurate.

Soul Food felt like the evolution of Mississippi Delta blues, sorrowful in both delivery and subject matter. In the very first song on the album, the group is burned by their struggles, even contemplating death over facing their reality. It's a portrait of men locked within a metaphorical cage.

These themes extend through the album. Poverty. Unemployment. Feeling trapped within our own homes. Even the fear of race wars. And it was always poor Black Southerners who felt the brunt of these harsh realities.

After living through 2020, I bet this all sounds frighteningly familiar. Goodie Mob must have had a crystal ball in that dungeon.

Don't get me wrong. While *Soul Food* is a very heavy album, there are moments of levity and, most importantly, hope. The album closer— "The Day After"—parts the clouds that loom over much of the album, celebrating the lives of elders who have passed on, embracing the fortitude that comes from enduring the harshest realities, and reminding listeners that freedom is always just footsteps away.

You see, *Soul Food* isn't an album about Southern sorrow. It's a survival kit. It grabs fear by its throat and shoves it to the dirt.

We're too proud, too strong, too Black to fail.

And that was the mantra for 2020.

Poor, Black communities were hit hardest by the pandemic. People of color make up over half of the uninsured population in the US, with Black and Latinx communities more likely to work low-wage jobs—jobs that usually lack strong health insurance options or paid sick time off.

Black Americans' struggles with diabetes, obesity, asthma, and cardiovascular disease also made them much more susceptible to COVID, and more likely to suffer complications.

But our people know adversity, and we know how to face it head-on.

Soul Food was prescient, and also a reflection of a community historically under attack. But it also provided the wisdom, the tools, and the inspiration to fight back.

Goodie Mob never received the mainstream acclaim that Outkast enjoyed, but they're just as important to hip-hop culture. Landing at No. 1 on the charts is great and all, but you can't use numbers to measure classic albums. To me, classics are measured in moments.

Soul Food was unquestionably a moment.

The year 2020 was shrouded in uncertainty. But in moments like those, we pull inspiration from all places. Nothing is more inspiring than the story of four brothers who defeated the odds.

They never turned their back on the homes that raised them. It wasn't about escaping; it was about uplifting. I love that journey.

Soul Food was our own personal GPS, a guiding light through the darkest of nights. And my mission, my motivation in 2020, was to get us back on that road called hope.

On March 13, 2020, Jefferson County received its first documented case of coronavirus. Just one day prior, Dr. Mark Wilson, health officer at the Jefferson County Department of Health and a trusted colleague during these trying times, issued a public statement asking public gatherings to be limited.

Cases of COVID began rising across our city. That naïveté I showed back in January and February was long gone.

COVID was here and I had to lead. And leadership comes with tough choices.

The first step in leadership is building a team. I won't pretend to be the smartest man in the room, but I'm smart enough to know that a leader surrounds himself with experienced, capable people.

We were facing a public health crisis unlike anything in our life-times. So, I leaned on the advice of medical experts.

Sounds like good ol' common sense, right? Well, in 2020, good sense wasn't always so common. I never understood the point of politicians attacking and discrediting our scientific community at a time when their expertise was needed most.

If you want to talk about the best producers of trap music, I can go for hours.

If you want to discuss Spike Lee's greatest cinematic achievements, I got you.

But if you want to talk about how to medically treat a global pandemic, don't ask me; ask a doctor.

You have to know your lane.

I made the very difficult decision to close nonessential businesses. Soon after that came the mask mandates.

Alabama's attorney general sent a press release to the media (before even sending it to me) saying that mandates were an overreach of my power and I was infringing on people's rights.

I said, "Bet. I'm a lawyer, too." I'll deal with the legal ramifications later. Birmingham is a city with a high proportion of seniors, many with underlying health conditions. I was terrified of people dying under my watch as leader.

If I had to take a hit politically to protect the people I serve, so be it.

The occupant of the White House at the time, the leader of the free world, saw fit to politicize a global health pandemic. Masks were painted as a source of shame. Even the virus itself was often mockingly called the "China virus," in an attempt to place blame on those outside our borders—which in turn made many US citizens of Asian and Pacific Island origin targets of hate in our own country.

That's not leadership. That's cowardice.

We were fighting a battle on many fronts—trying to safeguard the residents who were succumbing to this illness, protecting our small business community, providing support to overburdened first responders and public health teams, and attempting to block mass amounts of misinformation (from lawmakers who were injecting divisive politics into a health issue to conspiracy theorists sitting behind computer screens) that were flooding our airwaves.

Our strategy was simple—overcommunication. It was essential that the Black leader of a majority Black city be the primary voice for truth.

My office set up regular conference calls with faith leaders in our city, helping to keep them connected with resources and to build partnerships between congregations. Like government agencies, many churches and community outreach groups operate in silos and even get territorial about the communities they serve. But COVID erased the era of egos. We were all in this together, and I was happy to bridge the gaps.

We saturated the block with social media videos encouraging face coverings and pushing for vaccinations.

As stated earlier, many members of our community were skeptical of treatment—and due to the history of underserved communities being manipulated, I could empathize.

But as a leader, I'd never ask someone to do something I wasn't willing to do. If I'm pushing our at-risk community to be vaccinated, best believe I'm getting that shot, too. If I'm asking our residents to wear masks, I had to walk that walk.

No, I didn't want to wear the mask. But I also didn't want to kill someone's grandparent. If I'm deciding between my own comfort and the life of a loved one, I'm going to put on the damn mask.

Likewise, as COVID dragged on and businesses like barbershops were closed, my hairline was starting to look like Mr. Snuffleupagus from *Sesame Street*. As my hair began to resemble Florida Evans's 'do from *Good Times*, the memes started to roll in.

And you know what? I laughed. I wasn't upset. Sure, I could have called my barber to make a house visit to line me up, but that's not fair to the hundreds of residents who had to go without. I'm not better than them.

Leaders don't just lead from the headquarters behind the lines. They lead from the trenches.

That doesn't mean we didn't do everything we could to support our small businesses. In fact, it was a major priority. We couldn't wait on Washington to provide relief. We had to act quickly. With our partners, we established $5 million in aid, which would go on to save nearly a thousand jobs. We named it #BhamStrong, a tag that we had already used as a label for solidarity during 2020. Credit our public–private partnerships—support from public institutions, the private sector, and philanthropic organizations—for uniting for a greater good.

Once Washington did step in with resources, we were able to establish the Emergency Rental Assistance Program, which assisted residents who experienced difficulty in paying rent or utilities because of COVID-19. Aid was provided for struggling landlords, as well.

I'm very proud of the strides we made. In about a year and a half, our city was able to rebound from the financial toll of the pandemic. In comparison, it took nearly a decade for Birmingham to bounce back from the Great Recession of the late '00s.

Oh, and remember when the state got salty because of our pro-active mask ordinance? Thirteen days later, they followed our lead.

2020 brought out the worst in us. Crime was on the rise, not just in our city but also across the nation. Suicide rates were up. Mental health was strained.

But 2020 also brought out the best of us. Community organizations and faith leaders coming together to support residents. Nurses, fire-fighters, and other first responders literally putting their lives on the line daily, exposing themselves to illness to save strangers. The geniuses in our health community who turned to science, not politics, to combat a deadly disease. A big shout-out to our own University of Alabama at Birmingham's medical team—we're blessed to have one of the world's top medical institutions in our backyard. Their research, testing, and treatment during those uncertain times helped us turn the tide.

The year 2020 was an unprecedented time, and I'll be the first to tell you, I didn't have all the answers. Hell, at first, I had zero answers.

But I had to save lives.

The only way I could do that was to surround myself with people way smarter than me. I leaned on authentic, honest opinions from informed voices, not hollow rhetoric. I overcommunicated in every form available, from robo-calls, social media, and radio spots to TV ads, newspaper announcements, and virtual conferences. We had to touch every corner of our city to silence the misinformation.

I made very tough decisions. But I trusted my gut, and my gut told me to trust my medical advisors.

And like my favorite Goodie Mob album, we're *Still Standing*.

I've always had a connection to our seniors. It probably comes from being so close to my three grandmothers. And it's always comforting when I wrap up a conversation with an elder and they say, "Be sure to take care of yourself."

I wish I took their advice more often.

After nine months of being extremely careful—not just for my sake, but for those around me—I finally got caught slipping. December 2020, COVID knocked at my door.

Trust me (if you don't already know from experience), you don't want 'Rona as a houseguest.

I remember COVID naysayers claiming at the time that it was "no different than a cold." Well, I don't know what kind of colds y'all have had—this wasn't a cold; this was some biblical Pharaoh-level stuff.

I'll admit, I ignored the warning signs as the symptoms began to creep in. I was too distracted by city business. Headaches. Fatigue. Chills. The loss of smell and taste. Soon I would have difficulty breathing.

Black men often have an aversion to going to the doctor. I don't know if it's ego, the need to "tough it out" and put on a brave face for the family, or if it's just an inherent need to self-medicate when medical care isn't an option for struggling families. Regardless, once I realized that I probably had COVID, none of that mattered. I made treatment a priority.

After four or five days of steroids and other medication, I wasn't improving, and my breathing and chest pains were getting worse.

I was rushed to the same hospital where my grandmother had passed just a couple of days earlier. My physician, Dr. Joseph Wu, was most concerned by the breathing issues. He ran a scan.

The good news: No blood clots in my lungs.

The bad news: My COVID had advanced to COVID pneumonia.

I was hospitalized for days, receiving plasma and other treatment, and I felt horrible. Not just because of COVID; I could handle that. But I knew my family was in pain, grappling with the loss of my great-grandmother. I knew I had to get back to leading our city. Birmingham was on the mend—both financially and in terms of wellness—but there was still so much to do.

I didn't really fear COVID. I feared failure.

Finally, I recovered enough to be discharged from the hospital.

But that raggedy 'Rona. She still wasn't through with me.

About a week later, I began experiencing shooting pains in my leg. I soon felt a tingling sensation throughout my body. It literally took me minutes to hobble from the couch to the bathroom.

It's like I went from thirty-nine years old to three hundred years old overnight.

Once again, I headed in for treatment. I swear I was in the doctor's office more than City Hall at this point. This time I was diagnosed with neuro-COVID, a version of the disease that attacked the neurological system. In this case, the nerves related to the bones, joints, and muscles in my legs were the target.

But 'Rona STILL wasn't done. Ever heard of COVID tongue? If not, I'll make it simple for you—your tongue turns chalky white and feels like it's been shredded by a thousand razor blades. Fun times.

In total, I had COVID—in all its myriad, mutant, musty forms—off and on from the end of December 2020 until early March 2021.

So, the next time you try to downplay COVID as some sort of grand hoax created by the Illuminati, or whatever some random YouTube video claims, think about the lives this illness permanently changed—both physically and emotionally.

If you don't want to get a vaccine, fine, that's your choice. If you think wearing a mask goes against your freedoms, whatever.

Just stay out of my face. I'm over this COVID stuff.

———

I don't have to remind y'all—2020 sucked. COVID presented unprecedented challenges for our nation. It was a time filled with uncertainty and confusion. It was also an era rife with misinformation.

Two months after businesses closed in March, I released this letter to our residents to alleviate their fears, clarify our difficult decisions, and to ensure them that their health and safety were our priority.

This wasn't about politics. It was all about keeping our residents safe.

Dear Birmingham,

I feel obligated to speak directly with you on the road we've traveled the past eight weeks, and where we're currently headed.

From the moment COVID-19 began to take hold of our community, I have attempted to solve three key issues—to keep people from dying, to help reduce community spread, and to prevent our local hospitals from being overburdened.

My approach has been to equally address the public health crisis and the economic crisis created from this pandemic.

It has hurt me deeply to speak with residents who are now unemployed, who have lost their health insurance, and who have shuttered their businesses. We are in a situation shared by every city in America. That's why, as a city, we acted quickly to help stabilize small businesses through emergency loan funds. My team is working around the clock to figure out how we can best support businesses as they look to reopen.

As leaders, we have one major duty, and that's to protect the community we serve.

"Putting People First" isn't just a slogan. It is the strategy for how we govern.

It's with that in mind that businesses were closed March 24, following the order of the Jefferson County Department of Health. On that day, there were 215 cases of COVID-19 in Alabama, with just one death announced. Twelve days later when the State of Alabama shut down nonessential business there were 1,927 confirmed coronavirus cases and 48 deaths in Alabama.

Today, there are 9,486 confirmed cases and 388 deaths.

When it comes to the reopening of Alabama, we must choose data over dates. Here's the reality: the cases of COVID-19 continue to rise in our state. In fact, they increased by 20 percent in Alabama last week.

The state's amended Safer at Home order goes into effect on Monday, May 11. More businesses will open, including restaurants, bars, barbershops, and hair salons. These businesses are a hallmark of Birmingham's quality of life. It has pained me to see them close, especially those who have been forced to close for good.

But as you find it necessary to return to shopping, supporting small business, and to the workplace, I want to remind you of the importance of staying safe and healthy. If you are in Birmingham, please continue to wear face coverings. Right now, it's the law. Research has shown that many people are not showing any signs of COVID-19 but that they could be carriers. For those who are carriers or potential carriers, wearing a face covering helps reduce the spread. And that's all I'm trying to do—stop the spread of this deadly virus.

If you don't have to go out, continue to stay home. If you do have to go out, please practice social distancing, remember to wash your hands, and remember to wear a face covering. I've said this before and I will continue to say this: we are all in this together. And if we can all join in agreement to do whatever we can to stay safe and healthy but to also find safe ways to support each other, let's do it. Please remember to practice common sense during this ongoing crisis.

Public health leaders ask people to wear face coverings, not to protect themselves, but to protect those they are around. It is selflessness that defines community responsibility and self-interestedness that defines personal responsibility.

On this Mother's Day, when we take time to celebrate the women who have given so much for us, I'm reminded of one word—sacrifice.

Too many in our community have already lost loved ones to this deadly illness. There are families now experiencing their first Mother's Day without mom. It's for those grieving families, and for those strong women like my own mother who are currently at risk, that we make personal sacrifices for the wellness of our community. It's the least we can do for those who have given so much for us.

As a people, let's do the things we have learned to slow the spread of this disease. When you leave home, cover your mouth and nose. Keep a safe distance from others who are not part of your household. For businesses, adhere to the requirements put in place to keep your employees, your customers, and yourselves safe. That includes requiring face coverings for those entering store fronts in the City of Birmingham.

Let's put politics aside and simply do what's right to keep Birmingham healthy and safe.

Randall L. Woodfin, Mayor
Letter to Birmingham Residents
May 2020

CHAPTER 9

LIBERATION

E arly evening. May 31, 2020.

Hours earlier I led a peaceful rally protesting the brutal and unjust death of George Floyd in Minneapolis. The event took place in Birmingham's Kelly Ingram Park, which stands in the shadow of 16th Street Baptist Church—the site of one the most vile acts of domestic terrorism our nation has ever seen. It's the very church that was bombed in 1963 by four members of the Ku Klux Klan, killing four precious girls as they attended Sunday school.

Birmingham is no stranger to pain. Nor outrage.

Maybe it was due to the fury of yet another Black life snatched from a grieving family. Maybe it was because our country had spent months in quarantine, and this was an outlet to unleash their frustration. Maybe many felt it was finally time to right a wrong that stood for far too long in our city.

Maybe it was a combination of all three.

But when crowds directed their attention away from the peaceful protest in Kelly Ingram Park to the Confederate monument that stood in nearby Linn Park, everything changed.

On the night of May 31, they wanted to see this monument—this mockery of Black progress—finally fall. Crowds hammered away at the fifty-foot obelisk with pickaxes and sledgehammers. They defaced it with spray paint.

But still, it stood.

Eventually a red pickup truck showed up. Protesters attempted to use rope to pull the monument down—which only resulted in snapped ropes. Even if they had succeeded and pulled the monument down, it would have crushed that truck and, tragically, taken lives with it.

I empathized with that crowd. I hated that monument as much as they did. My administration had been working for months to remove that eyesore from our city. But this was not the way.

I marched into that angry crowd (a move my mom still probably hasn't forgiven me for) and asked them to disperse for their own safety. I told them to give me twenty-four hours and I'd tear that monument down for good.

But that wasn't enough to keep destruction at bay. Tensions were too high.

Crowds found new targets, including a nearby statue of Thomas Jefferson and another of Charles Linn, a captain in the Confederate Navy and the park's namesake. One of the protesters attempted to set the Jefferson statue ablaze; the fiery outrage was no longer metaphorical.

A mass of protesters moved into the heart of downtown—shattering windows, raiding storefronts, even assaulting journalists who were simply doing their jobs. My heart sank as chaos made its way through Birmingham's historic business district, a cherished area of our city that has always represented progress in the face of adversity.

As our first responders scrambled to regain control, I was awash in sorrow. I shared the same pain, the same anger, the same frustration as these protesters—but I knew this was not the path to redemption.

All the while, that damn monument loomed in the background of a burning city. Defaced and cracked but still standing—mocking us all.

I had twenty-four hours to heal my city—twenty-four hours to tear down that hateful pillar once and for all.

I asked myself one question—What would Freddie Lee Shuttlesworth do?

The history books tend to oversimplify things.

When it comes to the Civil Rights Movement, things boil down to two key figures—a villain in Theophilus Eugene "Bull" Connor, Birmingham's public safety commissioner and white supremacist who orchestrated coordinated attacks against the Civil Rights Movement, and a hero in the Rev. Dr. Martin Luther King, a name so iconic that it needs no description.

But there was another man whose boots were on the ground here, leading the fight against segregation with just as much fire and charisma as Dr. King.

National history books have done him a disservice, but we in Birmingham know better. He was a man who did more to shape our city's identity than any before or after.

That man is the Reverend Fred Shuttlesworth. My personal hero.

Shuttlesworth was born in Mount Meigs, Alabama, eventually making his way to Birmingham when he was called to minister at Bethel Baptist Church. He'd not only become involved with the local chapter of the National Association for the Advancement of Colored People, he'd also become a founding and key member of the Alabama Christian Movement for Human Rights and the Southern Christian Leadership Conference.

If someone put up the bat signal during the movement, the Rev. Shuttlesworth would come swooping in, superhero style. He was a fiery voice for change, even going toe-to-toe with Dr. King on occasion. Though they shared a healthy amount of respect there, Shuttlesworth was never afraid of giving his colleague a piece of his mind, telling Dr. King that his "flowery speeches" would mean nothing without action behind them.

Shuttlesworth didn't play, y'all.

But that brazenness made him a target. The night before he planned to lead a challenge against Birmingham's segregated buses, his house was bombed. His home was destroyed, but he was unscathed.

He was beaten with chains, baseball bats, and brass knuckles by Klansmen while attempting to enroll his children in a previously all-white school. His wife was stabbed in the melee.

Again, Shuttlesworth stood tall.

He was the Luke Cage of the Movement—a hero whose body refused to be broken by his enemies, and with an impenetrable spirit to match.

I believe every person should have someone to look up to. It's easier to find your own path when one's been blazed by someone you respect. I admire John F. Kennedy. We share a birthday. I look up to Dr. King. I find inspiration from many musical artists and colleagues.

But something about Fred is different.

His convictions. His defiance. His passion. His realness.

The Rev. Shuttlesworth was not merely a man of words. He lived his life on the front lines. He laughed in the face of fear. No death threat, no bombing, no attack on his family nor blows to his body slowed his stride.

He knew the sacrifice of leadership and was willing to pay the toll.

Many cities have claimed to be the cradle of the Civil Rights Movement. In my eyes, Birmingham will always be the heart of the Movement.

And the Rev. Fred Shuttlesworth? He's the heartbeat of our city. Pumping the blood through our veins to this day.

In times of crisis—what would Shuttlesworth do?

He'd do the impossible. He'd save his city.

• • •

The monument that stood in Linn Park represented a lie.

The Confederate Soldiers and Sailors Monument was erected in Linn Park by the United Daughters of the Confederacy—a group of women descendants of Confederate soldiers—in 1905. The intent was to honor Birminghamians' role in the Civil War.

OK, so let's run these dates.

The Civil War ended in 1865. Birmingham was incorporated in 1871. Birmingham wasn't even a city during the Civil War, so why is a second-place trophy sitting in our public square?

Revisionist history twists the Civil War as a dispute about states' rights, and the Confederate imagery that followed in its wake as a celebration of Southern pride.

Allow me to make it clear: The Civil War was about states' rights, all right—the right to own slaves. The right to subjugate my ancestors. The right to claim that I, my mother, my father, everyone who shares our beautiful Black hue—are merely three-fifths human.

In a city whose legacy was built on breaking down systemic racism, that monument's existence is outright treasonous.

That's why I empathized with every protester who attempted to chisel it down that infamous night.

It was far from the first attempt to erase it from our city's eyesight.

Three years earlier, my predecessor, Mayor William Bell, heard cries to remove the structure, following a deadly white nationalist rally in Charlottesville, Virginia. But when legal issues slowed the removal process, he instead built a plywood box around it.

Even though the monument itself wasn't visible, the shadow it cast remained. I give Mayor Bell credit for the quick fix, but we all knew that wasn't good enough.

It had to fall. For good.

In the years that followed, Bell's administration—and later, mine—engaged in an exhaustive court battle over the removal. Our position was clear—this city refuses to support a monument that honors a regime that aimed to oppress Black residents. However, the state attorney general filed a lawsuit against the city, citing the Alabama Memorial Preservation Act of 2017, which prohibits local governments from removing, altering, or renaming monuments that are more than forty years old.

Imagine telling a 74 percent Black city that they aren't allowed to touch a monument that celebrates their oppression.

Well, lawsuit or not, by May 31, 2020, the people of Birmingham were tired of the rhetoric and red tape.

In spirit, I couldn't blame them.

Like those protesters, I was tired of being told what should be in our city by people who don't even live here. I'd watched the same footage of George Floyd as they did—seeing a man scream for air while an officer's knee crushed his windpipe, draining the last ounces of life from him. I saw the same menace on that officer's face as he murdered a man in broad daylight on camera.

Birmingham knows police brutality all too well.

Before George Floyd, there was Bonita Carter.

In June 1979, twenty-year-old Bonita was with a male acquaintance at a convenience store in the Stockham section of Birmingham's Kingston neighborhood. The acquaintance got into an argument with the store clerk, who called police for assistance.

Meanwhile, Bonita, who was outside and not part of this argument, went to move her acquaintance's car. That's when an officer arrived, shooting her several times at close range. The officer, who already had six complaints of excessive force prior to this incident, was backed by then-mayor David Vann and the shootings were ruled justified.

Tensions rose, with residents of Kingston protesting Bonita's unjustified murder while opponents, including members of the Ku Klux

Klan, provoked and harassed residents. Things hit a fever pitch when Black residents armed themselves while white residents drove through the neighborhood, screaming support for the disgraced officer.

Justice would come, and his name was Dr. Richard Arrington.

At the time, Arrington was a member of the Birmingham city council. While others buried their heads, he stood firm in the cause for police reform, including introducing policies that required officers to take injured suspects to hospitals before taking them to police stations. He also pushed to move officers from the streets to desk jobs if they had a record of friction with residents.

Arrington's leadership contrasted with Vann's inaction, paving the way for Arrington to become Birmingham's first Black mayor.

Arrington transformed helplessness into hope.

Forty years later, that helplessness arose over our community once again.

I felt that same pain, that same helplessness, the same fear that chilled my bones—I saw that on the face of every protester that night.

For George Floyd. For Bonita Carter. For every Black soul struck down by oppression. We grieved collectively.

And that's why, despite the reservations of my team and the angst of my family, I marched directly into the crowd that night as they attempted to pull down that monument by force.

What would Shuttlesworth do? He would be with his people.

By this point, tensions were already heavy. The Bell-sanctioned box that originally hid the monument was already destroyed. But there was no way they would be able to topple that fifty-two-foot monstrosity with hand tools and somebody's vehicle as a makeshift tow truck. And if by some miracle they did bring it down, with a crowd that large and unorganized, there could be casualties.

So I marched into that sea of hundreds of protesters bearing the same pain they carried. Despite the haze of emotions in the air, I never felt unsafe. Their intentions were pure.

Bullhorn in hand, I had one simple request: "Go home. I feel your pain, I share your anger, but go home. Give me forty-eight hours, and I'll take care of this."

It wasn't enough. They wanted their leader to empathize with them. The crowd began to chant, "Stand with us."

I did stand with them, 100 percent. But I knew this wasn't the way. The emotions were too raw, the task too heavy—literally. One of the protest leaders challenged me, telling the crowd that they should allow the city twenty-four hours to take action. But overeager protesters began booing and rejecting that plan. Protest leaders lost control of the crowd.

Not long after, all hell broke loose.

This was not my Birmingham. And I mean that literally.

I believe that the protesters I spoke to at the monument were actual residents of our city. They knew the vile history that the structure represented, and they were sick of it towering over them.

But those who were facilitating the later chaos? Nah, that wasn't us.

These folks came downtown with coolers and pizza boxes filled with rocks. I mean, no one just happens to have a Molotov cocktail in their back pocket. Their motives were quite clear.

They even sprayed phrases like "pig" on the side of buildings. There's a lot of police-related slang used in our city, but we don't say "pigs" down here.

I'm convinced that the original protest was hijacked by people just looking to cause anarchy—people who probably weren't even from Birmingham.

They didn't want justice. They just wanted destruction.

As our response teams fanned out downtown to protect our residents, I went live on social media that night in an attempt to ease tensions. I'll be real with y'all, I don't even remember what I said—I'm sure someone can find the video somewhere. Everything lives forever on the internet.

All I remember is crushing, agonizing disappointment. As a leader, I felt like I could have prevented this. I should have been able to rally us in unison to stand together against our true enemy—that monument—not the destruction of Black businesses that for generations faithfully served our community.

That was the only night of my tenure as mayor that I didn't sleep one wink.

This was not my city.

But as the sun began to peek between the clouds the following morning and tensions eased, one thing became crystal clear—no city is as resilient as Birmingham.

That next morning, we saw the true face of Birmingham.

Residents and business owners stood side by side in cleanup efforts. There was no finger-pointing, no outrage, no victim-blaming. Instead, there were young people assisting seniors, folks from across town driving in to lend a hand in recovery efforts, Birmingham's diverse tapestry of cultures standing shoulder to shoulder to sweep, board up broken structures, rebuild, paint, and rebound. Those who couldn't join the efforts in person—remember, it was 2020; COVID was still a thing—contributed financially.

A phoenix rose from the fires that burned the night before. That day, we were a Birmingham united.

This is what Shuttlesworth fought for. This was my city. And I was so proud.

But there was a big challenge that loomed ahead of us. We had less than twenty-four hours to remove that monument.

And I wasn't going to break my promise.

The year 2020 was such a tumultuous time for leadership in our country, but it was Birmingham that, in the 1950s and 1960s, established the blueprint for successful protests. So I turned to the wisdom of the greats for direction.

I reread Dr. Martin Luther King's "Letter from Birmingham Jail," specifically taking note of his four steps for nonviolence campaigns: the collection of the facts to determine whether injustices are alive, negotiation, self-purification, and direct action. In fact, any published articles and speeches from Dr. King were required reading.

I also revisited my favorite book about the most influential hero in my life, *A Fire You Can't Put Out: The Civil Rights Life of Birmingham's Reverend Fred Shuttlesworth* by Andrew M. Manis. The Rev. Shuttlesworth was such a firebrand, unapologetic in his pursuit for justice. He gave me the motivation to be bold and unwavering.

The song that stuck closest to me during this time had to be Common and John Legend's award-winning "Glory" from the *Selma* soundtrack. Yeah, I know they played this song into the ground and back again, but that doesn't make it any less moving. It's a modern-day Negro spiritual, and we all needed that motivation.

One thing about racists . . .

They're complete idiots. Here's a call that 911 dispatch received after I announced that the monument would be removed:

DISPATCH: Birmingham 911, go ahead sir.

CALLER: If you take down that statue in Linn Park, Confederate soldier states, man, imma come down there with my AK-47 and start blowing the damn pigs away. And the protesters, everybody. I'm going to assassinate Mayor Randall Woodfin and kill that dead nigger. You hear me, punk? You better call that shit off right now. You think I'm playing? You find out. You'll be all over the news, you punk ass, you hear me? I'm coming down there right now and blow your fucking heads off, assholes. You hear me?

DISPATCH: What kind of car will you be driving, sir?

CALLER: FUCK OFF, ASSHOLE. I'll hang you from a tree, nigger. That Mayor Randall Woodfin will be dead before light. Before morning, you hear me, punk ass? Imma start blowing people's heads off down there.

DISPATCH: Sir, what's your name?

CALLER: I've got a bomb set right by that statue about to go off, you hear me? You hear me, punk ass? You little punk fuck nigger police fuckboy. I'll beat the living hell out of you, punk ass nigger. You better lay off that statue, you better back the fuck off, you hear me? Say something, coward!

DISPATCH: What's your name, sir?

CALLER: Say something, you coward punk-ass nigger! Imma gonna blow that damn nigger mayor's head off, you hear me? You hear me, punk ass?

DISPATCH: Sir, what's your name?

CALLER: Go fuck yourself. Fuck you. It's none of your business what my name is, asshole. Go fuck yourself, moron.

DISPATCH: Well, you're threatening folks, sir.

CALLER: People are gonna die tonight. I'm going out with my AK-47. I'm on my way right now, punk. You think I'm playing? I'm gonna go to NBC 13, CBS 42, and the stupid news stations, too. You can all kiss my ass and go to hell. Go fuck yourself, asshole.

This guy really thought he could threaten the lives of residents and a public official on a recorded line. Racism really does rot your brain. He was arrested and charged soon after.

In case there was any doubt, this is an example of the hate that this Confederate Soldiers and Sailors Monument nurtures.

Unfortunately, this wasn't the only threat we received. Public safety became an issue, and curfews had to be enforced, which was not an attempt to infringe on rights; it was all for the safety of our residents.

Of course, my family was terrified for my safety. Security was monitoring me at all times. But I had more important things on my mind. I promised our city that in twenty-four hours, I'd remove the monument that had haunted us for generations.

I had less than a day to do what lawmakers, activists, and lawyers couldn't do over the course of dozens of years.

No pressure, right?

My team and I had to find a way to physically remove that massive structure, which seemed like a Herculean task in such a short amount of time.

Meanwhile, I had to play politics with the state.

I called both the state attorney general's office and the governor's office. I made my stance clear: If I had to choose between a civil fine and civil unrest, I was taking the fine. Birmingham was not having another night of unrest, not on my watch.

I knew there would be consequences, but I didn't know how serious they could be. We were outright defying the Alabama Memorial Preservation Act. I thought to myself, *If I'm charged with a felony, I could be removed from office.*

I could be the architect of my own political demise.

Fear loves to whisper doubts into your ears. So what? I was too focused to hear it. I had to protect my city; that monument could not trigger another night of unrest.

The governor's office understood and didn't push back. The state attorney general, though, fined us $25,000.

Whatever. We'd put up the bread. As long as that monument came down.

I have to shout out my team right here. I gave them a nearly impossible task—move a not-so-metaphorical mountain in less than a day.

And they sprang into action without hesitation.

That morning, a structural engineer arrived to assess things. By that point, there had been a ton of damage done to the monument, so removing it safely was paramount.

The engineer knew the stakes were high. His hand trembled as he signed the contract.

Next up, we needed someone to knock the thing down, safely. And as we learned the night before, you can't pull down a massive monument with a couple cords and a pickup truck. We'd need a crane to support the structure, a diamond-toothed saw, maybe a wrecking ball, several large trucks, the works.

Raising money wasn't an issue—Birmingham's philanthropic community graciously chipped in. One church donated $50,000 to cover costs. The real issue was finding skilled hands to do the job.

Remember, we were one of the first cities after George Floyd's murder to declare that a monument was coming down. And in less than twenty-four hours. Many companies didn't want to deal with that type of pressure. Plus, there was a big fear of retaliation.

Eventually, we found our crew:

A general contractor from Mountain Brook, Alabama

A haul crew from Bessemer, Alabama

And a demolition crew from Cullman, Alabama

Unless you're a Birmingham native, it's hard to convey how vastly different those three locations are. Mountain Brook is a city known for its affluence, while Bessemer lies on the opposite end of that spectrum. And until the 1970s, Cullman was known as a "sundown town"—a tag given to cities where Black folks weren't allowed to live. We had to get out of town before sundown, or the consequences would be dire.

These three different crews had never met each other. Frankly, they were nervous. But there was something astounding about these three very different walks of life uniting for an important cause.

It's so very Birmingham.

By then, night had fallen, and time was ticking. We were racing against the clock.

We asked the crews to put cardboard over the logos on their trucks so they wouldn't be identified. Meanwhile, Birmingham police secured the perimeter.

Media outlets were pissed—they wanted a front-row seat. History was about to be made.

But again, my priority was protecting our teams. Tensions were still sky-high. Comments on social media were hostile. Anti-monument protesters were turned away; pro-monument protesters were turned away. There was another bomb threat called in.

The haul team was spooked. They hadn't signed up for *all this*. But we convinced them to finish the job.

And they did. By 11:30 p.m., the obelisk was broken into three sections and the first piece had been removed.

On the birthday of Jefferson Davis, the ex-president of the Confederate States of America, that damn monument, that fifty-two-foot lie, finally came to the ground.

Shuttlesworth would have had a big laugh about that.

It would still take many more hours to continue to remove the monument. By 3:00 a.m., the crowds began to dissipate. The majority of the structure was down by morning, but we needed an extra day to track down a diamond-toothed saw to cut down the pedestal and some steps. Shout-out to our friends in Montgomery for coming through in the clutch with that saw.

We bent a lot of rules that day. But I stand by the action. It was the right thing to do.

Now, I wouldn't say the removal of that monument instantly solved racism in Birmingham. Far from it—a member of the Cullman team shared a text thread that detailed people driving by his home and calling him a sellout. But his defiance, and his bravery, is what defined that day.

There's one moment from that very crazy week that always sticks with me.

Around Thursday or Friday, a rumor began that had the fastest legs I've ever seen. Word around town was that the KKK was upset about the monument's removal and they were planning to march downtown.

This rumor of a KKK takeover was absolutely unfounded. But that didn't stop dozens of folks coming to the site of the departed monument, standing ready to face off with the KKK. These folks were old and young, majority Black, but with dashes of diversity, hyped up with bullhorns and signs, ready for battle.

Of course, nothing came of it, and everyone eventually went home. But watching all those people united in defense of their city while standing on the remains of a broken symbol of oppression . . . That's what Shuttlesworth would do.

I deliver a lot of ceremonial welcomes and greetings in my role as mayor, but when Birmingham played host to the National Association of Black Journalists in 2023, I wanted to go a little harder than usual.

More than 3,500 journalists descended upon our city, making it one of the largest gatherings in the convention's illustrious history. It also wasn't lost on me that this would be the first time many of them ever stepped foot in Birmingham, a city they might only know from horrific images frozen in the Jim Crow era. I wanted those journalists to know that Birmingham's story is so much bigger than its past, and I challenged them to join us in talking about our future.

Good evening.

On behalf of the city of Birmingham—the city that raised me, and the city I'm so proud to serve as mayor—I extend a warm welcome to all of you for choosing the Magic City as home of this year's NABJ convention.

NABJ's mission of equality, fairness, and telling the true stories of Black communities is not lost on us.

In fact, you couldn't have chosen a better time to join us.

Because we need you. And, in turn, you need Birmingham.

If you haven't been to the South in a while, you might need to be reminded how hot it is. I'm not talking about the temperature. I am talking about the political climate. A climate where sitting governors, senators, and former presidents are leading a movement to erase the history, the stories, and the very lives of our people.

You need Birmingham. And Birmingham needs you.

The fourth branch of our democracy is the media. And I believe that media has the ability to speak truth to power.

Birmingham is a living example of this.

This year, Birmingham is celebrating the sixtieth anniversary of the events of 1963, one of the most pivotal years for social progress in our country's history.

It was the terrifying morning in September of 1963 when 16th Street Baptist Church was bombed before Sunday school, robbing four precious little girls of their futures and injuring so many more.

It was the year that Black activists embarked on the Birmingham campaign, leading marches and sit-ins to counter the racial segregation that plagued our city. The result was our homegrown leaders like the Rev. Ralph Abernathy and my personal hero, the Rev. Fred Shuttlesworth, being arrested for that defiance. Among those leaders was Dr. Martin Luther King, who would pen the "Letter from the Birmingham Jail," a powerful reminder that "injustice anywhere is a threat to justice everywhere."

It was the year that our greatest resource, our young people, decided to literally march into their destinies by becoming Civil Rights Foot Soldiers. These young people literally stood eye-to-eye with their oppressors—marching, chanting, and fighting so that every person in this room would be allowed the opportunity to vote.

When white publications turned a blind eye to these stories or rewrote narratives, it was the fourth branch of media—Black media specifically—that raised awareness about our people's fight for justice.

Media turned the tide.

And in today's age of misinformation, media again can turn the tide.

Birmingham is a living witness. That's why we need you, and you need us.

Though we celebrate our history proudly, please do not be mistaken. Birmingham is not a city frozen in its past.

We are a progressive, forward-thinking city that is building upon its legacy. While you're here visiting with us, you will experience nationally recognized, award-winning restaurants. Our newly

renovated arenas are establishing Birmingham as a sports and entertainment destination in the South. And, of course, exploring our
historic Civil Rights District is a must.

You see, our commemoration of 1963 isn't about self-reflection. We
aren't waxing nostalgic about past glory while staring at old photos.

Because Birmingham's history, our history, isn't in black and
white. It's in color, and 4K.

Sixty years later, we're reminded that injustice still lingers, but
Birmingham has provided the blueprint for victory. It's a reminder
of the role journalists like yourselves have played in telling the stories
that moved mountains. It's a reminder that, as a people, our strength
is matchless.

So, NABJ, this week especially, I challenge you to go out and tell
Birmingham's story—of the change we helped create, but just as
importantly, the progress we're helping to establish.

I'd like to personally thank NABJ leadership for your hard work
in creating this event, as well as a shout-out to our own BABJ—the
Birmingham chapter of NABJ.

We're so grateful for the tireless work of our homegrown journalists through the decades, which is why I'm so proud that our
own—Dr. Jesse Lewis, founder of the *Birmingham Times*, and AL.com
columnist Roy S. Johnson—will be among this year's inductees into
the NABJ Hall of Fame.

Master storytellers who have ensured that Birmingham's legacy
of progress is preserved, but just as importantly, they know that our
story is far from over.

So they write; they report. They walk the streets. They listen and
connect.

They give voice to the voiceless. And they trigger action in the
name of justice.

Journalism, at its most powerful, is another form of activism.

Lessons learned from the streets of Birmingham.

Thank you again, NABJ. Thank you for making Birmingham your home for the next few days. Thank you for moving forward with us, sixty years and beyond.

Thank you for telling our story.

Randall L. Woodfin, Mayor
National Association of Black Journalists Convention Address
August 2023

CHAPTER 10

MAKES NO SENSE AT ALL

True story, present tense: I'm working on this chapter about the plague of violence against our youth, and I receive this news alert—

Breaking: Three children are dead after a shooting at a private Christian school in Nashville, a hospital spokesman said.

I'm not just stricken by grief. I'm stricken by frustration. Because when it comes to mass shootings in America, our lawmakers hop on the merry-go-round of false outrage—going in circles, but never going anywhere.

Y'all know how the mass shooting news cycles go by now:

Violence strikes the heart of our communities.

There's an outpouring of emotion.

The usual #ThoughtsAndPrayers tweets from politicians.

Then, there are the calls for gun control, which immediately drown in debates about Second Amendment rights, mental health, policing, and more—all legitimate issues, by the way, but inaction turns these action items into no more than rhetoric.

• • •

In the specific case of the Nashville shooting, once some reports alleged the shooter was transgender, opportunistic lawmakers and talking heads moved the conversation to attacks against the trans community. Laying the actions of one person at the feet of an entire marginalized group is unconscionable.

Odd how these same lawmakers didn't keep that energy for white males, who between 1966 and 2024 carried out more than 80 percent of mass school shootings in this country. Funny how that works.

At the end of the day, we grieve, we tweet, we argue with strangers. We ride the merry-go-round, making no forward progress.

Meanwhile, mothers and fathers bury their children. Classmates are stricken with lifelong trauma. Communities are broken.

As an elected leader in a state with no home rule—meaning I have zero power to enforce gun control without the blessing of state lawmakers—I'm handcuffed. And no, no one is trying to take your guns. But we have to be more diligent about keeping weapons out of the hands of domestic terrorists.

People often ask me what keeps me up at night. There's only one answer to that question—the safety of our children. When I turn off those bedroom lights and I lay my head down, that's when fear seems to be at its most powerful.

My family knows the horrors of violence against loved ones first-hand. It's a grief that never leaves. I'd never wish that pain on anyone.

And few things have caused more collective heartache in our community than the tragic case of Kamille "Cupcake" McKinney.

I was attending an event in October 2019 when I got the call from our chief of police. His words were, "Mayor, we found her."

I knew from the chilling tone of his voice that it wasn't good. After a two week–long search, we finally had answers, but not the answers we wanted.

Three-year-old Cupcake—a beautiful, brown-skinned girl whose smiling photos captured the heart of our city—had been found dead in a dumpster.

How could any living, breathing human being be so callous, so devoid of compassion, so downright evil as to abduct and murder an innocent child, then toss her remains aside with household garbage?

I still remember the chilling walk through the corridors of police headquarters to meet with investigators after Cupcake's fate was clear. I'll never forget the scream Cupcake's father unleashed when he learned he would never see his daughter alive again. It was the most painful sound I've ever heard in my life. It pierced my soul.

I'll never be able to understand what he went through.

For two weeks, we had done all we could to reunite Cupcake with her family. I'm still devastated that we weren't successful.

On October 12, 2019, Cupcake and her mom attended a child's birthday party at their housing complex. That evening, video footage captured a man talking to a group of children who were playing outside.

According to the children on the scene, the man convinced Cupcake to get into his vehicle by saying he was going to take her to the store for candy.

That was the last time Cupcake was seen alive.

An Amber Alert was issued, and the search began. It didn't take long for Cupcake's search to become a national story. Celebrities like actress Kristen Bell used their platforms to call for support. I have to tip my cap to media, which did a great job of telling the story, blitzing our phones, TV screens, laptops, and radio airwaves with the latest news and updates.

But despite the best efforts of our community, the many tips that came in, and the donations that were made to our reward hotline, nothing could stop that horrible phone call that I eventually received.

I prayed so hard that we'd find Cupcake alive. But that wasn't our reality.

Our reality is that pure evil exists in this world. It rattled me.

Announcing the discovery of Cupcake's body to our residents was one of the hardest duties I've had as mayor. Scratch that, it was one of the hardest days of *my life*.

It was extremely hard to hold it together as I announced that our search for Cupcake had come to a tragic end. I was overcome with sadness for a life lost. Guilt, as well. Guilt that I, as a leader, couldn't save her in time.

And fear. Fear for the lives of our children.

Children are supposed to feel safe among their friends. I'm sure Cupcake felt that way while hanging out with other kids and family at that birthday party. And adults are supposed to be their protectors—that's why she felt comfortable enough to wander off with a stranger. She was too pure, too innocent, to know the evils of this world.

In March 2023, Patrick Stallworth and Derick Irisha Brown were sentenced to life in federal prison without the possibility of parole for the abduction and death of Cupcake.

Stallworth and Brown have conflicting stories about what actually happened when Cupcake was abducted. What we do know is that police testified that a plastic mattress cover found in their apartment contained bloodstains and DNA from Stallworth, Brown, and Cupcake. It was determined that Cupcake died by asphyxia. Methamphetamine, Trazodone, and Benadryl were in her system.

I hope both of them are locked underneath the jail. Forever. No punishment is too extreme for the harm they caused Cupcake's family and the pain they caused this community.

If there is one silver lining I can find in this very dark cloud, it's this: Birmingham rallied together to find this precious soul. The rhetoric that so often divides our country during its darkest hours was nowhere to be found.

I think it's because no matter who you are, your background or social status, if you looked into Cupcake's eyes, you saw someone you loved. A daughter. A stepdaughter. A granddaughter or niece.

There were no politics this time, no finger-pointing. We were one city—one family—praying for a miracle. I wish it didn't take such tragic circumstances to achieve that level of unity.

I've talked a lot in this book about my love for hip-hop. Those who might not understand what hip-hop truly represents might find it hypocritical that I'm constantly celebrating a culture that is so tied to violence in our communities.

I won't deny the fact that hip-hop glorifies gun culture on its worst days. But it does just as much to fight against it.

In July 2022, Birmingham had the incredible honor of hosting the World Games 2022—an international gathering of 3,600 athletes from more than a hundred countries competing in multi-sports disciplines. It was the first such gathering since the COVID-19 pandemic, and Birmingham was honored to welcome the world to our doorstep.

A gathering of such international magnitude is guaranteed to bring the stars out, and one of the many concerts we hosted was from Chicago rapper Lupe Fiasco, an incredibly talented lyricist and deep thinker who, in my opinion, never got his just due. He was Kendrick Lamar a few years before Kendrick became Kendrick Lamar, if you feel me.

Lupe blessed Birmingham's World Games stage just weeks after releasing his new album. That album, *Drill Music in Zion*, closes with a song called "On Faux Nem."

Traditionally a rap verse is comprised of sixteen bars, or lines. This one, though, has only two—"Rappers die too much. That's it. That's the verse."

There's so much power in its simplicity.

The title of the song adds an extra layer of meaning. "On folks nem" is Chicago slang that roughly translates to "what I'm saying is the truth." Replacing "faux" for "folks" is a double entendre—"faux" meaning "fake," as he wishes that rappers falling victim to violent crime were only make-believe; and "faux" as a homonym for "foe," which is pretty self-explanatory.

And y'all thought rap was just about guns and girls.

The murders of Tupac Shakur in 1996 and Christopher Wallace, a.k.a. The Notorious BIG, the following year are hip-hop's two highest-profile deaths, but they're far from the only ones. In 2022 alone, rappers Snootie Wild, Goonew, Trouble, JayDaYoungan, Pat Stay, PnB Rock, and Takeoff—one-third of the hitmaking Southern rap trio Migos—all lost their lives to violence.

Rappers die too much.

I agree with the cries that say hip-hop needs to work harder to address these tragedies. But to understand hip-hop's role in America, well, you have to understand hip-hop better.

In the late 1980s, the West Coast rap group NWA were labeled as the biggest villains in American pop culture. Their explicit lyrics detailed crime, drug abuse, racism, police brutality, and more in vivid detail, getting them banned from radio stations in many markets.

Despite that, they were one of the most successful groups of their era, selling more than ten million units in the United States to date.

Obviously, the skeptics among us will ascribe their success to controversy creating cash, but they're missing what hip-hop truly is. At its core, hip-hop is storytelling. In NWA's case specifically, they were the CNN of the streets, using their music to report on the conditions they viewed with their own eyes.

The extreme poverty they were subjected to; the inadequate medical care for loved ones; turning to the drug trade when employment options were nonexistent—and the violent crime that followed; the over-policing and brutality that sowed a deep resentment of law enforcement.

The American dream of white picket fences did not exist in these communities. Hip-hop was there to shine a light on the darkest parts of America. The violence that still festers in today's hip-hop is a sign that those generational curses still have not been broken in our most troubled communities.

Make no mistake, I'm not excusing *anyone* for committing violent crime. Every adult is capable of making their own decisions and owning up to the consequences. But blaming hip-hop for violent crime in our cities and towns is extremely shortsighted—it's just scratching the surface of a deeper wound.

Hip-hop isn't the root of our evil; it's the reflection of our pain. Don't shoot the messenger.

Want to end violence in hip-hop? End gun violence in America.

It's triggering when someone is shot and killed, especially when that someone is a child or young adult. Losing my nephew Baby Ralph at just eighteen years old was difficult. The moment I learned about his death is forever seared into my brain.

It's an issue that hits very close to home. That's why, as leader of Birmingham, I have to do everything in my power to save lives.

In February 2019, I stood next to Dr. Mark Wilson, Health Officer for the Jefferson County Department of Health, to declare gun violence as a public health crisis in Birmingham. We stood shoulder to shoulder with the mothers of gun violence victims—including my own mother, still grieving the loss of my brother.

An issue this massive and multifaceted needs a multifaceted leadership approach. Birmingham Police seized nearly 1,800 firearms in 2022 alone, but this is a problem we can't simply police our way out of.

Instead, we set up conflict resolution programs, aiming to teach younger people methods to de-escalate violence before guns are drawn. Health-based violence interruption programs were launched. We partnered with Birmingham City Schools to push mental health initiatives in our classrooms as a way to break the stigmas that surround mental health treatment in our communities. We locked arms with community organizations that championed reentry efforts for individuals looking to rebuild their lives after incarceration. We have to break the prison pipeline, y'all.

And with the help of those brave mothers, we launched the Increase Peace awareness campaign. In a series of vignettes that ran on social media and local TV, those women gave heartbreaking accounts of their lost children, the holes left by their absence, and an impassioned plea for peace.

We're also fighting the uphill battle against "no snitching" culture by pushing law enforcement to be more present and active members of the communities they serve, as well as turning to the OGs—those seasoned street-smart veterans of gang life—to build bonds of trust with our youth.

The streets are always talking—they just rarely talk to us. Law enforcement and politicians are excluded from those convos, and I get it. Remember, NWA taught generations not to trust the police. But with more trusted voices on our streets, we can resolve heinous crimes more quickly if the community is empowered to speak up.

"No snitching" culture has gotten way out of hand. When you reveal information about a crime you witnessed, you're not "snitching"; you're protecting your community. So many crimes go unsolved simply because members of communities refuse to speak up. Justice cannot survive in an information vacuum.

But again, public safety goes both ways. We as an administration have to sow the seeds of trust in our community if we want that love reciprocated.

If you're reading this chapter looking for the key to erase violent crime, sorry to disappoint. You can't wipe away generational issues with one quick fix. That's why we're approaching this public health crisis from as many angles as possible.

No matter your approach, I ask you to keep one thing in mind—the lives lost to crime and violence are not just numbers. They're not merely statistics on a ledger. It's why I get so disgusted when fellow lawmakers bury their heads in the sand while grieving families bury their loved ones after a mass shooting. The deceased aren't talking points or political chess pieces—they are real people, who lived real lives and left behind real loved ones who may never recover from their loss.

They are Snootie Wild, Goonew, Trouble, JayDaYoungan, Pat Stay, PnB Rock, and Takeoff. They are Baby Ralph Woodfin III. They are Kamille McKinney. They are missed and they are loved.

My people—our people—die too much.

———

The 2019 abduction of three-year-old Kamille "Cupcake" McKinney was a turning point in my administration. The community collectively held its breath while working in unison to locate that precious girl. When her body was found, it ripped the heart out of our city. As a leader, I was charged with bringing comfort and hope to a broken family and a grieving community. These words that I spoke at a vigil for Kamille were some of the hardest I've ever had to deliver.

But it was important that, in the midst of tragedy, I highlighted how our community united for a common good. Birmingham is no stranger to tragedy, but it also knows how to uplift those at their lowest.

Good afternoon.

Our hearts are so very heavy today.

Today we stand here in memory of a three-year-old girl. A girl who would never know the joy of graduation. Or getting her driver's license. Or starting a career or starting a family.

A girl ripped from her family far too soon. A girl whose absence leaves a hole in all our hearts.

Kamille McKinney.

We will never forget your name.

To Kamille's parents, we understand that there is nothing we can say that will fill the void by her absence. There's nothing we can do to heal your aching hearts.

But I do ask this one thing. Just look around at these faces gathered here today and know that all ninety-nine of Birmingham's neighborhoods, as well as our friends and neighbors statewide and nationwide, stand beside you in these troubled times.

The weight you are feeling right now is unimaginable. But please know that our hands are here to help lift that pressure. Our shoulders are here for you to lean on. Our arms are here to embrace you.

You are not alone.

As a community, we're left with many questions. Who would be so callous, so barbaric as to rob a precious three-year-old girl of her future?

We ask the same heartbreaking questions about Stanley M. Turner II, a Ramsay High student who was found dead in a parked car early Sunday morning. Our souls are shaken by the same cold reality regarding the death of five-year-old Nevaeh Adams of South Carolina, whose remains were found in a landfill.

This week is symbolic of a time of celebration in Birmingham. And I'll be honest, it's a little tough for us to do that right now. Not when we're constantly reminded of the evils of our world.

But there is a spirit that seems to resonate in our streets every year around this time.

It's because every year, at the end of October, Birmingham is awash in a spirit of camaraderie.

The bonds of friendship.

Family and community united as one.

Birmingham, that's the spirit we must continue to embrace today. It's more than a game; it's who we are.

It's the same perseverance we showed in the face of Jim Crow.

The way we locked our arms and sang "We Shall Overcome" to the heavens.

The way we fell to our knees and prayed for comfort in our darkest days.

The way we fought, as brothers and sisters, for the betterment of our community.

These are the lessons Birmingham taught the world.

About faith, about courage, and about rising up in the face of evil.

That's our charge today.

Birmingham, we are a family. And as a family, we must move as one—teaching our young people the importance of valuing life. Speaking up when we have information that could help alleviate the pain of our neighbors. Putting the needs of others before self.

And recognizing that every life is precious.

So that no other family can endure the pain that Cupcake's family is enduring.

We pray for strength. We pray for comfort. We pray for answers. We pray for an end to the senseless violence that hurts our communities.

Kamille McKinney.

Say her name. Hold it close to your heart.

Because we're all family.

Randall L. Woodfin, Mayor
Prayer Vigil Address
October 2019

CHAPTER 11

DA ART OF STORYTELLIN' (PT. 2)

Diving ten thousand feet out of an airplane puts a lot of things in perspective.

Just five months after I stood onstage at Linn Park and was sworn in as Birmingham's thirtieth mayor, the US Navy reached out and asked if I'd join them in skydiving with the Navy Leap Frogs during Navy Week.

I would say I jumped at the chance, but, nah, come on, that's too easy.

So let me give you this one instead: I've often said that my first year in office was like building a plane and flying it at the same time.

The challenges of the previous administration were now at my doorstep: A community in dire need of revitalization. Low morale from city employees. Years of under-resourced communications from City Hall to its residents.

And I was still trying to shake off the doubters who saw my election victory as a fluke and were waiting for this "inexperienced kid" to fail.

We had to rebuild city government—and the city itself—from the inside out. Immediately. It was the ultimate on-the-job training.

That vision becomes a lot clearer when your body is hurtling toward Earth.

I saw that dive like I saw the challenge of governing: scary, fun, and exhilarating all at the same time.

On that plane, just like in City Hall, I was surrounded by veterans experienced in their craft. I knew I couldn't dive headfirst into these issues alone. They were by my side, guiding me the whole time.

I knew I had to take risks. My campaign was built on creating a more progressive approach to governing. Legendary New York rapper Nas once said "a caterpillar can't relate to what an eagle envisions." I had to look at every problem with a big-picture perspective. That bird's-eye view isn't relatable to everyone at the time of assessment and decision-making, but the picture becomes clearer in time.

And here's one that took me a very long time to comprehend—I had to enjoy the ride. During the first couple years of my term, I was working fourteen- to sixteen-hour days. I was leaving home before the sun came up and returning long after it had retreated. I was determined to make municipal government work, but I couldn't be an effective leader if I was running myself down.

Sometimes, it's OK to take a breath and soak in your surroundings. Having your head in the clouds ain't so bad.

When my parachute unfurled and I slowly began to descend above the city's center, it was so peaceful. And it was beautiful to see my family coming into view as I slowly approached the earth.

Leave it to mom n' them to keep you grounded.

A lot of people thought jumping out of that plane was an unnecessary risk. Others thought it was the coolest thing ever. And some just said I was crazy to attempt it.

From the development of Protective Stadium after decades of debate, to paying high school graduates' tuition to any state university via the Birmingham Promise, to pardoning more than 15,000 people for minor marijuana convictions, I've received all those reactions—and more.

But I wasn't elected mayor to rest on my laurels. I was brought in to soar.

And I was going to take every resident of our ninety-nine neighborhoods on that ride with me.

I had one priority after stepping into City Hall as Birmingham's new mayor—I had to build my team.

Thankfully, I didn't have to look far. I had been surrounded by incredibly talented men and women during the last decade of my career. That wasn't going to change now.

I first reached out to Cedric Sparks, who opened his doors to me at the Division of Youth Services. Long before I was elected mayor, I told Cedric that if I was ever chosen to serve my city as its leader, I wanted him to be my right hand, my chief of staff.

I came back to him to honor that promise. But he was hesitant.

To understand why, you must truly understand Cedric Sparks. He's the most selfless man you'll ever meet. Though he quietly supported my campaign for mayor, he was never visibly active. He rightfully worried that his support might be seen as a conflict of interest within the previous administration's ranks—making my campaign a target for mudslinging.

Ced wasn't so much worried about his current job; he was working to protect my future job. I respected that.

In fact, during the campaign, I caught up with Cedric at a tailgate party. As I approached him to say hi, I could see the worry on his face.

He asked me, "How are you doing? I mean, how are you *really* doing?"

Cedric knew the rigors of Birmingham politics. These pillars of our community, whom I had grown up respecting, were now using all their resources to plant false stories and make up lies to demean my character and belittle my experience.

How can you spend a lifetime telling our young people that they can grow up to be anything they want but when they pursue those dreams, you knock them down with every low blow possible?

I kept it real with Cedric, as I always do.

"For a second, they knocked me off balance," I said. "But I got my footing and now I'm good."

Cedric didn't realize I was leaning on shoulders like his to regain that footing. And that's why I needed him as my chief of staff.

But Cedric was uneasy, concerned that if he accepted the position, it would look like he was scheming to rise up the political ranks the entire time. It would reflect poorly on me and DYS.

That's fear raising its ugly head again, twisting opportunity into opposition.

Cedric found solace in both his brother, who reminded Cedric of our past and the future we could build together, and his wife, who told him that his heart for service made him the perfect man for the job.

There's no greater sight than watching courage rise from the ashes of fear. Cedric embodies that. He accepted the role and has become an even more dynamic leader in the years since. I rest easier at night knowing that he has my back.

Ed Fields also remained by my side, transitioning from campaign manager to senior advisor and chief strategist. To round out this triple threat of leadership, I appointed Kevin Moore as the city's chief operating officer. At that point, Kevin had more than two decades of experience at the City of Birmingham, serving as director of the Parks and Recreation Department in his most recent role. That level of institutional knowledge was invaluable.

Rounding out the OG leadership team was City Attorney Nicole King, who had served in the city's law department for a little over a decade; Director of Intergovernmental Affairs Kelvin Datcher, an everyman who wore dozens of hats, serving everywhere from city council to economic development organizations to Alabama state director for Bernie Sanders's 2016 presidential campaign; and Executive Administrator Sylvia Bowen, another veteran of the city council and the woman you turn to when you need things done.

Over the years, this executive leadership team would nearly triple in size.

Good leaders know that they don't have all the answers, but they know to surround themselves with experienced employees, industry experts, and supergeniuses who do.

Every dope rapper has a signature catchphrase—that defining ad-lib that serves as a personalized stamp on every great bar.

For Young Jeezy, it's that dry, raspy YEAHHHHHH he loves to pepper tracks with.

Lil Jon's WHAT and OK! have transcended the 2000s crunk rap era and became pop culture staples.

Gucci Mane sounds like he's got ice cubes down his pants when he unleashes his BRRRRRRRR while Rick Ross grunts HUH and BAWSE and ROZAY like clockwork.

Lil Wayne has a billion of them—whether he's screeching his nickname TUNECHI, shouting out YOUNG MONEY, or fiddling with his ever-present lighter, you know he's arrived before he jumps into his verse.

But here at the City of Birmingham, our phrase is a little more universal.

We're Putting People First.

It's much, much more than a catchphrase, though. It's a reminder of what drives our administration.

Not long after I made the first round of appointments, I sat down with Ed, Cedric, Kevin, and Kelvin to start preliminary planning.

Cedric hit me with a great question: "Mayor, what do you want your administration to stand for?"

We already had a mission statement: Building community through servant leadership. It's the same mission I used for my administration at Morehouse. But we needed a theme, something that really defined what we were about.

DYS had been using the theme of Putting Youth First. It was his idea to flip it and expand it beyond youth and include every resident—every neighborhood—that we served.

Putting People First.

It was that simple. Three words that would be the hallmark of our administration. While on the campaign trail, concerns from our residents all revolved around the same issue.

Whether it was improved development in their neighborhoods, the removal of blight and restoration of long-ignored community landmarks, more job opportunities for students, or support for small businesses, it all came back to one issue—residents didn't feel like their concerns were being heard.

Those three words, Putting People First, was our public vow that our ninety-nine neighborhoods wouldn't be ignored. They would be heard and served.

But I wanted to go even deeper in our commitment to service.

I believed it was vital that we develop a set of core values that would be as recognizable as our theme.

So, again, we went back to the lessons of the campaign. What did residents want from their government? What were they not receiving previously?

We came up with five values:

Customer service. Whether it's a life-or-death call to 911 or a request to pick up missed trash in a neighborhood, our residents deserve to have their needs addressed swiftly and professionally. It's the backbone of how we deliver services.

Efficiency. One of my biggest frustrations after taking the reins at City Hall was learning just how slow and inefficient many of our governmental systems truly were. I don't believe in doing things because "that's how it's always been done." Streamlining services to deliver the quickest and most hassle-free experience for residents is always a priority.

Effectiveness. This one ties directly into efficiency. Our services must make a real, tangible impact in the communities we serve. If our residents can't see or feel the impact of those services, we're not doing our jobs. To bring real change to communities, we must develop strategies that are immediate and long-lasting. No fluff over here.

Accountability. No more passing the buck. Accountability means owning up to what we say and do. Yes, there will be times when a policy or initiative doesn't hit the mark. And yes, our residents are justified in speaking up when that happens. But instead of immediately going into defense mode, our administration must open its ears, hear those concerns, and possibly realign our approach. Though it didn't always feel like it under previous leadership, municipal government and the residents we serve are all on the same team. Accountability helps us become better servants.

Transparency. This might be the most important value of them all. People don't trust government because, often, they just don't understand it. It's our mission to demystify government and make it more accessible for our residents. It's why we re-created an "open checkbook" website so residents can see where their tax dollars are going, as well as a "mayor's travel" site to show that I'm not chillin' in Aruba on the taxpayers' dime. We serve at the pleasure of our residents—if they have questions, we owe them answers, plain and simple.

Those core values aren't just for public consumption. We had to make them take root in our city employees, as well. When I arrived at City Hall as mayor, morale was below sea level. We had to retrain staff on the importance of these values, but we also had to make it fun.

Cedric noted that having staff memorize all five words would be too much. It seemed like homework. Folks would reject that right away. Instead, he decided on an acronym.

We came up with CEETA, pronounced "Cita"—like the loud cartoon woman from the old BET show.

Internally, CEETA became a way of life. We repeated the values at every weekly staff meeting, had CEETA posters plastered in offices, and we've even held two CEETA Games professional development outings. It's like a field day for grown folks, all wrapped in the values of CEETA.

CEETA and Putting People First might not roll off the tongue as easily as Lil Jon screeching YEAH over and over on an Usher song, but for city employees, they've become a way of life.

But don't think I won't yell CEETA on a track if one of these rappers ever lets me inside the booth.

Jumping headfirst into governing was a whirlwind. I spent so long working toward this dream but once I arrived there was little time for celebration.

What does the dog do once he finally catches that car he's been chasing?

For me, I had to reimagine government.

My top priority then (and to this day) was neighborhood revitalization. It was the bedrock of my campaign, so it had to be the main focus of my administration.

Improving decades of urban decay was first on the menu. We invested heavily in street repaving, pothole repair, and removing abandoned and blighted buildings. To pay for these projects, I came up with an inventive but controversial plan of generating funds.

More on that later.

But it's not just about tearing down; we had to build up, develop new single-family homes and subdivisions across underserved areas of town. We partnered with Alabama Power to restore streetlights in neighborhoods that had been shrouded in darkness for years. We did our best to keep up with the growing demand for trimming weeds in empty lots.

And, of course, the Birmingham Promise, our vow to provide last-dollar scholarship and apprenticeship assistance to Birmingham graduates, was the initiative I'm most proud of.

We also made lots of changes internally.

One of my first goals was to beef up the city's communications team. It was very important that not only were we listening to residents, but that we were relaying information swiftly and accurately to them.

Since social media was such a major part of my campaign, it was a no-brainer that the City of Birmingham's social media presence be just as informative. The previous administration's communications team was pretty lean. I built our team out to not just cover traditional public information roles, but to include a videographer, social media managers, and community liaisons who could meet with residents personally. We prioritized the growth of Facebook, Twitter, Instagram, LinkedIn, YouTube, and TikTok and brought the city's graphics department into the fold to assist in creating content for those channels. We added a weekly digital newsletter, the *Magic City Spotlight*, to fill residents in on news and notes; we launched a podcast, also called the *Magic City Spotlight*, and partnered with V94.9 for a radio broadcast called *Radio Randall's Rap Sheet*.

Nah, I'm just playing. The radio show is called the *Magic City Spotlight*, too. Can't you tell we love that name?

And for those who aren't as tech savvy, we have a print mailer that goes to mailboxes every other month.

Our communications team has tripled in staff and content produced over the previous administration. We had to evolve with the times.

Meeting people where they are—it's the CEETA way.

From upholding the city's legacy as a champion of civil rights, we had to be more proactive. Yeah, it's important to celebrate our past, but how are we moving our city forward? That's why I brought on the Division of Social Justice and Racial Equity, which not only finds ways to celebrate our civil rights icons and historic sites, but develops strategies for violence reduction and addresses inequalities in underserved neighborhoods.

From repairing the formerly tenuous relationship between city council and the mayor's office through increased transparency, while also supporting our small business community with the help of our Department of Innovation and Economic Opportunity, we were upholding our promise—the promise to build a better Birmingham.

But it didn't always come easy.

While I was on the campaign trail, I was the underdog, the symbol of hope to shake up a stagnant city.

But once I was sworn in, I was something different. I was now the establishment.

That changed the game in more ways than one.

One of the most disheartening things I faced when becoming mayor was watching folks who supported my campaign immediately throw stones.

And before y'all come for me on social media—because I've definitely had to deal with that time and again over the years—hear me out: There's nothing wrong with healthy debate. I welcome that. And I have no problem with anyone holding me or my administration accountable for shortcomings in policy.

Shout-out to CEETA.

But it was clear that some activists, faith leaders, and business partners were only along for the ride because they were looking for a come-up. When it became obvious that I wouldn't rubber stamp some of their programs, or when we challenged some of their approaches, they put me and my administration in their crosshairs.

If I'm being real, some of them were just in it for the bag. Once it was clear they weren't getting cut a check, they went on the offensive.

We also quickly learned there was a quid pro quo culture that didn't sit right with me. For example, we cut way back on distribution of free tickets for high-profile events when we learned that some businesses, employees, and even city leadership were using them as currency for political favors.

You should have seen the tantrums that were thrown when we adjusted those policies.

Even my own mom occasionally got caught in the crossfire.

Once I became mayor, my mom became Mama Woodfin, matriarch of the Magic City. It wasn't a title she asked for; it was bestowed upon her by our residents.

During the inauguration night celebration, everyone called her "first lady"—a title she constantly rejected. That's my mom, not my wife. Y'all chill.

At some point, a guy yelled out, "That's Mama Woodfin!" And the name stuck.

My mom is proud to be held in high esteem by her city. But she never asked to be a political figure.

Before long, folks were approaching her off the street looking for favors. Some wanted her to convince the city to mow their lawns. Others went to her in an attempt to sidestep coding laws. She was given gifts to pass along to me for favors; she was even offered a beach trip at one point.

She really wanted to take that trip, y'all. But she knew better.

My mom has a strong desire to assist people in need, but I had to warn her that in the game of politics, not everything was what it seemed. It was very tough on her, especially those days when she had to watch my social media channels get bombarded by trolls. She's my mom, so of course she wants to clap back when folks start talking crazy about her son. But I had to tell her—if you go off publicly, you're putting me and yourself in a dangerous position.

My mom is incredible and she's proud to be a mother of Birmingham. But sometimes, she just wants to be Cynthia.

She learned to pull back. But don't get caught slippin', 'cuz Mama Woodfin still don't play about her son or her city.

You know that famous GIF of Donald Glover from the TV show *Community* when he walks into a room smiling, carrying pizzas, only to see fire and chaos before his eyes?

Replace Donald with me and insert those flames over Birmingham's city employees' pension system.

During my transition into office, we set up a team to run through the previous administration's finances. We found a major, *major* problem.

The city's $1.4 billion Retirement and Relief Pension System was short by about $378 million.

If this problem was not addressed immediately, the city would run out of money in thirty years, destroying the retirement of countless employees.

This was not a problem I created, but it's one I inherited.

I had two options: I could continue to kick the can down the road and let it be a mess for a future administration to fix. It's not like I'll be mayor in thirty years, so someone else could figure it out.

Or, I could do what I was elected to do and lead.

Apparently, the pension was fully funded in 2001. But by 2003, the city couldn't keep up with its contributions. By the time the Great Recession hit in 2008, things got even worse.

There was no way I would allow city employees to suffer because of someone else's mistakes. A decade and a half of mismanagement was not going to continue.

It took nearly three years, but we doubled the city's annual pension contribution from $14 million to $39.6 million. We also implemented a new state law that mandates our city to fund our pension fully every year. This not only put us on course to make sure our pension was solvent, but it also increased the city's credit rating.

For as long as I can remember, Birmingham has debated the need for a stadium.

Mayor Larry Langford was always viewed as a visionary in our city, mainly because he constantly pushed against Birmingham's "can't do attitude." He dreamed big and expected others to do the same.

Fear of progress has often made Birmingham its own worst enemy.

In the early 2000s, Langford pushed to build a domed stadium downtown in hopes of attracting the 2020 Olympics. But like so many big projects floated in that era, little came of it.

When I started my term as mayor, I made it very clear to my team—we're not going to spend another generation debating a stadium. Either it's happening or it's not.

And I wanted it to happen.

I saw the value in upgrading our venues. One of our biggest secrets is that Birmingham is a big sports town, as evidenced by the massively successful Magic City Classic event that we host every year. More than sixty thousand HBCU fans flood our city to watch Alabama A&M's Bulldogs and Alabama State's Hornets battle it out on the gridiron. It also draws a wide array of weekend events and concerts.

The Classic is great, but why not expand those experiences even more?

Not only would we be able to draw more sports and concerts, we'd have a built-in system to fund the scores of neighborhood revitalization projects that were on our plate.

I threw my support not only behind expanding our Birmingham-Jefferson Convention Complex but also building a brand-new, open-air stadium.

This was our chance to become a destination city in the South, as well as generate much-needed revenue.

Many residents didn't see it that way, and they were very vocal about it.

The biggest concerns revolved around historic Legion Field, a nearly hundred-year-old site that has been the longtime home of the Magic City Classic. Opponents of the new stadium wanted to see the city invest money in upgrading Legion Field instead of creating a competing site.

Eventually, our city council approved the new development, and a loud portion of the community directed their anger my way. They believed that, once again, their interests were being ignored in favor of new downtown development—a huge criticism of the previous administration.

But here's what made this development different.

Along with the passage of the stadium development, the council also passed the Neighborhood Revitalization Fund, which takes money directly generated from the stadium and places it back into communities. That's about $9.9 million a year for paving, pothole repair, sidewalk construction, and more.

The stadium was a twofold investment—for the well-being of residents and for the draw of tourism.

It didn't take long for the new Protective Stadium to be a hit. We hosted nearly fifty thousand screaming fans for a Garth Brooks show in June 2022. Protective became the home for the Birmingham Legion FC soccer franchise and the Birmingham Stallions, the 2022 United States Football League champions.

Birmingham welcomed the world to our doorstep for the World Games 2022, an international gathering of 3,600 athletes that competed in more than thirty different sports. Parkour, wheelchair rugby, Muay Thai, archery, powerlifting—it was an incredible display of athleticism and we were honored to share our Southern hospitality with 377,000 spectators.

Imagine all the revenue, all the excitement, and all the history our city would have missed if we hesitated to be visionaries.

Leadership is filled with calculated risks. Even when folks are screaming for you to keep your feet on the ground, sometimes you need to take that leap of faith.

My administration had to teach Birmingham to soar.

My first term in office was successful, but I'll be real with y'all: It just wasn't enough time.

There was so much more work to be done. Generations of neglect couldn't be corrected in four years.

The first term laid a solid foundation, and we had to keep the momentum rolling.

I needed another term. Which meant it was time to go back on the campaign trail.

But the world of 2021 was nothing like the world of 2016. Our city was still grappling with the long-term effects of the COVID-19 pandemic. Hell, I was still dealing with the effects of COVID-19, as my 2020 diagnosis was still wreaking havoc on my body. When I announced my candidacy in early 2021, simply walking was a challenge.

Businesses were struggling, crime was rising, and uncertainty loomed.

Still, there was no way I was going to leave the job undone.

Time for round two.

My campaign announcement for re-election was much different in 2021 than 2017, mostly due to COVID-19.

We called it a drive-in campaign kickoff.

It was held outside at George Ward Park. Supporters drove into the park, sat in their cars, tuned into the radio frequency we were on, and listened to the presenters. We even had campaign-branded face coverings.

It was good, clean, socially distanced fun.

I like to think I had grown as both a speaker and a leader since the first time I declared my candidacy. My remarks then were handled by a speechwriter. This time, I did my own version.

During the first campaign, I did a brain dump with friends to outline policies and direction. This time, my team presented me with a massive document, I reviewed it, and I handled business. Once I had the finer points down, I workshopped the platform with my team.

In the early days, it was more about trying to develop a direction. But now, I had a direction. I just needed everyone else on board.

My confidence had grown. My personality and style were more apparent. I might just drop a rap line from T.I. or a quote from a Spider-Man movie in a speech just to see if the real ones were paying attention.

At this point, I owned my own message. It made a world of difference.

Fundraising also was a lot easier this time around.

In the first few months of campaigning, more than two thousand people contributed $1,003,783—a record for the city. It was powerful confirmation that Birmingham had our back.

But we refused to get cocky. I still wanted to run this campaign like the one before it.

Grassroots. People-centric. We're the big dogs, but we have to move like underdogs.

Daniel Deriso came back on board, this time over operations. I named E. J. Turner as our new field director. E. J. was one of our most dedicated door-knockers during the 2017 campaign and proved himself to be a more than capable leader. By 2021, he was just twenty-four, but he had the poise and wisdom of brothers twice his age. I knew he'd be an invaluable asset.

I'm so grateful to all the mentors who opened doors for me in my early twenties. I had to pay it forward for young men like E. J.

E. J.'s role was vital because, while we had no problem getting folks to open their wallets, it was a lot harder to get them out in the streets with us due to pandemic fears. E. J. turned to college students to bolster our volunteer ranks and linked up with young local superstar Rylen Dempsey to connect us with a pipeline of high school volunteers. Rylen himself was a high school student at the time and, like E. J., has shown more character and leadership skills than anyone in the White House from January 2017 to January 2021.

You heard it here first, Rylen is going to change our world.

The previous campaign taught me the importance of surrounding myself with young minds. They aren't weighed down by the cynicism that comes with adulthood, nor have they been poisoned by political agendas.

They just want their city to be better.

It's no wonder why Birmingham's foot soldiers—those infinitely brave young men and women who were on the front lines of the Civil Rights Movement—are the unsung heroes of our city.

Energetic. Courageous. Unshackled to the past. The young will fight for their future.

If they're willing to fight for the rest of us, we must be willing to fight for them. It's why I work so hard to provide options for their future, whether that means scholarships or internships through the Birmingham Promise, mental health programs through our schools, or violence-reduction measures in our communities.

Want change? Turn to our kids.

During my first campaign, I was dismissed by my fellow candidates in the early stages. It wasn't until we started participating in debates that I became a target.

This time, though? They had the bullseye on my back from day one.

William Bell jumped into the race in an attempt to regain his seat. Chris Woods returned, too, along with Jefferson County Commissioner Lashunda Scales, whom I had a history with from her days on city council.

But none of them, nor any of the other candidates who stepped up, had a detailed plan on how they'd run the city. Their platforms revolved around what I was doing wrong, not what they would do for the city.

It was a fatal mistake.

We had four years of tangible evidence of what we had done and what we planned to do. We talked about infrastructure improvements, business development, how we got that disgusting Confederate monument out of our downtown, and public safety initiatives.

We talked about how we chipped away at years of blight, demolishing 524 vacant structures in 2018, 542 in 2019, 467 in 2020, and 239 in 2021 (and 176 in 2022, in case you were wondering).

We didn't deal in hypotheticals over here. We showed receipts.

We also created some fun, artful campaign ads—sort of in the spirit of the "If" video, but different. My favorite might be the one featuring my mom, where she has me taking out her trash and cutting the lawn, proving that basic services like trash disposal and landscaping are top priorities for us and our residents.

We also had an ad that featured my own teachers from Putnam Middle School, to reaffirm our commitment to education, and to prove that you can't forget where you came from.

Despite our wins, I must admit—campaigning while governing is a much different beast than devoting 100 percent of your time to the trail. I still had to run the city, push initiatives, and put out fires while also making time to fundraise and get in front of voters. It was an extreme case of time management.

During the previous campaign, Bell got in hot water for making overtures to paid employees about what they should and should not be doing in support of his campaign.

Much like my man Cedric did way back then, we had to have a clear divide between city staff and campaign workers.

We hired Rene Spellman from Los Angeles as campaign manager. Rene is an absolute bulldog when it comes to pushing for perfection. She was not afraid to push me, or anyone else, for the good of the campaign.

Obviously, I couldn't travel as much during this campaign, so I spent a ton of time on the phone to make connections and build support.

But best believe, any time I had a spare moment, I was out in our streets, knocking on doors.

During the first campaign, we knocked on fifty thousand doors. Our goal this time was sixty thousand.

We smashed that. When it was all said and done, we had visited eighty thousand doors.

Like before, we weren't just going out to tell people our story. We wanted to hear theirs. We listened to residents, and took notes about what issues were still of concern in their communities. We took the opportunity to shut down the half-truths and misinformation being spread by my opponents, too.

My message was simple. We called it Vision 2025 and it was a forward-thinking look at how we planned to lead our city in four key categories—Investing in Our People, Reimagining Public Safety, Renewing Our Commitment to Neighborhoods, and Realizing Our Economic Potential.

That was the game plan.

I participated in three debates with my fellow candidates. During the first debate, I feel like I was too nice; I let them talk too recklessly. I learned my lesson. In the following debates, I had to smack 'em with receipts.

Big shout-out to Mississippi's own Big K.R.I.T. for being a major inspiration during my re-election campaign. The defiance of "Mt. Olympus," the motivation of "Glorious," and especially the mission statement of "Confetti." "What's a crown if you don't protect it?" Krizzle asked. I knew this election was bigger than me; it was about building upon the foundation we laid in term one, protecting our residents.

K.R.I.T.'s "Rich Dad, Poor Dad" made me think about the state of our ninety-nine neighborhoods. K.R.I.T. used this song to share the life lessons his father imparted upon him, uplifting a young K.R.I.T. through challenging circumstances. It made me think about the many young men in our community who desperately need direction from a trusted OG, and the importance of using my platform to fight for them.

This was also a time when I began to reread all my favorite Malcom Gladwell books from my time on the school board. Revisiting those themes helped settle my mind during those long, stressful days.

• • •

We had to deal with our share of mudslinging during the previous campaign, but the attacks felt more salacious—and desperate—this time around.

As usual, since no one could claim that I was stealing taxpayer money or doing anything politically nefarious—"No Scandal with Randall" is the slogan some supporters created in the first campaign—the opps had to go back to the usual nonsense: I'm gay and only love white folks.

Seriously, this again? Is this all y'all got?

No, I'm not gay, but yes, it's a widely known fact that I'm a proud ally of all our marginalized communities—and that includes LGBTQ+. Anyone who isn't should be ashamed of themselves—especially if they call themselves a native of the city that wrote the book on tolerance for all people.

And yes, my campaign was blessed with lots of generous donors, but to pretend that I was secretly funded by the evil white Illuminati is a horrible disservice to the residents of all colors who contributed their hard-earned money to our cause.

Let me calm down before I go off the rails too much and write a diss track.

Because in the midst of all that campaign drama, I would find my forever.

I met Kendra in May 2021. Her beauty was striking—she was super bad, y'all—but after exchanging pleasantries and talking for a bit, I didn't think much else of it. The interaction was short, I was on my way to another event, and, besides, the last thing on my mind was starting a relationship. I had a city to run and a campaign to win.

One month later, we ran into each other at another charity event. At this point, it couldn't be a coincidence.

Another month later, we decided to meet up for drinks. When she walked into the Paper Doll in downtown Birmingham, I immediately went in for a hug. The emotions that rushed over me when we embraced . . . man.

This was something special.

We talked and laughed for hours. We decided to grab dinner that evening and have been inseparable ever since.

I've never had someone match my energy the way she does. We can talk about our favorite shows and movies endlessly. We'll turn on music in the car and have our own personal *Verzuz* battles—she plays a song, and I hit her with an even better one.

She's not just a pretty face attached to my arm at formal gatherings. She's a driven Black woman with a successful business, a beautiful family, a heart full of love for her community, and the best taste in ratchet trap music.

I hit the lottery.

When you have a diamond, you love to see her shine. I came up with what I thought would be the perfect date night.

Instead, it would be the night everything changed. Our quiet little love story would soon be much more public than we anticipated.

I hit up my friend Ursula Smith, owner of an incredible dance studio in town. I asked her to come up with a routine for us. I'd bring Kendra by the studio as a surprise, and we'd learn this routine together. I saw it as our time to bond, creating an intimate moment that we could both hold on to forever.

We did the routine in the studio and nailed it. Kendra loved it so much she had us repeat the whole thing in the parking lot outside her place. It was so much fun, and so passionate that we decided to do it even bigger. We got dressed up in our flyest outfits and hired a videographer to capture us dancing outside of Birmingham landmarks.

We had no plans to share this video. It was just supposed to be our moment, a representation of our growing love.

But those political arsonists attempt to destroy everything we build.

The photographer sent us a few photos from the dance shoots. Kendra, like anyone would, shared some of the pics with her girls. Well, I guess those friends shared those photos with friends and eventually they wound up in the hands of my opponents.

I won't bother naming the culprits—they don't deserve the free publicity in this book—but someone posted the photo of Kendra and me to their Facebook page, and used it to play into the "is he or isn't he gay?" rumor mill funded by the opps.

I. Was. Pissed.

A very private, intimate moment was shared without our consent to the entire world. I wasn't tripping about the attack on my sexuality; I was above that by then. I was more upset about Kendra, who was now caught in the crossfire. Kendra and I hadn't publicly announced our relationship at this point; social media was flooded with questions and rumors about Woodfin's mystery woman.

And please don't come for Kendra and say she shouldn't have shared the photos with her friends. This wasn't her fault. She was brand new to the world of dirty politics; she didn't ask to be put in this position.

It was a last-minute, pitiful attempt to sway voters hours before they went to the polls.

It wasn't going to work.

As the results started flowing in, one thing was clear—the people of Birmingham had my back.

I won re-election with 64 percent of the vote.

For comparison, Scales came in at 20 percent, Bell at 9 percent, and Chris Woods at 4 percent.

No runoff here.

But here's the most powerful story from that night—across all ninety-nine neighborhoods, we won *every single* precinct. Every one. I don't believe that feat has been matched in my lifetime.

To win that decisively in an eight-person race that included long-time political players, well-known activists, and community leaders said so much about the trust that Birmingham had in me and in my administration.

We spent four years listening. Working. Connecting. Every promise we made when I first hit the campaign trail in 2017 we spent the next four years fulfilling.

We held town halls to have direct conversations with our residents. We launched programs like ACE, the Academy for Civic Engagement, to invite residents into City Hall to learn the inner workings of government, empowering them to be community leaders. We uncovered long-hidden problems like the city pension shortfall and patched them up, so our workers would have a future. We took major risks, like the construction of Protective Stadium, because, despite the naysayers, we knew it would pay off.

Customer service. Efficiency. Effectiveness. Transparency. Accountability.

We didn't just win. We soared.

But this time, it was even sweeter to have a dance partner by my side.

Before the race was officially called, I decided to put the photo rumors to rest by releasing the full video of Kendra and myself dancing around Birmingham on social media (with Kendra's permission, of course).

If these nosy people really wanted a relationship reveal, they were gonna get it on our terms.

I guess you could say it was kinda cocky to drop that video before results were finalized, but I wasn't sweating it. The old Randall would have been too insecure, too shaken by fear.

But fear didn't have nothin' on us.

So instead, we danced the night away—in front of Birmingham's beautiful Rotary Trail, among the shimmering neon lights of downtown, and underneath the stars of the city I was so privileged to lead.

Though we're a city of nearly two hundred thousand people, in that moment it felt like there were only two.

I received another huge vote of confidence nearly two years later when I asked Kendra if we could spend the rest of our lives together. She said yes.

We're dancing into our forever together.

———

Birmingham is a city with a renowned history of civil rights advancement. Unfortunately, in years past, that fight wasn't always extended to our LGBTQ+ community. My administration vowed to change that.

Our city made history in 2024 by earning a perfect score on the Human Rights Campaign's Municipal Equality Index, a measurement of our commitment to LGBTQ+ rights, including our use of inclusive policies and practices.

I had the honor to speak to the Human Rights Campaign in 2022 about Birmingham's legacy as an advocate and the importance of standing as an ally in turbulent times.

Good evening.

On behalf of the City of Birmingham, it's my great honor to be here, surrounded by friends and passionate changemakers.

As you know, this month has been designated as Black History Month, a time where we reflect on the folks who made incredible strides in our world.

Make no mistake, this country was built by Black hands. Shaped by Black minds. Moved forward with Black talent. And I'm so proud to be mayor of a city whose roots run deep in strengthening civil liberties for marginalized communities.

But can I be real with y'all for a second?

As a son of Birmingham, one thing that has always frustrated me is that we are so often defined by our past but not celebrated enough for our progress.

Here's what I mean.

When folks unfamiliar with our city think of Birmingham, they think of those old black-and-white photos of protesters getting attacked by dogs and drenched by hoses. They hear names like Bull Connor that represent hateful, oppressive leadership. They recall church bombings where the precious lives of girls attending Sunday school were stolen.

Simply put, they think of the trials of Birmingham. But they don't think of the triumph of Birmingham. How our streets were filled with children who marched for change. How legendary activists pushed for voting rights on a national level and inclusive leadership on a civic level.

That is the real face of Birmingham, greater than our past, marching toward our future.

As mayor, I work every day to reimagine Birmingham as a place of progression, not oppression.

Not long ago, I read an article that named Alabama as the worst state for LGBTQ+ Americans. I won't deny it. That hurts and it's proof that our state must do more to make its residents feel accepted. But let me assure you, we don't roll like that in Birmingham.

That's why in 2018 I appointed Josh Coleman, who is here with us tonight, as the City of Birmingham's LGBTQ+ Liaison, a first for both our city and the state of Alabama.

From there, we formed the city's first LGBTQ+ advisory board, which provided LGBTQ+ training to city workers, expanded fully inclusive healthcare coverage to our trans employees, and provides intentional visibility to the community.

And that brings us to last November, when the City of Birmingham proudly achieved its highest-ever total raw score on the Human Rights Campaign Municipal Equality Index—a score of 108.

It was affirmation of the hard work we're doing to build a more inclusive city. And when you think about it, why shouldn't we?

How dare I serve as the mayor of Birmingham, a city whose legacy has been built on the audacity of hope, and not extend that fight to our LGBTQ+ community.

How could we not push for change in a city where Dr. Martin Luther King Jr. sat in a Birmingham jail and penned a powerful letter that explicitly said: "Any law that uplifts human personality is just. Any law that degrades human personality is unjust"?

In his words, "Injustice anywhere is a threat to justice everywhere."

Though the paths of those civil rights pioneers and the paths of today's LGBTQ+ community are different, paved with different needs, different approaches, and different obstacles, the destination is the same:

Daring to create a more inclusive country, one that actually lives up to the rights and freedoms guaranteed by our Constitution.

How do we do that? It's simple—follow the blueprint set by Birmingham.

We build a community of like-minded activists and leaders who can elevate the issues affecting the LGBTQ+ community. The Human Rights Campaign is doing a masterful job of leading that effort.

We engage our youngest to feel empowered to fight against injustices and guide them toward more inclusive thinking.

And we push back against unjust laws that threaten to tear at the fabric of the LGBTQ+ community. Hear me clearly—the mounting anti-trans bills that are spreading across our nation right now are a product of toxic misogyny. The rights of our youngest and most precious must be protected.

Dr. King reminded us of the fierce urgency of now.

HRC, as leaders, as advocates, as allies, friends and family, we are on the edge of history, and as Dr. King said, there *is* such a thing as being too late. We cannot delay when lives are at stake.

This is not a time for apathy or complacency. This is a time for vigorous and positive action.

No matter how insurmountable the odds may seem, change is attainable. Look no further than Birmingham. Those old black-and-white pictures of chaos and upheaval from the '60s, yes, that is us. That's who we were.

But we're not victims. We're fighters. We're survivors. We're changemakers.

HRC, you stand at the doorstep of change, as well. For the trans kids fighting for acceptance at school, to the elderly couple finally being able to show the world who they truly are, and all points in between, their fight is our fight.

Allow me to leave you with this thought from one of the greatest authors of our time, James Baldwin: "Love does not begin and end the way we seem to think it does. Love is a battle. Love is a war. Love is growing up."

HRC, in the spirit of love, we must fight for justice. Only then can we finally grow into our full potential.

Randall L. Woodfin, Mayor
Human Rights Campaign Address
February 2022

CHAPTER 12

ELEVATORS (ME & YOU)

E very bride, every bridegroom, feels stress about their wedding. Why wouldn't they? It's one of the most important days of anybody's life, a moment they've been dreaming of since they were young.

But this stress was different for Kendra. I could see it in her eyes. The frustration. The anxiety. The fear.

It was the fall of 2023. We had decided that December 31 would be the public declaration of our love, closing the year with a beautiful wedding ceremony surrounded by friends and family.

But that invitation list soon expanded to coworkers and constituents and church members and play cousins and my mama's friends and her mama's friends and neighbors and legislators and . . .

I've gotta stop there. Wedding day PTSD is hitting me, too.

Literally every day, random people were stopping us in the street asking, "Where's my invite?" and saying things like, "I'm not going to miss the city's royal wedding."

Bruh, let's set the record straight—we are not royalty. And even though I'm truly blessed to have a deep connection with my community, the entitlement so many people had over our day was too much.

Absolutely too much.

As Kendra was going over the invitation list for our wedding, which had ballooned to more than five hundred people—and we still weren't done adding names—she sat me down and asked a question that still sticks with me: "Is this wedding for us, or is it for everyone else?"

I faithfully serve as leader of nearly two hundred thousand people in the Magic City. But at that moment, the only number that mattered was two.

I didn't hesitate one bit—I told her this day was about us, not anyone else.

It was the first test of what a real, genuine partnership is.

I see marriage as the next step in my growth into manhood, leadership, fatherhood—everything that will define my legacy.

That growth takes all of us into unexpected places.

Even hip-hop.

In 2023, rap artists spent the entire calendar year celebrating Hip-Hop 50—the five-decade anniversary of the phenomenon that would change the world, and my life specifically.

While I'm still a few years away from hitting fifty myself, I've had the opportunity to follow hip-hop culture almost from its inception. And one of the coolest things I've witnessed in the past decade is the maturation of rap.

Hip-hop is growing up.

Hip-hop has always been characterized as a youth movement, a reflection of the Black ethos. But like every culture, hip-hop refuses to be stagnant. It evolves with the times, with each branch representing a different aspect of the Black identity of its era.

The carefree block parties of the '80s eventually gave way to more sociopolitical commentaries later in the decade. The '90s morphed into a reflection of harsh realities of underserved Black communities, detailing both the struggle and violence of those eras. The 2000s began to embrace flash and excess once hip-hop hit mainstream and became big-time business. And by the 2010s, everything that was old became new again, as a new generation of artists steered the genre back to commentary that fit their youthful experiences.

But some of those young artists definitely have old souls.

Jermaine Lamarr Cole, better known as J. Cole, is one of those young cats who, as the old heads would say, has been here before.

Unlike many of his peers who embraced style over substance, Cole was a deep thinker and an intricate storyteller, often being compared to legendary '90s griots like Nas and Common.

And as hip-hop matured, it was clear that those decades of lessons had seeped their way into younger artists as they began embracing adulthood.

Cole's 2016 album *4 Your Eyez Only* featured one of the most unexpected songs of his career. "Foldin' Clothes" was a track about the little joys of adulthood—specifically, doing laundry with your wife.

Cole celebrates the joys of watching Netflix with his wife, eating Raisin Bran with almond milk (he makes a really big deal about that almond milk)—it's a slice of life that seems foreign in a culture that far too often puts so much worth in extravagance.

Sure, artists like the aforementioned Nas and Common—even Jay Z and Snoop Dogg—have embraced elder statesmen roles in hip-hop, but rarely do we get that level of commentary from the current generation.

As you might guess, "Foldin' Clothes" was met with very mixed reviews at the time. I get it. As a music lover, as a hip-hop aficionado, you need a few years under your belt to understand that life's beauty isn't confined to noisy clubs or in the seat of an absurdly expensive car.

The first concert Kendra and I attended was a J. Cole and 21 Savage show at Atlanta's State Farm Arena in 2021. Despite being diametrically opposed on paper—Cole as the laid-back, intricate thespian, and

21 as the more brazen and materialistic spitter—the two find common ground both in concert and as collaborators. Their 2018 track "A Lot" is probably 21's best song to date.

I think there's a lesson from Cole here—finding serenity with his wife at home, while also being the yin to 21 Savage's chaotic yang. (Cole also had the levelheaded maturity to bow out of the 2024 feud between Kendrick Lamar and Drake before things got too out of hand. He had the foresight of Miss Cleo on that one.)

As hip-hop matures, its greatest artists prove that they can't be defined by just one aspect of their lives. The culture is multifaceted, and so are the artists. Cole is as much of a superstar rapper as he is a Netflix-bingeing family man.

Being a man—mayor or otherwise—means serving multiple masters. Being the best son I can be. Being a public servant, working tirelessly in the best interests of the constituents I serve. Representing Alpha Phi Alpha. Representing Morehouse College. But I bet Cole would agree with me when I say family comes first. It's one of the many lessons learned from the love of a Black woman.

A household cannot thrive without partnership. When two become one, that bond is unbreakable.

Pass the almond milk.

Back when Kendra and I were dating and the video of us dancing went viral, it symbolized so much more than a political victory. From that moment on, the world would know that we were partners, perfectly synchronized in our thoughts and movements.

The months that followed would be some of the happiest times of my life.

I found my equal in every way.

Some days it was five-star restaurants; other days it was fried bologna sandwiches. One night we might be rocking to the grooves at a Frankie Beverly concert; the next week we would be screaming ad-libs at a Jeezy show.

I had a travel partner, a wedding date, a permanent plus one.

I was her cheerleader as she dominated the world of real estate, forming her own company, making her own deals, and flaunting her boundless creativity. Likewise, she showed endless support through late nights and early mornings as I worked to make my city better.

A lot of that came down to her faith. Kendra is deeply spiritual and helped strengthen my spiritual walk by relating biblical stories of leadership, sorrow, and hope when my journey became difficult.

And it was the little things—forcing me to put down my phone and unstrap my Apple watch when I walked in the house to completely focus on her—on us. She encouraged me to take on thirty-day challenges when I'd abstain from distractions like sweets or social media for a month. Both did wonders for my physical and mental health.

She has truly made me a better man. Continues to do so.

But let's backtrack, because after recounting all these amazing things that she has done for me, I have to admit that for too long before our wedding-invitation conversation, I was unwilling to give her what she deserved—I couldn't give her forever.

After nearly two years of dating and falling deeper in love, marriage seemed like the obvious next step, but those steps weren't ones my feet were willing to take. Forget cold feet—mine were lodged in a pair of icebergs.

I knew Kendra was the only woman I wanted to be with. I knew she was the woman God designed for me. I knew she was my future.

But I could not commit.

Why?

Fear. That's always the reason.

Kendra and I have very different upbringings.

When Kendra's father passed away, her mom remarried. Kendra's mom and stepdad have been happily married for decades. Kendra's the product of a married family. Stability is pretty much all she knows.

The game was much different for me. My parents split when I was young, which caused a deep-seated fear of divorce in me. I always wanted to be married, always wanted to be a dad, but I knew how hard divorce could be for children. I did not want to be the cause of that pain for my future kids. So I ran from commitment.

I didn't want to be some woman's baby daddy. I didn't want to be in a failed marriage.

But I also knew that God put this very special woman in my life for a reason.

My own family picked up on the cues before I did.

Long before Kendra and I were engaged, my dad gave her a card during a Sunday dinner. There was no particular reason for the gift. It was just one of those "showing you love just because" tokens of affection.

The card called Kendra "daughter" and I wasn't happy. I felt like he was pushing marriage on us before we were ready.

Here's the funny thing—I was ready. I was just in denial.

Fear is like a faulty GPS, intentionally steering you away from your intended destination. I knew where I wanted to end up, everyone who was traveling with us knew we were on the right path, but that lying GPS kept telling me to recalculate my route.

Nah. This was the road we were meant to travel. Together.

Hear me when I tell y'all this: If you can afford it, get a good therapist. It helps. Thanks to a really dope relationship counselor, I recognized all that was holding me back. And I soon learned that I had to look those fears square in their eyes and confront them. The fear of failure. The fear of abandonment. The fear of rejection. All those tiny little monsters that nipped at my heels since childhood—I had to squash them.

And this time I had a dance partner who helped trample them underfoot.

Kendra was too beautiful, too kind, too fun, too perfect to allow her to slip away.

I wasn't going to let the fears of the past define my future. I was going to make Kendra my wife.

I'll admit that I'm not much of a "surprise" guy, but when I decided to finally pop the question to Kendra, I went all in.

This surprise was a three-act play, and I spent days getting all the players into their positions.

And on that fateful Sunday, the performance was award-winning, if I say so myself.

I'm gonna pause here. Before we get to the main event, allow me to set the stage: In the weeks leading up to the proposal, Kendra and I were discussing buying a home together. Kendra, of course, has her finger on the pulse of the market. One day, she went to check out a place, opened the door, and immediately said, "This is my house."

She was blown away by its beauty, and quickly hit me up so I could check it out, too. She wasn't wrong—the house was amazing, and I fell in love with it, too. I was ready to move forward with purchasing the house, which confused Kendra—at this point she still saw me as the guy who was too afraid of commitment, and marriage seemed like a pipe dream. She was very unsure about committing to a house with a guy who hadn't committed to a ring yet.

But we moved forward. We got all the way to closing day on the house and Kendra remained nervous. Everything still felt so *up in the air*.

Oh, but I had big plans.

The day before closing, I gave her a call and said, "Hey, tomorrow's a big day. Let's go out for a nice dinner before we move. Oh, and wear something nice."

We headed to the Paper Doll, the very bar where we had our first date, for drinks. The bar was completely empty and the lights were dim. (It completely went over her head that it was a Sunday and they should have been closed. Props to the owner for allowing me to set up this sneaky surprise.)

The server sat us at a table and Kendra said, "Oh, this is the same spot we had on our first date!"

What a coincidence!

I told her I had to go to the bathroom but I really went to get mic'd up and to tell the bartender to play "Honesty" by Pink Sweat$. That song has double importance for us—not only was it the song that was playing when we met, but its lyrics are about a woman too afraid to commit to her man.

Okay, flip the roles, and it's our story.

I came back to the table, and I'll admit, I was visibly nervous, even shaking a bit.

As Pink Sweat$'s opening lines rang out—"Baby, I'm afraid to fall in love / Cause what if it's not reciprocated?"—a camera crew appeared to capture the moment (shout-out to my folks at Bold as a Lion Studios for making this memory last forever). Kendra still didn't get the hint—it's not unusual for cameras to be around us.

But then, it was time. Time to put fear on the back burner. Time to make forever our destiny.

"I want to talk about something more important than the house," I told her. "I want to talk about our lives. Together. I want to spend our lives together."

Man, she started ugly crying like Viola Davis in *Fences*.

She gave me the three letters that—with the help of therapy—I realized I'd been dying to hear since we attended those Isley Brothers and 2 Chainz concerts, that one word that I hoped to hear on those nights we spent dozing on the couch while attempting to watch action movies on Netflix and days watching her write in her journal.

That one word that would change our lives and cement our forever.

She said it.

She said *yes*.

But that was Act 1 of our three-act story.

Next up on our agenda, I tell Kendra that we're walking over to El Barrio to grab some Mexican cuisine for dinner, just as we did during Date No. 1. Remember, it's Sunday, so technically it should be closed, but Kendra's head is swimming so she doesn't realize it.

Once we entered, she came to her senses—our parents and Kendra's sons were waiting for us inside.

She had meltdown No. 2. It was a beautiful thing to see.

At this point, Kendra was shaking; she was so overwhelmed by the outpouring of love. But we weren't through yet. For the finale, we strolled over to the House of Found Objects. When we walked in, it was wall-to-wall friends and family. A playlist of our favorite songs rang out in the background—UGK, N.E.R.D., Outkast, and more.

Act 1 was just us, our moment to revel in our love. Act 2 was immediate family, spending time with those who will walk closest on our journey. And Act 3 was celebrating the moment with the friends and family who were destined to be our support system.

Kendra's reaction—from confusion to joy to overstimulated glee—will forever be etched into my soul.

She later told me that the entire experience made her feel worthy. Although she was much more sure of our relationship earlier on than I was, she had wrestled with her own fears.

Her previous marriage had failed. It made her feel very unworthy of love. Fear makes even the mightiest giants feel small. But that special Sunday afternoon—from the surprises, the callbacks, the friends and family, the special musical touches—she says it helped her to regain her sense of self-worth.

She deserved love.

As we both danced in the House of Found Objects, surrounded by those we loved the most, two people finally found what they'd been looking for all these years.

Each other.

I know some brothers have a tough time transitioning from bachelor life to their boo'd up era, in the words of singer Ella Mai. It's even tougher once a man commits to putting a ring on it.

For me, it was smooth as silk.

That's probably because everything just felt so right. I had begun to overcome the fears of commitment and failure that had me in a chokehold for so long, almost causing me to miss my blessing.

But it also helped that so many people around me really wanted to see us happy. Didn't matter if I was preparing to speak at a neighborhood town hall or hitting up Yo Mama's in downtown Birmingham for some chicken and waffles (or that Tuesday pork chop lunch special), the outpouring of love was so heartfelt. I'll never forget having a conversation with a state senator who said, "This new life looks good on you."

I felt lighter. Less stressed. And so optimistic.

Unfortunately, the road wasn't as smooth for Kendra.

Now keep in mind, Kendra is no stranger to the public sphere. As part of her real estate business, she's very active and visible in the community.

Now, though, she was on her way to becoming the first lady of Birmingham. That came with a lot—a lot—of attention, a lot of stress. And a lot of intrusion.

Our country has been hard on Black women. The pressure from outside of our community is intense. America asks too much for too little. Black women are overworked and underpaid, making sixty-nine cents for every dollar made by white, non-Hispanic men. Growing up, Black men are always told that they have to be twice as good, twice as educated, and twice as creative as their white male counterparts. For Black women, that bar is even higher. And that's just the professional pressures, saying nothing of the generations of beauty and identity standards that are thrust upon them.

Straighter hair. Fewer curves. More European, less Black.

And within our community, the pressures of perfection are even stronger.

From the days of the plantation, to the horrors of the Jim Crow South during the rise of the Civil Rights Movement, and well into the twenty-first century, Black women were positioned as the stalwarts of the Black family.

Black women had to be infallibly strong to uphold the family unit.

Black women had to be soft, but not show weakness. Unbreakable but not too masculine.

They had to be dependable problem-solvers but not allowed to set their own sights too far beyond the household.

It's a curse that has seeped into every bit of our culture. Hip-hop is no exception.

No offense to Sexyy Red, Ice Spice, or whoever else is on your playlist, but I can't think of a woman in hip-hop history as talented as Lauryn Hill.

After breaking in with the legendary group the Fugees in the '90s, she broke out on her own, releasing her one and only solo studio album in 1998, *The Miseducation of Lauryn Hill*. (Before the hip-hop purists come for my neck, yeah, I know she had an *MTV Unplugged* album three years later. I didn't forget.)

Lauryn's rise to the top of the charts was astronomical, winning five Grammys in 1999, including the first hip-hop album to win the award for Album of the Year. Those wins secured its legacy as one of the greatest albums of all time—in any genre.

As years passed, we never got a follow-up album (yeah, yeah . . . the *Unplugged* album). Lauryn basically went into seclusion, derailing her projected path to being one of the greatest artists of all time. Lauryn's disappearance was no mystery—she was disillusioned with an industry that was taking more from her than it was giving.

But sadly, the longer she was gone from the spotlight, the more her history was rewritten. No longer was she celebrated as a cultural touchstone for women's voices in hip-hop. The narrative now included words like "flaky," "has-been," or "one-hit-wonder."

Cleary, the critics weren't paying attention to her lyrics.

The fourth track on *Miseducation* is entitled "To Zion," an incredibly moving song dedicated to Lauryn's son of the same name. In that song, she discusses her pregnancy and how some people around her told her to think of her career over her child. To them, terminating a pregnancy would be the best choice for her future.

But as Lauryn says at the end of the first verse, she chose her heart over the whims of others.

And people wonder why Lauryn got out of the music business. She was not willing to put her family second to industry politics and branding.

She didn't want perfection. She wanted peace.

That's all Kendra wanted. Peace. In the early days of our engagement, she didn't get that.

Kendra was immediately thrust center stage; the spotlight was blinding.

Wherever she went, people were constantly stopping her to take pictures. The pressure of always being camera-ready was tough. She felt like she had to be photo-shoot fresh whenever she stepped out of the house.

If one hair was out of place, if her smile wasn't wide enough, if her energy couldn't match those who greeted her, it could be a bad look.

The plague of perfection.

And then, the favors. Similar to what my mom continues to experience, residents began treating Kendra as proxy for me. Need something done in your community and you can't find the mayor? Ask his fiancée. Need promotion for your business? Ask his fiancée. Looking for tickets for the Chris Brown show coming to town in a few weeks? Ask his fiancée.

By the way, I never have concert tickets. Don't talk to me; talk to Ticketmaster.

It even spilled over to the kids of our blended family, with teachers and lunch ladies relaying business requests through them.

Kendra's a good woman—a great woman, in fact—but the pressure to be Birmingham's proxy mayor was overwhelming.

Now this is the part of the book where I tell y'all how she overcame those mounting expectations and found peace among perfection.

If the answers were that easy, Lauryn Hill would be on her eighth solo album by now.

Here's the reality: Fighting through unrealistic expectations of perfection is a daily battle. Kendra is coming to terms with that. She serves faithfully on boards around town. And if you see her, best believe she'll greet you warmly and with enthusiasm.

Perspective comes with time. Instead of believing that she must be all things to all people, she'll tell you she's quickly learning that it's most important to be herself. She'll always be an incredible partner, a stellar mom, a successful businesswoman and servant leader, but she's doing it for herself first and foremost.

On a related note, my girl Lauryn Hill recently returned to the spotlight that she'd avoided for so long, gracing the 2024 BET Awards with a showstopping display of her talent. Back like she never left.

Her chronic lateness and whispers about her work ethic will constantly linger, but at this point in her career, Lauryn is living life on her terms. It's a song I hope all Black women can one day sing.

Why be perfect when it's so much more fulfilling to be yourself?

. . .

These days, people often ask how my leadership style has changed since marriage.

I honestly don't think it has changed at all. In fact, years of leadership helped me to become a good husband, a good father—a good partner. (Of course, you'd have to ask Kendra for confirmation.)

Public–private partnerships. If you've ever heard me address a crowd, you've probably heard me use that term.

It's one of the most important building blocks of any successful administration.

Believe me, no project will thrive without buy-in from multiple community partners. Without strong, committed partners, even the best-laid plans are little more than bare-bones scaffolding, sure to topple like a rickety Jenga tower.

For instance, look at the success of the Birmingham Promise. It's the shining example of strong partnerships changing lives.

In order to offer every Birmingham City Schools student last-dollar tuition to any public college or university in Alabama, as well as funding for business apprenticeships, we had to have lots of dollars in play.

Lots and lots of dollars. Way more than our municipal budgets could afford on their own.

So we turned to our business community. My pitch was simple—in order to improve graduation rates, to grow our workforce, to keep our talented young people in our borders, and to restore hope to communities that long gave up on it, we need your help.

Simply put, put your money where your mouth is. Be the change we need.

And they stepped up. In 2020, the Promise received $1 million contributions from the Alabama Power Foundation, the Altec/Styslinger Foundation, and Regions Bank.

The next year, Protective Life, Blue Cross and Blue Shield of Alabama, and Alabama Power gave another $1 million each.

Bloomberg Philanthropies came through with $1.8 million in 2021, while Shipt made a $1 million contribution spread over five years starting in 2023. Also, the Birmingham Board of Education, my old stomping grounds, provided $240,000 in 2023 to expand the internship program.

And then in April 2024, PNC Foundation came through with an incredible ten-year, $10 million grant for the Promise.

The result: More than $9 million in scholarships to more than 1,300 students in 2024. That's life-changing money in the most literal sense.

And that's the power of partnership—communication, finding common ground, and working in unison to establish a better foundation for the future.

I thought the same ideology would serve me well in my upcoming marriage, even if that meant disappointing a lot of people. Around five hundred people, to be exact.

The original plan for our wedding was for it to be held at my home church. But as Kendra and I got bogged down with the planning, it felt more like a chore than a celebration. We quickly realized why—nothing about the ceremony was intimate.

The guest list was ballooning every day, growing from friends and family to people we felt obligated to add to the list for various reasons. Family ties, friends of friends, work connections—it was too overwhelming. And that's not including the random people who often popped up and outright demanded invitations.

My brother in Christ, I don't even know your last name, how am I supposed to mail you an invite?

We became so concerned with pleasing other people that we forgot to focus on ourselves.

It was time to stop listening to everyone else and start listening to my partner.

Communication.

Finding common ground.

Working in unison for our future.

We talked. We came to a consensus. We determined our future.

That year-ending mega-bash? Nah, that wasn't happening.

We were getting married imminently. Just us, immediate family, and a couple of friends.

A lot of people weren't happy with this decision. But that's cool; it wasn't their day.

The partnership is all that matters.

The wedding day itself was storybook, the intimate backyard affair we imagined. We were joined by our parents and kids, grandparents and siblings, their significant others, and a few friends—many of whom helped out with the wedding proceeding. Somewhere around forty people. Our good friend Dr. Thomas Beavers officiated the ceremony; he and his wife also provided pre-marriage counseling.

I'll never forget the image of Kendra walking down the aisle. She was so radiant, totally breathtaking. The nervous energy I experienced didn't make me anxious; it gave me more of a silly energy.

I was giddy. This beautiful woman was going to be my wife.

So much of the day is a blur, but I remember the sounds. Ella Mae's "This Is," Robin Thicke's "Angel," and Jeezy's "I Do" were the soundtrack of the biggest day of my life. I remember the laughter. The hugs and being dapped up by friends. I remember Kendra being in my arms.

That fear of failure and commitment? The frustrations of wedding planning? The insecurities that Kendra wrestled with as a first lady?

They all just washed away that night.

And, oh yeah, there's no partnership without compromise. Although the December 31 event was no longer the wedding ceremony, it still happened—this time as an extended wedding reception.

It was much easier planning this revamped event, since we didn't have to be held to the constraints of a wedding ceremony. It was just a big ol' New Year's Eve party, surrounded by the city that loved us, and that we loved back.

I've had a lot of journeys in life—from Morehouse to the courtroom to City Hall. But all those roads lead right to the old Red Mountain Theatre, where we celebrated the joys of Black love among those who guided me along the way.

Best of all, this celebration was on our terms.

That's the best part of growing up. Whether it's shutting out distractions for the sake of your inner peace like Lauryn Hill, or finding joy in the mundane like J. Cole, we've learned to write our story on our own terms.

I'm a mayor, but now I'm a husband first.

I love having the opportunity to speak to young graduates as they head on to the next phase of their lives. It means even more when I can deliver words of wisdom at one of Alabama's HBCUs.

But one thing I've learned—especially in marriage—is that things don't always go as planned. So you have to pivot.

In 2022, I was excited to address the graduating class at Alabama A&M, until a storm cut the outdoor commencement short. Once those chairs started flipping over, I wrapped things up fast.

But here's the full transcript of what I had planned to deliver that day. I hope it can still provide meaning and motivation.

What's up, Bulldogs?

I bring greetings from my hometown, the city for which I'm honored to serve as mayor, Birmingham, Alabama, and I'm so humbled to join you here today as you step out into the next phase of your lives.

I'm also grateful that during my two terms as mayor, I've had not one but two very proud A&M grads on staff, two brothers who literally walk beside me in all of my duties.

So I know firsthand the incredible people this institution produces.

But in recent years, as times change and our country evolves, one intriguing topic of conversation seems to come up time and time again:

Are Historically Black Colleges and Universities still relevant?

In a world where diversity is slowly being embraced; in a time where students of color are getting much more opportunities than the days prior to the Civil Rights Era, when doors were constantly closed for us, are HBCUs still important?

To those who doubt the impact of these historic intuitions, to those who may question your journey or discredit our heritage, I say this.

In the words of the great philosopher Moneybagg Yo: I just looked at my wrist—I got time today.

When I look into this crowd and see eyes filled with hope, wisdom, enthusiasm, pride, what do I see? I see the future.

A future built upon the foundation set by HBCUs. And although 2022 looks a lot different than when A&M was established in 1875, know this—you're a reflection of that legacy. Walk in it. Embrace it.

Embrace the struggles.

Whether you are a first-generation college graduate or your family has a long history here, know that your story is *your* story. It's a story worth celebrating and telling. Doesn't matter if you were on the four-year track, the five-year track, or, whew Lord, even the six- or seven-year track—the fact is you are now *on* track. You made it.

You made it despite COVID-19 throwing the world a major curve-ball, forcing us to adjust the long-standing educational process. You adapted, and you made it.

You made it despite personal challenges that were thrown your way. Long nights studying, exams you thought were impossible to get through. Trying to balance work and class. Even waking up early enough to make it to class—I remember those days, trust. Every obstacle you overcame on this campus has prepared you for greater battles ahead.

Think of the strength Vivian Malone Jones had when she faced down Alabama governor George Wallace as she attempted to enroll in the University of Alabama. What is often left out of that story is that years before that historic confrontation, she spent her formative days right here on this campus.

The strength she showed in the face of all of that hate was built and molded right here. That's the stock you also come from.

Know this: Like her, you are also built to win. You're built to change the world.

I also want you to embrace your heritage. You are the product of a state that literally fought and shed blood to deny our ancestors our God-given rights of equal education. Freedom to vote. Freedom to have a seat at the table and make change.

You are the personification of the faith that the dark past has taught us. You are the reflection of the hope that the present has brought us. It's why we continue to march on until VICTORY is won.

And despite all the years of social progress and change that have been made, all the battles that have been fought and obstacles knocked down, victory is still not here yet.

We can't claim victory when communities of color are still underserved and denied employment and denied the financial and educational opportunities of white peers.

We can't claim victory when young Black men continue to be literal moving targets for an unjust law enforcement system. When lives, hopes, and dreams are snatched away by a coward's bullet.

We can't claim victory when, in this very state, lawmakers work to suppress the truth about Black history, keeping it out of classrooms and burying it in favor of their own narratives.

There is no victory when those same lawmakers use young trans children as political pawns, denying them healthcare and their humanity.

And that's where you come in. As a proud HBCU graduate, you understand the importance of uplifting underserved communities. You know the importance of being a voice for the unheard. You know no one should be denied the rights established under this country's Constitution.

HBCUs were established as a haven for Black students to become changemakers. It's on us to continue to plant those seeds, to be the shoulders that future generations stand upon.

Because, Bulldogs, you are the reflection of William Hooper Councill, an enslaved man sold on the land where Green Bottom Inn once sat. That very same enslaved man would come back one day to buy that very same land—land that he would later use as a site to educate his people.

That's how you uplift your people. That's how you change your destiny.

That's why you are Black history.

So, Bulldogs . . .

Embrace the struggles. Embrace your legacy.

Most importantly, embrace the future.

No matter how difficult the road ahead, no matter the challenges that you and your family face, remember this: You are an overcomer.

When our ancestors were taken from their land against their will and forced to endure inhumane conditions, we still rose.

When our cries for equal rights were met with bombs, water hoses, and attack dogs, we still rose.

When systemic racism denied our forefathers and foremothers a chance to provide for our families, we still rose.

When bullets tear through our communities, robbing us of our friends and family members, we will rise.

And we are still here.

The fact that our people continue to achieve, continue to aspire, continue to change our world despite those insurmountable obstacles makes each of you before me today one thing: a living miracle.

To ask if HBCUs are still relevant is silly. It would be like asking if *you* are relevant.

And let me tell you, you've never been more relevant to our present, and to our future.

You are a reflection of the mothers and fathers who raised us, the activists who motivated us, the athletes who inspired us, the singers and rappers who captivate, the Black hands that built this country.

So, A&M, continue to build. Continue to inspire. Continue to lead and motivate.

Continue to be relevant.

Thank you.

Randall L. Woodfin, Mayor
Alabama A&M Commencement Address
May 2022

CHAPTER 13

BEHOLD A LADY

One day you're chillin' in the den, relaxin', while your wife is in the bathroom doing whatever it is women do in there.

And then your life changes forever.

Kendra was posted up in the bathroom when she called me over.

"I want to show you something," she said.

Kendra's in the *bathroom*; I'm not sure I want to see whatever it is she has to show me. But I'm a good husband, so I pull up.

What she showed me was a pregnancy test stick. "*Look!*" she shouted. The stick read positive.

I only had two words: "Oh, shit!"

I embraced her for what felt like an eternity. The range of emotions were crazy. Shock. Disbelief. Happiness. All simultaneously.

When we found out that our first child together would be a girl, I'll admit that it threw me. Kendra always wanted a girl—she's already mom to two fantastic young boys—but, honestly? I was apprehensive.

Fear is very good at finding cracks in the happiest of moments, ready to infiltrate the most intimate experiences.

I grew up around sisters and was always close to the women in my life, but, still, I just figured that a connection would come easier with a boy.

That wasn't the case, though. As the weeks went on, as I saw the ultrasounds and felt her squirming inside her mom, I began to feel a connection with her before she even arrived.

It finally hit me: I'm gonna be a girl dad. And I'm going all in. I'm talking buying onesies with Spelman College's logo emblazoned across it. I even started making monthly donations to the school. Gotta get her ready for those "pearly gates."

And yes, I'm gonna be playing the role of both Martin Lawrence and Will Smith from *Bad Boys II* when my girl's first date shows up on my doorstep. I can't wait.

Fear, move over. This was all joy. We were about to bring a child into this world. And I knew I had to do my part to make sure that she would enter a world worth living in.

Serious question: When did America lose its civility?

If you ask me, I have to put a lot of the blame on social media. And that's not just me being an old head.

A 2023 survey released by the American Bar Association found that 85 percent of respondents felt that civility in today's society is worse than ten years ago.

A leading 29 percent of respondents placed the blame on social media—see, I told y'all—with 24 percent blaming traditional media and 19 percent blaming politicians.

I guess I'm less concerned about who is to blame and more concerned about the ramifications.

Social media is an incredibly useful tool, not just for recreation but also for building community and sharing ideas. But what many don't realize is that social media's algorithms are tailored to your specific interests. If you're obsessed with cute cat videos, for instance, it's very likely that social media platforms will take note of the videos you watch, like, and share—and they will send more of that content your way. Therefore, you spend more and more time on those platforms, keeping their crucial engagement numbers high.

This also means you'll be more likely to interact with more users who share your interests and ideals. That's how community is created—and, unfortunately, such shared-interest communities can be a means to be exploited.

Here's an example: In my heart of hearts, there's only one way to eat grits. That's with sugar.

The sugar-grits community and their superior taste buds would stand tall with me.

But there are those among us who, for some reason, prefer salty grits. Why you'd want your grits to taste like the sand in Orange Beach, Alabama, I'll never know. To each their own.

In a perfect world of breakfast meals, we can agree to disagree. I'll have my delicious sweet grits; y'all can eat your salt stuff.

But in a world driven by social media one-upmanship, debates can become downright diabolical. Lines are drawn, tribalism takes hold, and on platforms where users can hide behind anonymity and there are rarely repercussions for attacks, even the most mundane topics can become outright wars.

The worst politicians among us know this. And they've been using civil discord to their advantage for years now.

Don't misunderstand me—social media by design is not a negative. Far from it. I believe in its power. One of the first actions of my administration when taking office was to vastly grow our city's social media presence. Facebook, Instagram, Tik Tok, Twitter, LinkedIn, NextDoor, e-newsletters—all these avenues became ways to keep our residents updated and connected. And not just on basic city services like trash pickup and holiday closings, but also to regularly highlight staff members and the unsung heroes of our ninety-nine neighborhoods.

There's power in community. But when misused, that power can break down society.

I believe the loss of civility starts with the result of social media's design to constantly please its users, and it carries over into debate culture, where there must be one winner and one loser. Nothing in between.

Alabama football fans vs. Auburn football fans. Marvel comic book movies vs. DC comic films. Kendrick Lamar vs. Drake. Liberal ideas vs. conservative views.

Only one side can be right. You have to stand tall for your home team—i.e., the social media silo you represent. No backing down, no compromise, no finding coming ground. That would be weakness.

You have to be right, because you have to win. Your opponent has to be wrong on all fronts; they have to lose.

The main thing we lose is civility.

Social media was originally designed to be a digital town square that could allow differing ideas to meet and find common ground. On its best days, that still happens. However, it's become easier for users to retreat to digital silos, patiently waiting for voices with more clout and status to back those toxic keystrokes. That provides validation.

When closed minds receive validation, the seeds of division are watered.

That harvest has borne the fruit of political tribalism and downright extremism in its worst cases.

When I read horrifying policies like Project 2025 and ask, "How did we get here as a nation?" I realize that it's a result of extremism slicing through civil discourse.

Project 2025 is a collection of devastating proposals developed by the Heritage Foundation, a conservative think tank, that, if enacted, would erase generations of progress in our country.

Among other things, the project threatens to ban contraception and take away women's abortion rights; raise prescription drug prices; eliminate the Department of Education; push to remove African American and gender studies, along with curriculum on slavery;

abolish DEI (diversity, equity, and inclusion) programs; and much, much more.

No, this isn't a megalomaniac's master plan from a '90s action movie. This is real life.

In a world where civil discourse was still encouraged, there's no way we'd get this far. Stern conversations and cooler heads would have struck down disgusting policies like these before they saw the light of day.

But it saddens me—actually, it pisses me off—to see conservative support for such unjust, abhorrent rhetoric. They know it's wrong, but they're so obsessed with supporting their side, their team, that they'll cover their eyes for as long as it takes them to reach the finish line.

I wish they'd turn around and see all the bodies they've trampled along the way.

This is not the world I want to raise my children in.

I thought about my kids a lot in the summer of 2024 when Birmingham played host to Major League Baseball. Our city is home to Rickwood Field, the oldest professional baseball park in the country. Rickwood was home to the Birmingham Black Barons, a member of the Negro Leagues and a team often called the jewel of Southern Black baseball. The Black Barons produced four Hall of Fame players, Mule Suttles, Willie Wells, Satchel Paige, and Willie Mays, who sadly passed away the day before our planned tribute to him in Birmingham.

While the eyes of the world were tuned in to the game between the St. Louis Cardinals and San Francisco Giants, it was the legendary Reggie Jackson who captured our ears.

During a televised interview, Mr. October told of his harrowing experiences traveling as a Black player in the Jim Crow South.

He was denied entry into restaurants and hotels, with the N-word thrown freely in his face. He was thrown out of country clubs.

He was dehumanized due to the color of his skin.

Of his experiences, he said in chilling tones, "I wouldn't wish it on anybody."

This is not ancient history. Reggie Jackson is in his seventies. This is *lived* history. And if you listen to the Heritage Foundation and their authoritarian supporters, it's history they want us to forget.

Birmingham taught us better than that.

After Mr. Jackson's comments, several people reached out to me and my team discreetly, to apologize for his words, worried that they cast a dark cloud over what was to be a joyous conversation.

Birmingham was not offended by his truths. In fact, we uplift them.

We don't hide from our history here. We know the evils of Jim Crow firsthand. Our parents and grandparents didn't have to read about them. Like Mr. Jackson, they experienced them.

To silence their experiences and to whitewash that history makes a mockery of the progress they fought to attain. They brought change to a very dark world. Why would we ever dim their light?

That's why Project 2025 and all other extremist doctrine must be eradicated. Our forefathers and foremothers literally risked their lives so that DEI policies would ensure communities of color had seats at tables that were often denied us. Banning African American studies means scores of lessons like Mr. Jackson's would be lost to time—a dark history that we would be doomed to repeat.

I want my children to know how horrible Birmingham was for faces that looked like ours. I never want them to take voting rights for granted or the fact that they can explore interracial relationships without winding up hanging from a tree. They need to see the scars so they can understand the healing process. I want them to know that their city—Birmingham—changed the world.

I understand that there's a temptation to pretend evils like slavery never existed in this country. It hits hard for white folks when a photo shows great-granddaddy standing there smiling while lynched

Black bodies hang lifeless. But today's children need to know that great-granddaddy's actions were monstrous. Pretending that this country is without its flaws will not save it—in fact, it will produce a repeating cycle.

America needs to stop running from its shadowy past. We need more ugly, hard conversations. We need to learn how to share ideas without attempting to shut down opposing views.

We need to learn how to talk to each other again.

Bring back civil discourse. Give us a world we can be proud to raise our kids in again.

It's hard enough being a kid in this world.

Now imagine suddenly being thrust into Birmingham's spotlight.

Everyone knows who you are. Everyone wants to be your friend. Everyone is asking you for favors. Everyone is piling pressure on your shoulders.

That was reality for Aubrey and Mason, Kendra's sons. Our new marriage meant that I was now a bonus dad, and that's pretty cool.

It also meant that everyone knew who my stepsons were. Everyone. I wasn't always so cool with that.

Aubrey is a mid-teenager, and he's the coolest teen you'll ever meet. He's smart, he's mature, and the sudden attention that came with being the "mayor's kid" rarely bothered him. When Kendra told him about our upcoming marriage, he replied, "If you're happy, I'm happy."

No sweat for him. It was light work.

Mason is ten and, as you'd guess for any ten-year-old, the transition was much more difficult for him.

Kids like stability and don't always respond well to change, especially rapid change. Mason's life transformed in the blink of an eye, and I can't blame him for freaking out.

Let's visit his first school year immediately after we moved into our new home:

Since his family moved from Hoover, a nearby city, to Birmingham, he was implanted into a new school system with unfamiliar faces. But because he was the "mayor's kid," everyone knew him before he knew who they were. It felt intrusive to him.

One day, he walked into class and all the students started bowing to him, like he was one of those spoiled kids from *Game of Thrones*. He was upset; he hated the attention.

When he won student of the month—no different than the accolades he received at his school in Hoover—he immediately questioned it. He had the same skepticism when he was in Beta Club or when he got on the honor roll: "Did I only get this because of Randall?"

He had teachers and school administrators asking him questions about Mayor Stepdad. And when he started getting involved in sports, he asked me to stop coming to his games. All the attention was on his relationship to me, not on Mason himself, and it made him extremely self-conscious.

Hell, he doesn't even like when we go to restaurants. Same reasons. He just wants to be a kid with his own identity, not a Woodfin stunt double.

He felt like a background character in his own story. That's not cool.

Of course, it put a strain on our relationship. This was all new to him, and step-fatherhood was new to me, too.

My dad is a great father to this day but, as I've mentioned before, marriage and fatherhood intimidated me. My mom and dad lived separate lives in separate households. They did their best, but the fear of failing in a fatherly role loomed large for me.

There's a prevailing myth in our country . . . nah, scratch that, let's call it what it is—an outright lie that Black men are less capable and even less caring than fathers of other ethnic groups.

A fatherhood study from the Centers for Disease Control and Prevention found that, among Black fathers of children under age five, 96 percent ate meals with their children every day or several times a week, 98 percent played with kids, 90 percent bathed them, and 60 percent made sure to read to them.

For Black fathers of school-age kids, 93 percent of dads ate meals with kids and 92 percent talked to their children several days a week about school and life.

That's a far cry from the media portrayal of the absentee Black dad.

However, it's a stigma that's often ingrained in our community. In the world of hip-hop, you don't have to look too hard for songs about men celebrating their moms. 2Pac's "Dear Mama." Kanye West's "Mama." J. Cole's "Apparently." Rick Ross's "Smile, Mama, Smile." There's no shortage of mama love.

But songs celebrating dads and fatherhood? You have to dig much deeper.

Will Smith's "Just the Two of Us" is a reimagining of the classic from Bill Withers and Grover Washington Jr. that serves as an ode to his eldest son. (Fun fact for the hip-hop heads in the house: Will's wife, Jada Pinkett Smith, was pregnant with their son Jaden in the music video.)

Jay-Z's "Glory" features his daughter Blue Ivy Carter (making her the youngest person to date to appear on a *Billboard* charting single), and is a celebration of her life, even touching on his wife Beyoncé's earlier miscarriage and worries that Blue would suffer the same fate. But as Jay said, "Nah, baby, you magic."

On the different end of that spectrum, Nas's "Daughters" talks about the stress of being a parent of a teen girl, from school issues to coming to terms with her dating life. He even questions himself, wondering if this is God's revenge on him for being a heartbreaker in his youth. But despite all of his honest talk, the love for his daughter is unquestionable.

Don't believe the media hype—Black men love their kids.

And since I was thrown into this Bonus Dad world, I had to find a way to show that same love to Mason.

I dug into books, specifically Ron L. Deal's *The Smart Stepfamily*, to get a better grasp on family dynamics. I listened to Kendra, who helped show me that I could be less of a disciplinarian and more of a comforting presence.

During those revelations, Kendra also told me that I was teaching her, as well—in this case, to be more firm. She's very nurturing but realized that sometimes that tender care opened the door for enabling. Together, we were finding that balance.

And a big shout-out to the boys' birth father, who has been supportive through this whole journey. He told Kendra: "Randall's raising them, so they're going to have to listen to him." Men supporting men. It goes a long way.

He's right: The boys are in our house; their eyes are on me. I have to be the mentor, the protector, the example.

I'm a stepdad, yes, but I have to be a dad, full-on.

Of course, being Dad leads to fun times, as well.

Before Mason's ninth birthday, we told him that we had to make a trip to Atlanta. We arrived, parked, and we walked around a giant structure—a setting that was somewhat familiar to him, but he didn't quite notice his surroundings.

Then, it clicked. We were at Mercedes-Benz Stadium and he was going to see the Atlanta Falcons vs. the Cleveland Browns.

He burst into tears. He was shocked, so surprised, so happy.

It was so cute.

It's just one of many adventures we've experienced as a family. We've visited Washington, DC, together, and even stopped by the White House. But we've also just had fun, quiet times at home. Those intimate evenings mean just as much as a rowdy stadium filled with Falcons fans.

Being the mayor of a mid-sized city is tough, but being a dad ain't far behind. I'm still learning every day.

Celebrating the magic of life like Jay. Creating connections like Will. Even adapting to the maturing process like Nas.

Kendra's boys—*our* boys—made me a better man. And very soon, they'd be joined by a brand-new baby sister.

Our journey is just beginning.

When your pregnant wife is uncomfortable and up all night watching TV to pass the time, that means husbands follow suit. Most nights, we'd turn on Netflix, scroll through the top movie picks, and click on something for the night.

But nothing beats the classics—The four-hour *Temptations* miniseries from 1998, a loose retelling of the legendary band's story, will never get old. Same goes for *The Five Heartbeats*, which follows the story of a fictional R&B group of the same name.

Speaking of, here's a mind-blowing fact for *Five Heartbeats* fans: Michael Wright's character is named Eddie King Jr., *not* Eddie Kane. Could have fooled me, too.

Kendra and I also have a fun way of bingeing Marvel movies—we select a character and watch all the movies related to that character. So if it's Thor week, we watch the four solo Thor films and the ensemble films that also feature the thunder god: *The Avengers, Avengers: Age of Ultron, Avengers: Infinity War,* and *Avengers: Endgame.*

Oh, and if we wanted to cry like Eddie King (not Kane), we catch up on the always-depressing drama *This Is Us.* "Nights like this I wish that raindrop would fall. . . ."

As the day of my first daughter's birth drew near, I asked myself an important question: There are leadership coaches to help leaders adjust to a life of service and there are marriage coaches to support partners on their journey—wouldn't it be cool to have a fatherhood coach?

Even better: What if there was an entire fatherhood summit, where brothers could gather and support each other?

Well, sometimes if you want something, you've got to make it happen.

And that's what I did. Just a handful of months before my daughter's birth, I invited all the friends, family members, and colleagues in my life who were also great fathers to a fatherhood summit.

Now, this wasn't the usual uptight conference where everyone is wearing blazers and sitting at assigned tables. This was a much more informal gathering of a few dozen men at Denim on 7th, a super cool downtown bar with an inviting ambience.

The rules were simple. We didn't talk about work, or drama—not even about being a husband. The conversations were solely about fatherhood. Having all those men—guys of different ages, cultural backgrounds, and economic statuses—pour their knowledge and support into me was an enlightening experience.

Kendra had jokes, of course; she tried to say it was just a baby shower. Call it what you want, but having that village in my corner for one of the most important moments of my life was so empowering.

And although I was filled with nervous energy as the due date drew closer, I realized that all the way up to the moment I walked into Denim, I had been preparing to make my city a better place for not just my daughter, but for all children.

Every parent wants their child to live in a better world than the one mom and dad experienced. That's why I'll never understand lawmakers who ignore the warning signs of climate change or neglect to replenish programs like Social Security. What parent would ignore the problems of today and allow their children to suffer down the road from today's inaction?

Couldn't be me. I want a better Birmingham for my daughter. For both my sons.

I want better for every child in this city.

Long before I met Mason and Aubrey, and well before I was rubbing Kendra's feet with our daughter in her belly, my administration was working to break the generational curses that kept our youth from fulfilling their potential.

I wanted to break the cycle of poverty and build financial freedom.

Few things piss me off more than check-cashing sites in the hood. When I realized that they were as present as liquor stores on our corners, I had to take a stand.

Essentially, those sites are dens of predatory lending, giving poor residents quick cash in exchange for sky-high interest rates that they may never be able to pay off.

They're preying on our most vulnerable. And it's disgusting.

I often pondered how I could strike back against those places. Sure, we could picket outside those buildings, but that means nothing to the families who need immediate cash. If you're on your last legs, you don't care about a protest. You need to feed your family.

Instead, I decided to turn our attention to the youngest generation, giving them the tools to free themselves from predatory chains before they're cuffed.

I met Isaac M. Cooper, a financial consulting expert, about a decade ago. He had a knack for talking not just to young people but also to parents about finances in a clear, often culturally relevant way.

We worked to bring his program, the Birmingham Financial Freedom Project, into Birmingham City Schools to teach students, teachers, and staff about needs like savings accounts, stocks, and other investments. His program helps students access bank and investment accounts. What started as a six-school pilot program has grown to nearly two dozen.

We aren't abandoning ship on the families who are currently struggling. But we want to break the cycle of debt so their kids can have a better life.

I wanted to break the cycle of gun violence by emphasizing conflict resolution.

During my days on the school board, when students were caught fighting, they were suspended—i.e., removed from school. I didn't like that. If they weren't in school, they weren't learning. They saw it as a badge of honor, basically a free vacation.

While on the board, I pushed for in-school suspension, so students could continue learning. As mayor, I wanted to take that further.

In the summer of 2024, the surgeon general declared gun violence a public health crisis. Birmingham was way ahead of that game—we had made the same declaration in 2019. But I know firsthand how political the gun control conversation can be. At the municipal level, my hands are tied. And in a state like Alabama, there's not much I can do to keep guns out of people's hands.

But here's what I can do—teach our children to make better decisions.

In 2022, we launched the Common Ground strategy, a plan that uses the Habilitation, Empowerment, and Accountability Therapy curriculum—known as H.E.A.T.—in our schools. The program uses a holistic approach to handling anger management and conflict resolution.

Simply put, we're teaching young people to address problems with methods besides guns and violence.

But Common Ground goes even further, providing mental health support for city schools; a juvenile reentry program known as RESTORE to provide support for youth ages sixteen to nineteen who are currently committed to the state's Department of Youth Services; and Birmingham Re-entry Alliance, which aids individuals after incarceration to provide basic needs and services and reduce recidivism.

Our goals are to teach our young people a better way to respond to conflict, and for those who have made mistakes in the past, to bring them back home on a path that steers them away from repeating those mistakes.

I wanted to break the cycle of hopelessness and encourage servant leadership.

People often get so frustrated with government. And it's easy to see why. Even if you want to help, how can you fit in? Where is your entry point? How do you change your community?

I want our young people to know that democracy is a participatory sport. ACE, the Academy of Civic Engagement, exists to get our residents—young, old, and in between—in the game.

When I take my car to a mechanic, I sit in the waiting area while the automotive experts ply their trade in the shop. The car comes out of the bay doors, as good as new. But 95 percent of the time, you don't know what went into fixing it.

ACE gives our residents a look under the hood.

ACE is a six-week crash course to help residents age sixteen and up understand how government works. From learning about the processes at City Hall to getting involved in neighborhood organizations, ACE participants get to meet the major players in government, make connections, and get tools to make effective change in their own communities.

Leadership isn't about hoarding power for oneself. It's about empowering the next set of leaders for service. That's the core of servant leadership.

I don't want our young people to feel beholden to faulty leadership. I want them to be changemakers on their own. ACE opens the door for knowledge and application.

I wanted to break the cycle of broken families and support single mothers.

When I was a prosecutor, I encountered so many women who were broken. Some were victims of domestic abuse. Others were overwhelmed due to raising multiple children alone. Some didn't have enough for bus fare when they left the court.

But all those mothers just wanted what was best for their children.

I wanted to help.

In 2022, we launched Embrace Mothers, a guaranteed income program for single mothers. More than eight thousand women applied, showing the dire need for this assistance.

In partnership with Mayors for a Guaranteed Income, a network of mayors advocating to give Americans an income floor, 110 Birmingham women received $375 a month for twelve months via a random drawing by a third party. No strings attached.

And before someone talks out of their mouth sideways, let's be clear—this was not a handout. This was a hand-up.

Women are more than eight times as likely as men to work in jobs that pay poverty-level wages. Women are half of America's workforce, but they are 70 percent of the population whose jobs pay less than $10 per hour.

With our partners The Penny Foundation, we also sponsored Mom's Night Out movie events, just for fun and fellowship. We also built a network around those women, connecting them with wealth-building resources and with one another.

When our families are stronger, so is our future.

I wanted to break the cycle of academic failure and give our kids a head start.

Obviously, the Birmingham Promise is my heart, and I am so proud that it has changed the lives of so many Birmingham City Schools graduates.

But what if we could set those students up for success even earlier?

In 2017, I gave a TEDx Talk on early childhood education. My parents are educators; my sister is an educator, too.

Everyone in the Woodfin household will tell you this—the earlier our children embrace education, the better.

Small Magic, originally known as Birmingham Talks, was founded in 2019 with aid from Bloomberg Philanthropies and The Overton Project. Their goal is simple: Help preschool kids increase their vocabulary.

Most children who participate in Small Magic hear fewer than the 21,000 words a day researchers say are needed for optimal brain development. But children who started the program increased the amount of conversation they were exposed to by 50 percent in twelve weeks.

I have such respect for founder Ruth Ann Moss, whose heart is really for these children and their parents. In communities where poverty is high, illiteracy is high, and mothers are working multiple jobs, community partners and government have to stand together to give our children a fighting chance.

It's not a handout. It's a hand-up.

The most important thing we can do for the next generation is make sure that they're better than we are. Less crime, more home-ownership. Less debt, more opportunity. Less conflict, more pride in their community.

It's not up to toddlers and teenagers to make those opportunities. That's what adults are here to do.

What kind of mayor would I be if I'm not fighting every day to build a better Birmingham? What kind of dad would I be?

When Kendra and I celebrated our engagement and wedding, we did it publicly in grand fashion.

For the announcement of our first child together, we kept it much more low-key. We shared the good news with our immediate circle of family, friends, and coworkers, but otherwise kept things on the low during that first trimester.

We wanted to make sure the baby was OK first.

As time moved on, it was getting harder to keep things under wraps—almost literally for Kendra. Our girl was gonna make sure she was seen, whether mommy and daddy wanted her to or not.

The day after the annual UNCF ball, a fundraiser for the United Negro College Fund, we were going through photos of the previous night's event. Kendra was quite obviously showing—people were even inquiring about it that night—and she just said, "Let's share a pic."

Almost on a whim, we shared our news with the world.

Just as we shared that photo with the world, I want to share with you all this open letter to my daughter, written a few weeks before her birth.

It takes a village to raise a child, right? So we're in this together.

I hope when she reads this book years from now that she understands the importance of good character. I hope she listens to her inner voice, those whispers that will help her make the right decisions when times are uncertain.

I want her to know that fear is powerful, but it holds no permanent power over you.

There is peace on the other side of fear. There is joy. There is hope.

It's where you'll find your true self.

Here's my dedication to you, my Love.

Love,

We love you. That's why it's in your name. It's a message you will always carry with you, one we never want you to forget.

Your mom and I have to wait a few more weeks before we can hold you in our arms. But until that day, you're still with us.

I see you when I look into your mom's eyes. I feel you when I touch her belly and feel you squirm around inside. When we lie in bed and watch Avengers movies because your mom can't sleep and I hear Tony Stark's daughter say, "I love you, 3000," it's like I hear your sweet voice.

You're a daughter of Birmingham. It's important to know that our city has a lot of scars. It's gone through some tough times—times that made life very difficult for people who look like us.

But you can't have scars without healing. And slowly, but surely, we're helping our city heal from its past. You can help heal our city, too, by being kind, considerate, and thoughtful. Think about ways to help the people around you. I want you to dream big and challenge yourself.

I want you to love others like your parents, your brothers, and your family loves you.

I want you to live up to your name. Love, Love, Love.

I can't wait to share ice cream with you. To watch movies and go to the park. I can't wait to introduce you to Daddy's favorite music. I hope you like Outkast.

Love, you are everything to me. I love you, (Andre) 3000.

———

Reggie Jackson's brutally honest retelling of his experiences in Birmingham struck a chord with our country during MLB's Tribute to the Negro Leagues in Birmingham in 2024.

During this crucial time in our country, when extremists are attempting to whitewash the Black experience by making terms like critical race theory *political bogeymen, Black America must be louder than ever to make sure our story is heard and remembered.*

While some wanted to run away from Mr. October's comments, I refused to cower. I welcomed his truths. I want my daughter to know his story, to understand how rough the road was for Black Americans, to celebrate the progress made, and to remind her that the fight continues. Here's my open letter to Mr. Jackson, a vow that his story and scores like them will never be erased.

Last week, Birmingham was honored to play host to not just Major League Baseball, but also to fans around the world, in a moving tribute to the Negro Leagues.

A celebration of the Black players who revolutionized the sport and helped to chip away at the color barriers that divided our country.

But during that celebration, we were all struck by the very candid comments of the legendary Reggie Jackson and his experience playing here in Birmingham in the 1960s.

He talked about being denied service at restaurants. Being kicked out of hotels. Being accosted at country clubs.

During a time of celebration, Mr. October brought harsh truths about our country's dark past to light.

And to Mr. Jackson, I have two words.

Thank you.

Thank you for your honesty.

Your strength.

Thank you for your truths.

Decades removed from the Civil Rights Movement, Birmingham is no longer a city defined by hate. It's because of our homegrown heroes like the Rev. Fred Shuttlesworth, as well as icons like Dr. Martin Luther King and our fearless foot soldiers who marched Birmingham out of the darkness and into the light.

It's that very legacy that drives us today to tear down monuments of hate, to bring hope to underserved neighborhoods crippled by inequality for generations, and to ensure every resident, regardless of race, religion, gender, or orientation, feels welcome in the city they call home.

But make no mistake, Reggie Jackson's experiences here and across the Jim Crow South were far too common. We don't run from that past.

These are stories that must be told.

Because history that is forgotten is doomed to be repeated. And to whitewash his experience is an utter form of disrespect.

The story of Reggie Jackson, of the Negro Leagues, of every Black family that survived the segregated South, is a story of triumph.

We don't hide from history in Birmingham. We are motivated by it.

Motivated to be better than our past. To build a stronger future.

And like the icons who made history here, we are motivated to continue to change our world.

Randall L. Woodfin, Mayor
Open Letter to Reggie Jackson
June 2024

CHAPTER 14

THE WAY YOU MOVE

I n the fall of 2022, I had the great honor of testifying at a congressional hearing on Developments in State Cannabis Laws and Bipartisan Cannabis Reforms at the Federal Level. Earlier that spring, on 4/20, of course, I issued a pardon for anyone in our city convicted of misdemeanor marijuana possession charges in municipal court. That was more than 15,000 people.

Marijuana possession convictions have taken a disproportionate toll on Black communities. Although marijuana use is about equal among Blacks and whites, Black residents are almost four times as likely to be arrested for marijuana possession. As of this writing, twenty-four states have legalized marijuana and thirty-eight have made some form of medical marijuana legal.

I thought it was important to take my voice to Washington to fight for the decriminalization of marijuana, not just for the medicinal benefits but for the sake of Black communities.

But once I was challenged by a Republican congressman, the UGK jumped out of me.

Let me break it down.

The UnderGround Kingz, aka UGK, were comprised of Port Arthur, Texas, rappers Bernard "Bun B" Freeman and Chad "Pimp C"

Butler, whom we tragically lost in 2007. Much like my boys Outkast, UGK had two vastly distinct rapping styles—Pimp C was the aggressive trash talker, while Bun was the laid back cat. (In fact, UGK and Outkast would combine forces for "Int Player's Anthem" in 2007, the most crunk wedding song of all time.)

UGK would quickly become Southern rap staples. Their 1992 debut, *Too Hard to Swallow*, is an all-time favorite and they were a constant presence in my music collection for the next twenty years.

Now, remember our discussion about Outkast from a few chapters back? In the '90s, hip-hop was very regional, and with that came built-in biases. While we here in Birmingham were very familiar with UGK, they were a nonfactor outside of the South—much less than even Outkast. They lived up to their names—kings of the underground, but unproven on mainstream airways.

That is, until 2000, when they linked up with New York native Jay Z.

By the end of the '00s, Jay was firmly established as the biggest name in rap. Where Jay went, so did hip-hop. So, it was a huge coup for UGK when they were the featured guest on Jay Z's hit "Big Pimpin'." Produced by Timbaland—a Southern boy himself—the song thrust UGK into a world unfamiliar to them, a bouncy, radio-friendly track.

But here's the beauty of it all—UGK did not compromise who they were. Pimp C was skeptical of the collaboration in the first place (he had turned down a previous collabo with Jay Z about a year prior) because he felt he'd have to water down his trademark sound. No worries here, as the duo made sure to keep their contributions as rooted in the Dirty South as possible. Bun outright calls himself a "Southern rap impresario" while Pimp C brags about the leather and wood in his "candied toys"—his brightly painted cars of choice.

Sure, by 2000, Outkast had already introduced their brand of psychedelic Southern culture to the mainstream, but this was different. Outkast was in a constant state of evolution, especially Andre.

They were fun and flashy. When the mainstream spotlight finally shone on UGK, they were the same gruff, matter-of-fact Southern superstars who wowed us back in 1992. It was a different side of the South, and even though they were in unfamiliar territory, they weren't compromising.

So, during the House Oversight Committee, when a congressman had the nerve to compare the marijuana industry to slavery, the spirit of Pimp C overtook me.

"The product is being marketed. The product is being sold. The product has been advocated by people who were in it to make money. Slavery made money also and was a terrible circumstance that this country and the world went through for many, many years," he said.

This congressman was arrogantly using slavery—slavery!—as a talking point to defend laws that have unfairly targeted Black communities for generations. The irony was infuriating.

And that congressman represented Texas of all places. Bun B would be pissed.

This representative of Birmingham, Alabama—yours truly—was not having it.

It was not the time to compromise. I had to be just as authentic, just as real—actually, just as trill—as UGK.

"While I'm on the record, I would just like to say to you directly, your committee members, that putting cannabis and slavery in the same category is patently offensive and flagrant."

Though "Big Pimpin'" was a half-decade removed from Outkast's coming-out party at the Source Awards, Southern artists still had to fight for respect. UGK's contributions to "Big Pimpin'" were mostly celebrated—much more so than in the 1995 era of rap—but there were still doubters who turned their noses up.

They didn't get the slang. Their rap style was too different. Their swag was unfamiliar.

You don't have to get us. But you absolutely need to hear us.

Southern leaders continue to fight to have their voices heard on the big stage today. The challenges in our communities are different from those of our counterparts: health disparities, voter redlining, inadequate funding for everything from education to infrastructure, and so much more.

Being a young, Black leader grappling with those issues in unfamiliar spaces, in front of audiences largely unfamiliar with Southern complexities, makes it even tougher.

But leadership has never been presented as a smooth ride. We build teams, we make tough choices, and we raise our voices—as loudly as possible—for the communities we represent.

Whether it's a New York rap track or a DC hearing, the South still has a lot to say.

Being a leader means reckoning with the sins of the past. Birmingham's past is well-documented, but the ramifications of our journey run deeper than you probably realize.

Birmingham was founded in 1871. Our claim to fame was the rich minerals hidden within our earth. Iron ore, coal, and limestone—three essential elements in making steel—were found here, all in one place.

That made us very attractive for industry.

The explosive growth Birmingham experienced after that raw-material discovery gave us our nickname, the Magic City. Surrounding towns were absorbed into our city and our meek downtown suddenly became much more urban, with high-rise buildings jutting into the skyline.

The demand for Birmingham steel skyrocketed during World War II, and prosperity continued after the war ended, as development boomed.

Birmingham was eatin' good. For a while, at least.

By the 1960s, things began to change.

The Civil Rights Movement picked up steam, with some of the most transformative battles in American history occurring right on our streets. At the same time, Birmingham was beginning to transition away from steel as the bedrock of our economy.

The '60s is also the era where Birmingham began to experience "white flight," with white residents moving outside of the city. Initially this exodus was partly due to rising activism in our city, but it increased as Birmingham became the site of homegrown terrorism—the bombing of 16th Street Baptist Church in 1963, among other incidents.

It accelerated during the federally mandated integration of public schools in the late 1960s and early 1970s, increased even more after the election of Dr. Richard Arrington as Birmingham's first Black mayor in 1979, and continues even today.

Numbers don't lie; check the scoreboard: In 1960, Birmingham's population was more than 340,000; as of the 2020 census, it's at 200,733. In 1960, the city's population was roughly 60 percent white and 40 percent Black; today, it's nearly 74 percent Black and about 21 percent white.

Here's what that means from a municipal government perspective: Our population shrank, but our city's boundaries didn't. Considering decades of property annexations, Birmingham covers a much larger area than it did in 1960—now with far fewer residents as a source of tax revenue.

Also consider the era of segregation, when Black residents were not allowed to patronize white businesses. Many communities had two sets of libraries, two parks, two recreation centers, etc. Segregation may have ended but many of these duplicate structures still exist in our neighborhoods, which means the city struggles to care for two sets of amenities, in spite of a reduced population.

That's especially true for schools: In the '60s, the city ran one school system for white students, and a separate (and unequal) school system for Black students. During integration, many facilities that served Black students were abandoned or became blighted. They're not just drains on city resources, but demoralizing eyesores in our communities.

It's the same story for many communities of color, especially in the South, where you can drive a handful of blocks in one direction and go from healthy, vibrant urban development to abandoned structures and dated construction straight out of the '70s.

This is the cost of segregation—the very real, very demoralizing divide between the haves and the have-nots, with cash-strapped municipalities struggling to balance the scales.

As a leader, this is what I've inherited. And it's my sworn duty to bridge the gap in our communities.

I often think about that mother who has a child in one of those underserved neighborhoods. The woman who stands on her porch, looks to her left and sees a dilapidated, abandoned home. She looks to her right and sees a vacant lot with weeds that come up to her kneecaps. She has to step over broken pavement to walk her child to the playground, which is filled with rusty, neglected equipment. That's the reality for so many of our residents.

That's why I've made neighborhood revitalization the No. 1 goal of my administration. Leveling longtime blight, going vertical on new homes. We've allocated millions of dollars for street resurfacing and pothole repair. We launched Birmingham Xpress, the first bus rapid transit system in Alabama, to expand the city's public transit options.

Just a few days before writing this chapter, we brought a new grocery store to an area of town with no access to healthy foods. Food deserts are another ugly byproduct of segregation, and I was so happy to see hundreds of residents line up as early as 5:30 a.m. to celebrate this new store.

To accomplish this revitalization, efforts like our new Protective Stadium have been key. The stadium and other new initiatives generate revenue that we're putting directly back into struggling communities.

We're a long way from where we need to be. But this is why I came back to my hometown after Morehouse College. To lead.

Make no mistake, Birmingham is not a broken city. Going back to its iron-ore origins, it's always been a city of potential. There are times when we capitalized on that potential, and there are times when it went to waste.

I'm ready to move beyond potential and embrace progress.

The cost of segregation is high. But our persistence is beginning to pay off.

I miss my brother Andre 3000 making hip-hop. If it were up to me, we'd have a new Outkast album every year. While his partner Big Boi continues to wave the flag of the Mighty O, still performing live shows and occasionally giving us new songs to rock to, Andre has become hip-hop's most enigmatic recluse.

Like a true ATLien, his appearances are fleeting, almost magical. Every blue moon he'll descend from the heavens, delivering a guest rap verse here or there—like his contribution to Kanye West's "Life of the Party" in 2021.

It was funny to hear younger fans say, "Hey, this Andre 3000 guy is good!" Um, yeah, he's dope; we've been saying that for thirty years now—catch up!

Otherwise, you're likely to catch Andre wandering the streets of America, playing his flute. Seriously, it's like a game of Where's Waldo, with fans taking pics of Andre everywhere from Philly to Venice Beach. He's even popped up in Portland, Oregon, for open mic night.

Imagine getting ready to read the poem you've worked on for weeks when a diamond-selling rap legend beats you to the mic. Man, I'd just go home—after I listened to him and applauded, of course.

When asked why he doesn't want to return to the spotlight and release a big comeback album, Andre's reason was simple—times have changed. Hip-hop has evolved, and he feels like his time at the top has passed.

Even though he says that, I believe his actions speak louder than his words. He may not want to be a star but he's still creating music, he's still writing lyrics.

The world is changing, but he can't change who he is.

What does leadership look like in this evolving twenty-first century? Well, as much as I admire the trailblazers of the past—many of whom I've celebrated in the pages of this book—I realize that times change. And we have to evolve with them.

When the White House successor to President Obama rose to power in 2017, many said it was a sign of changing times. The country was done with stuffy, aloof politicians who lorded over them. They wanted someone relatable, someone who told it like it is.

Or, more accurately, they wanted a leader who told them what they wanted to hear.

I think the observers were half right. In terms of the forty-fifth president, I believe he represented a sizable portion of our country that was afraid of change. Our country was quickly becoming more diverse and progressive, and he represented a return to how things used to be.

Reminder: Depending on what side of the fence you stood, things weren't always that great in the good ol' days.

However, I do believe that times were changing, and that Americans wanted a leader they felt comfortable identifying with. In that ex-president's case, voters confused "telling it like it is" with divisive, hateful rhetoric and "being great again" with erecting figurative and literal barriers to block the advancement of Black and brown people in our country.

What Americans really want is honest, transparent, inclusive leadership. I don't believe they want a template of a leader; they want someone real.

That's why I've become very comfortable in my skin as a leader. Some days I'll rock a three-piece suit, but most days you'll see me around town in some Jordans and a T-shirt. I might throw on a blazer if I feel like it—but only if I feel like it.

And it took a long time for me to come to that *real* realization.

I was very hard on myself as a child. It wasn't external pressure; it was from within. I had to get good grades; I had to clean up the kitchen and ensure it was spotless; I had to be the best member of the band.

This drive wasn't a desire for perfection or a way to satiate my ego by proving to everyone that I was the best. Deep down, young Randall just wanted to make his mom and dad proud. But that need for reassurance became a hindrance. An anchor.

If I felt I failed at any time, fear would eat me alive.

Each decade of my life got a little better. My twenties were the wilderness—I was constantly chasing potential, and it always seemed to slip through my grasp. My thirties were a little better, but even as a professional, I was too concerned about what others thought of me. I remember nights scrolling social media, reading all kinds of lies and attacks; it got to me more often than I care to admit.

The fear of letting my city down loomed large.

But now I'm in my forties and I'm walking in my purpose. I'm living out my spiritual gift—I was put on this earth to make change. That was the gift God gave me. And I decided I was going to do it, unapologetically.

And I was going to do it with the help of the leaders who came before me. The fire of the Rev. Fred Shuttlesworth. The poise of Dr.

Richard Arrington. The compassion of my grandmothers. The family values of my parents. And yes, hopefully, just a little of the cool of my brother, Ralph. He wasn't perfect, but I carry him with me every day.

I know I'm not the leader that some expect me to be. But I'm me, and I'm finally OK with that.

My insecurities, my past mistakes, my doubters, my fears—I can't run from them. They will always exist. I've realized, though, that none have the power that hope brings.

I will never avoid them. But I will always beat them.

I want Andre 3000 to make albums. But that's not how he wants to lead right now. He has stepped aside for a new generation of leaders to walk his path—incredible artists like Big K.R.I.T., Killer Mike, Earthgang, and JID who are keeping the South's story alive with the same creativity, insight, and boldness Outkast did thirty years ago.

You won't catch me on a Philly street corner with a flute, but you probably will see me in North Birmingham, fighting against industrial plants that have polluted the air of Black neighborhoods for generations.

You might holla at me at Yo Mama's restaurant downtown, grabbing some chicken and waffles.

Or you might see the kid in me riding my bike down one of our freshly paved streets. A different kind of Neighborhood Superstar.

No matter where I am, I'll be among my people.

Leadership looks like Rev. Shuttlesworth rallying activists to hit the streets. It looks like Mayor Arrington suppressing police brutality and ushering in a new era of Black leadership. It looks like Andre 3000 putting down his mic at a packed Atlanta concert in 2014 and picking up a mic in Portland to read the spoken word. It looks like Randall Lee Woodfin talking to a resident on the phone about a pothole in front of her driveway while on the way to see Mom for lunch.

The South will always have something to say, even when the messengers change.

———

In 2023, our city celebrated sixty years since the landmark actions taken during the 1963 Civil Rights Movement.

It also marked the anniversary of one of the darkest days in American history, when four girls were murdered when a bomb set by Klansmen devastated 16th Street Baptist Church.

On the eve of the dark anniversary, I spoke to our Chamber of Commerce about how that moment in time continues to shape us. My words included some frank talk about leadership challenges in our community.

The responsibility of leadership is heavy, but that's by design. There's so much at stake. For the sake of our city's legacy, and in honor of those four lives lost, leaders must put aside their differences for the betterment of those they serve.

The loss of those precious souls unified our community. We cannot allow that lesson to escape us.

This week marks a pivotal milestone in our city's history.

Tomorrow marks sixty years since a bomb tore through 16th Street Baptist Church, robbing four little girls of their lives and ripping the hearts out of our community.

Call it what it is: homegrown terrorism. A manifestation of the worst of evils.

And while are hearts will forever be heavy due to the sacrifices of Addie Mae Collins, Cynthia Wesley, Carole Robertson, and Denise McNair—here's what their loss taught us.

To be braver.

To be stronger.

To have more conviction for what is right.

To be better protectors of our children and better stewards of our community.

To never turn a blind eye to injustice.

To rebuild.

To be better.

Those four girls taught us that it is up to each and every one of us to build a better Birmingham. Not just in their honor, but for the little girls and boys who are here now. For the little girls and boys yet to come.

Sixty years of perspective tells us that we have the power to make change for the better.

And in the six decades that have followed, we have finally begun to turn Birmingham's perpetual potential into promise.

Look at how far we've come.

Birmingham has quietly served as an innovator in the healthcare space for years, but we're building upon that by attracting startups, becoming a major player in the tech space in our region.

Our arts and entertainment scene is flourishing. We've long been the home of the Magic City Classic, the largest HBCU football game of its kind, but with the addition of Protective Stadium, pub-lic–private partnerships, and mounting buzz across the nation, our sports imprint is growing. The Birmingham Legion, the Birmingham Stallions, the Birmingham Squadron—and let's not forget a little thing called the World Games 2022, which brought more than 140,000 spectators to the field to watch incredible feats of athleticism.

And you can't sleep on our growing culinary scene, bolstered by award-winning restaurants and national recognition.

As a city, we should celebrate these wins. Many of you had a direct hand in the upward mobility our city has experienced.

But let's take off those rose-colored glasses for a minute and keep it real. All those wins came with challenges. And as mayor, as leader of our city, allow me to be totally transparent.

The Birmingham Business Alliance has faced challenges. Serious challenges of leadership. And those challenges have had a direct effect on our city's growth, our momentum, our residents.

Quite frankly, our future.

Despite those challenges, I remain optimistic about the potential of this chamber.

But again, let's turn that potential into promise.

That starts with a back-to-basics approach. A great start is honing in on our support of women- and minority-owned small businesses. They're not just the lifeblood of our economy, they are the building blocks of our future. They are the innovators that deserve our attention and investment.

If we are to continue Birmingham's current momentum, if we are to maintain this upward trajectory, I'm asking you this one thing: We need our leaders to lead.

Without agenda, without spite, without conditions.

Lead. For the betterment of our city.

This week, of all weeks, is a reminder of that.

The responsibility of leadership is heavy. It comes with tough decisions and uncomfortable compromises.

But we must never waver.

Because of names like Addie Mae Collins. Cynthia Wesley. Carole Robertson. Denise McNair.

Names that represent the innocent we work to protect. Names that, tragically, represent unfulfilled potential.

Names that we hold dear to our heart. Because, leaders, we cannot let their loss be in vain.

How dare we be divided when their sacrifice taught us to be stronger together.

Their memory deserves more of us.

And in 2023, sixty years later, the leadership of Birmingham must give its residents more.

Focus on our small business community. Build bonds both inside and outside these walls. While you're at it, volunteer to sign up to be a reading mentor to our third graders, who are struggling to meet their reading goals.

Leadership takes many forms, but a servant's heart is always filled with humility and the drive to be better.

I'm so optimistic about the future of our city, and I'm equally optimistic about what this chamber is attempting to accomplish. Sixty years have taught us that Birmingham is built to last, able to rebound from the darkest of adversity.

Those four girls continue to be our light.

Chamber, continue to lead bravely and boldly. Shine brightly for your constituents, for your city.

And for those girls.

Randall L. Woodfin, Mayor
Chamber of Commerce Address
September 2023

ACKNOWLEDGMENTS

Back in 2001, Soulja Slim had a pretty good album called *The Streets Made Me*. Twenty-four years later, if you want to know who made me and my story, look no further than these incredible people.

They are the architects of my path.

I owe a huge amount of gratitude to the following folks, who shared their stories in interviews so that I could share my story in full with the world: Kendra, Mom, Dad, Rick Journey, Ed Fields, Henry Goodgame, Dr. Lisa Herring, Daniel Deriso, Mary Boehm, Josh Carpenter, Edward "EJ" Turner, Kelli Caufield, Cedric Sparks, Joe Carlos, Dr. Joseph Wu, and Dr. Mark Wilson.

Thank you, Western Supermarket—Dale, who hired me; Darrell, who trained me; and countless customers who taught a bag boy the meaning of service.

Thanks to Sixth Avenue Baptist Church's InStep Ministry. I'll always be a Christian Soldier.

Thanks to my alma maters, Morehouse College (especially my roommates Joe and John) and Samford University Cumberland School of Law.

Thanks again to my family—my parents (and my bonus mom), Cindy, and Candice.

Shout out to Miles to Go, Alpha Phi Alpha, Alpha Rho, Synergistic 22, One Face, Bloomberg–Harvard second cohort, the Birmingham Change Fund, the 'ahl cohort, and the Collective.

I'm so grateful for Birmingham City Schools, Putnam Middle School, my sixth-grade teachers Mr. Washington, Mrs. Snow, Mrs. Archie, and Mrs. Flowers—the Avengers of Education.

Shades Valley High School Class of 1999, what up!?

ACKNOWLEDGMENTS

Many thanks to the 2013 School Board Election Team.

Thank you, thank you, thank you to the 2017 and 2021 mayoral campaign team and the army of volunteers who helped us make history. I have to acknowledge the 2017 field organizers, whose enthusiasm and perseverance still motivates me today: Nakia Browner, Keundrea Felton, Ethan Harris, Austin Noble, Laura Binford, Taylor Packer, Arnee Odoms, Damian White, EJ Turner, Tricia McMullen, and Rashad Grimes. Special thanks to Daniel Roth for capturing the journey with his camera!

Thanks to my entire appointed team at Birmingham City Hall. CEETA-certified leadership!

Extra special thanks to John, Joe, Jaqueline, Kelli, Jennifer, George, and Randall G for making my wedding day magical.

Much love to the wordsmith himself Edward T. Bowser for making this memoir so special. Thanks to Ian Kleinert and the entire team at Diversion Books for their partnerships in this project.

And as always, thank you to my hometown, Birmingham, Alabama. I love you more than you'll ever know. I hope I make you proud.

I put on for my city.

RANDALL WOODFIN was born in Birmingham, Alabama, and after four years at Morehouse College has lived in Birmingham ever since. He worked at City Hall (in jobs for both the mayor and the city council) and for the Jefferson County Committee on Economic Opportunity, attended Cumberland School of Law at Samford University, and, after obtaining his law degree, accepted a job in the City of Birmingham Law Department. As an assistant city attorney, he also became an organizer, working on campaigns at the local, state, and federal level. After serving on the Birmingham Board of Education, he ran for mayor, won an upset victory in a runoff, and is seeking his third term in 2025. He was a keynote speaker at the 2020 Democratic National Convention and has been endorsed by President Joe Biden, Senators Bernie Sanders and Cory Booker, and Representative Stacey Abrams.

EDWARD T. BOWSER is an award-winning journalist, founder of the music and pop culture website Soul In Stereo, and currently serves as the deputy director of communications for the City of Birmingham Mayor's Office, where he helps shape the city's voice and vision.